King Arthur Through the Ages

Volume 2

Garland Reference Library of the Humanities
Vol. 1301

King Arthur Through the Ages

Edited by
Valerie M. Lagorio
Mildred Leake Day

Volume 2

Garland Publishing, Inc. ◆ New York & London ◆ 1990

Library of Congress Cataloging-in-Publication Data
(Revised for vol. 2)

King Arthur through the ages.

(Garland reference library of the humanities ;
vol. 1269, 1301)
    Includes bibliographical references.
    1. Arthurian romances—History and criticism.
    2. Arthurian romances—Adaptations—History and criticism.
    3. Literature, Medieval—History and criticism. 4. Liter-
ature, Comparative—Themes, motives. I. Lagorio,
Valerie Marie, 1925– . II. Day, Mildred Leake,
1929– . III. Series.
PN685.K46   1990   809'.93351   89-17223
ISBN 0-8240-7144-1 (v. 1: alk. paper) 1269

Printed on acid-free, 250-year-life paper
Manufactured in the United States of America

Dedicated to the Memory of

ROBERT W. ACKERMAN

and

ROBERT M. LUMIANSKY

KING ARTHUR THROUGH THE AGES

Valerie M. Lagorio and Mildred Leake Day
Editors

Volume I

Contents of Volume II

INTRODUCTION TO VOLUME II

Following the rich production of Arthurian works during the Middle Ages, the period from the sixteenth to the early nineteenth centuries was the nadir for Arthurian literature. The Victorian Age, however, gave rise to an Arthurian renascence which has continued through the twentieth century and reached new heights from 1950 onward, both in academia and in the popular culture. In the introduction to Volume I of *King Arthur Through the Ages*, we posited the need to evaluate the results of this renascence, particularly since thirty years had elapsed since the appearance of *Arthurian Literature in the Middle Ages*, the paragon handbook for Arthurian medievalists. Following suggestions first made by R. W. Ackerman, we formulated the following four goals: 1) to update, expand, or present a new overview of major entries in *ALMA*; 2) to introduce new areas for study and research; 3) to feature innovative methodologies and critical approaches to the Arthurian canon; and 4) to enlarge upon *ALMA*'s scope to encompass postmedieval and modern Arthuriana. As *ALMA* dealt with the medieval period exclusively, the area also covered by *KATA* I, *KATA* II is concerned with the Arthurian renascent continuum. Following our practice in *KATA* I, we consulted with a large number of Arthurians regarding the content of this second volume, which accordingly reflects our collaborative thinking.

In trying to analyze this spectacular Arthurian efflorescence, we can only offer some tentative conclusions: The Arthurian Grail legend is both timeless and contemporaneous, with a protean capacity to reinforce the aspirations and respond to the aesthetic, moral, and spiritual needs of humankind in succeeding ages. As questers facing the second Millennium, surely a time of great crisis and anxiety, we may experience, consciously or unconsciously, a retrospective nostalgia for the Arthurian Golden Age, with its certain, praiseworthy values and universal truths, the same verities which are threatened in today's world. Perhaps we long for the promised return of Arthur, the apocalyptic Last World Emperor, who will initiate a new age of peace and promise. Whatever the reason, this Arthurian revival has produced an astonishing number of works of poetry and fiction which have enriched the Victorian and ongoing literary Arthuriad. Moreover, in the latter part of this century, Arthur has permeated every facet of our culture, a phenomenon especially apparent in North America and Britain. This must be acknowledged and assessed in conjunction with its heritage from the past. Here, then, is the purpose of *KATA* II, as each contributor examines some aspect of the modern Arthurian revival in relationship to its medieval origins.

Janet Goebel takes issue with the critical shibboleth that the adaptation of Arthurian materials by the *Frühromantiken* of the Jena Circle was negligible and advances evidence for the Circle's Arthurian medievalism. She concentrates on the polysemous character of König Arctur in *Heinrich von Ofterdingen* by Friedrich von Hardenberg (known as Novalis). She maintains that König Arctur represents a conflation of the star Arcturus and King Arthur, and she also suggests the possible influence of the *Romance of the Rose* and Chrètien's *Erec et Enide*.

In a tribute to Sir Frederic Madden (1801-73) as the leading Arthurian scholar of the Victorian Age, Gretchen Ackerman, working closely with his personal journals, appraises the volume, variety, and quality of Madden's work as a scholar, and, more importantly, as an editor responsible for recovering and editing *Sir Gawain and the Green Knight* and Layamon's *Brut*, Ackerman credits Madden with effecting the change from antiquarianism to scholarship.

With this introduction to the Victorian Arthur, the next three collaborators are apologists for the works of Alfred, Lord Tennyson, A. C. Swinburne, and William Morris. Comparing audience reception and critical responses to Tennyson's *Idylls of the King* in the Victorian era, Linda K. Hughes scrutinizes the poem's nonsequential composition and publication, Tennyson's domestication and democratizing of his Arthurian matter, and his professed affirmation of humanity and the individual as it was perceived by his urban, middle-class readers. She proposes that a similar contextual grasp of the *Idylls* would balance both positive and negative modernist reactions to the poem, and recapture the freshness of characterization and other strengths which were admired by its original audience. Continuing with the Victorian revival, Rebecca Cochran examines Swinburne's Arthurian juvenilia, with its Pre-Raphaelite influence, and his mature works, *Tristram of Lyonness* and *The Tale of Balan*, in terms of his selection and treatment of sources, adherence to the essential spirit and letter of his medieval models, and poetic artistry. This essay contrasts in a striking way with Hughes's study, as Tennyson's *Idylls of the King* was Swinburne's special *bête noire*. Florence Boos praises William Morris's "The Defence of Guenevere" and the character of its defiant, unrepentant queen. After ranging over other modern critical opinions of the poem, she offers her own feminist interpretation of the work, which for her coalesces with Morris's "vindication of a limited but admirable female psyche."

In dealing with Richard Wagner's *Tristan und Isolde*, Henry Hall Peyton III goes to Thomas, Bèroul, Eilhart von Oberg, Malory, and Wagner's main source, Gottfried's *Tristan*, in order to clarify the composer's transformation of King Mark into a wise and sympathetic monarch. By contrast to the ethereal, all-consuming love of Tristan and Isolde, Mark serves as a musical and dramtic touchstone, a reminder to the audience of the "temporal order of earthly morality."

Muriel Whitaker conjoins the far-off past and modern present in her perceptive, word-painting study of the illustration of Arthurian romance, demonstrating how the pictorial representation of these works, like the works themselves, are informed by the artist's creative vision, medium, contemporary societal values, and intended audience.

Also bridging past and present, Jane Curry investigates a new genre — Arthurian literature written for children — and points out how this specialized audience dictated the authors' selection of stories, modernization of language, and didactic intentions. Interestingly enough, juvenile Arthuriana did not flourish during the two World Wars (1914-19 and 1940-45), when "lessons in right violence must have seemed superfluous."

The adaptability of the Arthuriad for pacifistic, anti-war purposes in seen in the *Merlin* and *Lancelot* of Edwin Arlington Robinson, who, according to Valerie Lagorio, taps into this rich apocalyptic vein, as did his medieval forebears and later twentieth-century authors like T. H.White.

Judith Kollmann handles one of the most challenging subjects in the modern Arthurian canon, the labyrinthine poetry of Charles Williams. She evolves a multifaceted analysis of the structure, plot, themes, and intellectual and spiritual substance found in his *Taliessin Through Logres* and *The Region of the Summer Stars*. These works form an amelioristic diptych which evinces Williams's hopeful vision for the future of humankind.

KATA now turns to modern Arthurian prose fiction, which is introducing the legend of King Arthur, the Round Table, and the Holy Grail to an ever-widening general audience. As it departs from the more defined medieval genres of chronicle and romance, it necessarily entails arbitrary taxonomies. Maureen Fries outlines major twentieth-century trends in the Arthurian novel: comedy, as exemplified by John Erskine, James Branch Cabell, John Steinbeck, and Thomas Berger; tragicomedy, in T. H. White; the mysticism of the Grail, with Charles Williams, John Cowper Powys, and C. S. Lewis; the social sciences of history, anthropology, and archaeology; and feminism, prominent in Marion Zimmer Bradley's *The Mists of Avalon*. Raymond H. Thompson adopts a broad-ranging taxonomy of science fiction and fantasy for this varied body of works. According to his categorization, science fiction is concerned with the impact of change on humanity, usually projected into the future, and coinheres with the Arthurian legend's cyclic pattern of rise, fall, and the promise of renewal. Fantasy employs Arthurian elements of the heroic and marvelous, along with the comic and feminist, to create a better alternate world or universe. Thompson clearly articulates the special affinity between Arthur and the SFF genres.

While T. H.White's *Once and Future King* is universally acknowledged as the most influential and enduringly popular of modern Arthurian fiction, two American novelists, Thomas Berger and Walker Percy, are receiving critical acclaim for their Arthurian contributions. Brooks Landon lauds Berger's *Arthur Rex*, which has been hailed in the *New York Times Book Review* as "the Arthur book for our time," and reveals how the author's strong "allegiances to literary, linguistic,and legendary traditions coalesce with his modern treatment of the Matter of Arthur." This double focus preserves the heroic essence of the myth and concomitantly explores its abiding universal truths. In "Walker Percy's Grail," J. Donald Crowley and Sue Mitchell Crowley demonstrate how, in the "densely allusive texture of his fictions," Walker Percy employs a broad spectrum of Arthurian characters, legends, metaphors, motifs, and moral and spiritual values as ironic, even antithetical paradigms, mirroring forth the emptiness and despair of a postmodern, desacralized culture. Their study centers on *The Moviegoer* and *Lancelot*, an antihero in search of an Unholy Grail, which, like Percy's other novels on the theme of *homo viator*, ends on an apocalyptic note of Christian hope.

In the final segment of this anthology, our contributors examine the modern-day phenomenon of Arthur and Camelot in the popular culture. Two deal specifically with the multimedia Arthur. Kevin Harty provides a comprehensive view of twentieth-century films based on treatments of the legend in opera, medieval and continental works, and nineteenth- and twentieth-century literature. His survey concludes with a useful filmography, to which the editors would add the recently released *Indiana Jones and the Last*

Crusade, which recounts a modern-day search for the Holy Grail, identified as the cup of the Last Supper, which contained the Precious Blood of Jesus Christ, collected from the crucified Savior by Joseph of Arimathea. The Grail effectively reinforces the film's central theme of the triumph of good over evil, and the picture's success guarantees the broad dissemination of the traditional Arthurian Grail story.

Sally K. Slocum and H. Alan Stewart look at the medieval heritage and modern presentation of Arthur and Camelot in comic strips and books. They spotlight Harold R. Foster's *Prince Valiant, in the Days of King Arthur,* as well as the fantastic *Mage* and *Camelot 3000,* which portray Arthur as a super hero. It is interesting to note the parallel development of Arthurian adaptations in the novel, science fiction and fantasy, movies, and the comics in recent years, as all have exhibited increasingly sophisticated, imaginative, and original treatments of the Arthurian ideal.

In the final essay, Freya Reeves Lambides traces the deep penetration of the "Living Arthurian Tradition" into our culture, as revealed by the disparate, yet overlapping audiences for her publication *Avalon to Camelot* and their divergent interests. She further assesses the conjuncture of the Arthurian mythos and today's concern with the arts, feminism, psychology, ecology, ethics, and spirituality. Her study is a fitting climax to KATA's "hoole booke," as it eloquently clarifies, so far as possible, the continuing appeal and power of the Arthurian nexus.

We wish to thank our collaborators for their enthusiastic support of and participation in the *KATA* enterprise, and hope that our readers will find these essays, each of which represents the contributor's own views, as informing and challenging as we do.

Finally, we dedicate *King Arthur Through the Ages* to the memory of R. W. Ackerman (1910-1980) and Robert M. Lumiansky (1913-1987), distinguished scholars, medievalists, Arthurians, academicians, teachers, and friends whose erudition and humanity have enriched the lives of us all.

The Editors

Contributors to Volume I

Professor Heather Arden, University of Cincinnati, Cincinnati, OH 45221-0377.

Dr. Mildred Leake Day, Editor, *Quondam et Futurus*, 2212 Pinehurst Drive, Gardendale, AL 35071.

Professor Richard Dwyer, Florida International University, Tamiami Campus, Miami, FL 33199.

Professor Francis G. Gentry, University of Wisconsin, Madison, WI 53706.

Professor Donald L. Hoffman, Northeastern Illinois University, Chicago, IL 60625.

Professor Reginald Hyatte, The University of Tulsa, Tulsa, OK 74104-3189.

Professor Sharon L. Jansen, Pacific Lutheran University, Tacoma, WA 98447.

Professor Marianne E. Kalinke, University of Illinois at Urbana-Champaign, Urbana, IL 61801-3675.

Professor Lister M. Matheson, Michigan State University, East Lansing, MI 48824-1036.

Professor Jeanne T. Mathewson, University of Wyoming, Laramie, WY 82071.

Professor Charles Moorman, University of Southern Mississippi, Hattiesburg, MS 39406.

Professor Jeanne A. Nightingale, Miami University, Hamilton Campus, Hamilton, OH 45011.

Professor Jeff Rider, Wesleyan University, Middletown, CT 06457.

Professor Martin B. Shichtman, Eastern Michigan University, Ypsilanti, MI 48197.

Professor Robert Warnock, Brown University, Providence, RI 02191.

Volume II

Dr. Gretchen P. Ackerman, P.O. Box 26, Walpole, NH 03608.

Professor Florence Boos, University of Iowa, Iowa City, IA 52242.

Professor Rebecca Cochran, Kearney State College, Kearney, NE 68849.

Professors J. Donald Crowley and Sue Mitchell Crowley, University of Missouri–Columbia, Columbia, MO 65211.

Dr. Jane L. Curry, 10324 Chrysanthemum Lane, Los Angeles, CA 90078.

Professor Maureen Fries, SUNY Fredonia, Fredonia, NY 14063.

Professor Janet E. Goebel, Indiana University, Indiana, PA 15075-1094.

Professor Kevin J. Harty, LaSalle University, Philadelphia, PA 19141.

Professor Linda K. Hughes, Texas Christian University, Fort Worth, TX 76129.

Professor Judith Kollmann, University of Michigan–Flint, Flint, MI 48502.

Professor Valerie M. Lagorio, University of Iowa, Iowa City, IA 52242.

Freya Reeves Lambides, Editor, *Avalon to Camelot*, P. O. Box 6236, Evanston, IL 60204.

Professor Brooks Landon, University of Iowa, Iowa City, IA 52242.

Professor Henry Hall Peyton III, Editor, *Arthurian Interpretations*, Memphis State University, Memphis, TN 38152.

Professor Sally K. Slocum, University of Akron, Akron, OH 44325.

H. Alan Stewart, 1950 Felix Avenue, Memphis, TN 38104.

Professor Raymond H. Thompson, Acadia University, Wolfville, Nova Scotia, Canada BOP 1XO.

Professor Muriel Whitaker, University of Alberta, Edmonton, Canada T6G 2E5.

Fig. 1 "Lancelot jousting outside a castle." B.L. Add. MS 102 93 (Lancelot), f. 149ʳ. Courtesy, British Library, London.

Fig. 2 "The Crowning of Arthur." Lambeth Palace Library MS 6 (St. Alban's Chronicle), f. 54ᵛ. Courtesy of His Grace the Archbishop of Canterbury and the Trustees of Lambeth Palace Library.

Fig. 3 "King Uther, Igraine, and the Duke of Cornwall." Sir Thomas Malory, Morte Darthur, *ill. edition of Wynkyn de Worde (1498), First book. Courtesy of The John Rylands Library, University of Manchester, England.*

Fig. 4 "The Lady of Shalott", ill. Dante Gabriel Rossetti, in Alfred, Lord Tennyson, Poems (London: E. Moxon, 1857). Photographed from the original edition in the Bruce Peel Special Collections Library, University of Alberta, Edmonton, Canada. Courtesy of the Bruce Peel Special Collections Library.

Fig. 5 "The Remorse of Lancelot." Alfred, Lord Tennyson, Elaine, *ill. Gustave Doré (London: E. Moxon, 1866). Courtesy of Muriel Whitaker.*

Fig. 6 "The Lady Guinevere." Howard Pyle, **The Story of King Arthur and His Knights** *(New York: Chas. Scribner's Sons, 1984). Reprinted by permission of Charles Scribner's Sons, an imprint of Macmillan Publishing Company.*

Fig. 7 "How Sir Tristram drank of the love drink." Malory's **Morte Darthur,** *ill. Aubrey Beardsley (London: J. M. Dent, 1893).*

Fig. 8 "Prince Arthur slays the monster Gerioneo." Edmund Spenser,
The Faerie Queene, ill. Walter Crane (London: George Allen,
1894-97). Courtesy of Unwin Hyman Ltd., London.

Fig. 9 "The Giant of St. Michael's Mount."Malory's Morte Darthur, *ill. Robert Gibbings (London: Golden Cockerel Press, 1936). This photograph was reproduced from* The Wood Engravings of Robert Gibbings, *ed. Patience Empson (London: J. M. Dent, 1959). Courtesy of Patience Empson and the Estate of Robert Gibbings.*

Fig. 10 "Bercilak's lady tempts Sir Gawain for the third time." Gwyn Jones, tr. and ed. Sir Gawaine and the Green Knight, *ill. Dorothea Braby (London: Golden Cockerel Press, 1952).*

Fig. 11 "The Questing Beast." The Romance of King Arthur and His Knights of the Round Table, *abridged from Malory's* Morte Darthur *by A. W. Pollard, ill. Arthur Rackham (London: Macmillan, 1917).*

Fig. 12 "Sir Gawain's dream at Hautdesert." Keith Harrison, tr., Sir
Gawain and the Green Knight, *ill. Virgil Burnett (London: The
Folio Society, 1983). Reprinted by permission of the Folio Society, Ltd,
London.*

KING ARTHUR
THROUGH THE AGES

Volume II

The Hero as Artist:
Arthur Among the German Romantics

Janet E. Goebel

Neither Arthurian scholars, nor scholars of early German Romanticism depart very significantly from the summarial assessment of the movement's involvement with the Matter of Britain offered by Richard Kimpel in Norris Lacy's *Arthurian Encyclopedia:*

> Though there was an almost unbroken stream of adaptation of the *Nibelungen* material from 1803 on, adaptation of Arthurian materials in the Romantic Age was at best sporadic and not very original. Here, and among the Preromantics, it was generally limited to poetic allusions to Merlin the prophet, often independent of specific Arthurian associations, or else consisted of translations of the French versions of Arthurian stories, the prime source being Count Tressan's *Bibliotheque universelle des romans* (1775-89), or else attempted to translate or rework parts of Wolfram von Eschenbach's *Parzival* or Gottfried von Strassburg's *Tristan.* [1]

Kimpel's larger entry also neatly summarizes the bulk of the criticism regarding the earliest group of German Romanticists', the Jena Circle's, motivation for and failure at "medievalism." Their motivations for interest in medieval texts are characterized as primarily political and nationalistic. Richard Barber also contributes to this view: "For writers in France and Germany, the Arthurian legends, which had been truly international in the medieval period, were less attractive than to their English counterparts, because Arthur was regarded as a British national hero; and the nineteenth century was above all the era of nationalism." [2]

Though some credit might be given to the German Romantics' concern with what Kimpel calls "poetic spontaneity," stress is put on their nationalistic interest in their own Germanic past. Elsewhere, the Circle's motivations are erroneously confused with the philological motives of later German philologists.[3]

Apart from these limiting motivations, the failure of the German Romantics as medievalists, practitioners of medievalism, or contributors to Arthuriana is attributed to a lack of adequate critical manuscript work which would, according to Kimpel, make "this material accessible to a wider public as a potential source for creative writers." [4]

I contend that the German Romantics were far more and more critically involved with late medieval texts than they are usually credited with. This is especially true of the Jena Circle or *Frühromantiker:* the closely knit group including Wackenroder, Novalis, and, during the period 1795–1806, Ludwig Tieck and both August Wilhelm and Friedrich Schlegel.

And, while it is true that the climate for Arthurian scholarship in which they worked was limiting, there was a good deal more knowledge of the Matter of Britain and of King Arthur than has been recognized. Two German Romantic works which support this position are Novalis' romance, *Heinrich von Ofterdingen*, and E. T. A. Hoffmann's short story, "Arthur's Hall" — two instances in which King Arthur not only figures prominently, but stands at the symbolic center of the larger works in intimate relation to the their respective artist figures. In Hoffmann's case it is the figure of Arthur who urges the artist to pursue his painting, and Arthur's Hall where the painter finds not only inspiration, but learns the truth of his own soul and of art. The focus of this study is, however, on Novalis' Arthur.[5]

Before one can begin to appreciate the role of Arthur among the German Romantics and to recognize Novalis's Arthur, three impediments to this view must be briefly addressed: 1) the problems arising from failure to distinguish varieties of German romanticisms; 2) a distorted picture of the Jena Circle's scholarly involvement with *late* and frequently non–German medieval texts; and 3) the Jena Circle's primarily literary motivations for medieval scholarship and their success in this endeavor.

One must first join Arthur Lovejoy in distinguishing between "romanticisms." What Achim von Arnim or the Grimm Brothers attempted and accomplished is very different from the work of the earlier Novalis, and equally different from the aims of the eccentric loner E. T. A. Hoffmann. One major characteristic of Novalis and his circle is a decidedly *international* mindset. In so far as one can attribute something resembling a political motivation to them, that motivation is centered around the desire for the former *cultural* unity of Europe, evident during the medieval period. Hoffmann is apparently interested in neither of these positions; certainly he cannot be viewed primarily as a politically or nationalistically motivated writer, nor has he a scholarly interest in medieval literature or philology.

I have argued elsewhere that the Jena Circle can best be characterized as critical imitators of late medieval and early renaissance literature.[6] Tieck, Novalis, August Wilhelm, and, to a lesser extent, Friedrich Schlegel were intimately occupied with the study, editing, and translation of Dante, Cervantes, Calderon, the Provencal poets, and the German medieval texts of the twelfth to the fourteenth centuries. Tieck and the Schlegel brothers only turned to earlier texts such as the *Nibelungenlied* in later years, after the Circle had broken up.[7] The *Frühromantik* never shared the nationalistic fascination with pagan *Germanentum* with which the undifferentiated German Romantics are often associated. Gerhard Kozielek observes that even when members of the Jena Circle turn to "altdeutsche Literatur" such as the *Nibelungenlied*, as Tieck began to do after Novalis' death, the Jena Circle interest was literary as opposed to the patriotic interests of Arnim and Uhland.[8] Nor is Eichendorff's indictment of Gottfried's *Tristan* evidence of the Jena Circle's conservative stance in moral matters as a glance at F. Schlegel's *Lucinde* or Tieck's characterization of the "everyday" and "vulgar" in the *Minnelieder* quickly reveals.

The Jena Circle worked as translators and editors at a time when there existed actual antipathy toward many of these texts, and certainly very few even partially edited manuscripts from which to begin. But the absence of a body of critical editions did not cause the Jena Circle to confine itself to the *Nibelungenlied* or Tressan's paraphrases of the Matter of Britain. There was a wealth of unedited, but accessible late medieval and early renaissance literature within reach. As A. W. Schlegel once told Goethe of medieval literature: "It is unbelievable what treasures lie there unused and unknown." One of A. W. Schlegel's earliest reviews (1790) was of a twelfth–century manuscript of *Richard Löwenherz*, in which he observes the "disappearance of the magical with all its fabulous consequences" from the much later Matter of England, compared to "the earlier ones in which the matter of Charlemagne and King Arthur's knights excels."[9]   In an 1802 letter to F. Froman, Tieck laments the sketchy understanding of the "Gedicht von den Pflegern des Graals" which he is working on: "No one understands the language or even has the opportunity to read it, because the Titurel has not been reproduced: I have had the opportunity to study this and some other works at the local library."[10]   King Arthur was no stranger to Novalis' Jena.

A. W. Schlegel distinguishes late medieval literature from the earlier heroic medieval epic when he notes in 1799 that the "truly chivalric" is first seen in the *Minnelieder*.[11] Tieck goes further and supplies dates for the *höfische Zeit* which are still accepted today:

The time from which the transcriptions and revisions of the older works, as well as the original poems of the Germans, dates is earlier than the "classical" period of Italian poetry which opens with Dante; if we take out the so–called *Lied der Nibelungen* and the poems which must be counted among the collection of historic poems, it was undoubtedly the poets of Provence who were the models for the Germans, French, and Italians. The flowering period of romantic poetry in Europe was in the twelfth and thirteenth centuries; the famous German poets begin roughly with Heinrich von Veldeck, who lived during the reign of Friedrich Barbarossa, and among the last of the *Minnesänger* we must reckon Johann Hadloub, so that the timespan stretches roughly to Rudolf of Hapsburg, until about the end of the thirteenth and the beginning of the fourteenth centuries.[12]

Tieck again equates romantic literature with the late medieval in his observations on the Matter of Britain: "This time period to which all the tales of Parcival, Titurel, Arthur, and Daniel von Blumenthal belong, is the real golden age of romantic poetry."[13]

The scholarly quality of Jena Circle editing and translation of late medieval manuscripts can be surmised from a careful reading of Tieck's *Minnelieder aus dem Schwäbischen Zeitalter* (1803). Kozielek's assessment of this and other Jena Circle manuscript work suggests we judge them in the appropriate context:

A critique of their inadequate translations and a dramatic stand for philological accuracy — as was the case from the perspective of later Germanists — lacks justification. Demands of that sort illustrate that neither the research conditions of that time nor the true intentions behind such efforts were recognized.[14]

Recognizing the distinctly international quality of the Jena Circle and their seriousness as medievalists working on an international body of late medieval texts is crucial to an understanding of how they perceived the Matter of Britain and King Arthur. Crucial to an understanding of how Arthurian material worked in their own, to borrow Kimpel's term, "creative writing," is the recognition of the primarily literary motives of the Jena Circle and, more important, of the unique way this literary motivation for medieval studies manifests itself in their fiction.

While the *Frühromantiker* are often faulted for idealizing the Middle Ages with a holistic medieval Zeitgeist based on Catholic idealism, and for failing to recognize the apparently obvious "medieval dualism," my contention is that precisely the conclusions they reached about medieval literature for which they have long been criticized were, in basic ways, very similar to the conclusions that critics like Robertson and Muscatine came to much later. Neither the method nor the conclusions about this literature, which A. W. Schlegel, for example, delivers in his Berlin Lectures, would seem out of place at a contemporary conference on medieval studies.

A major motivation in translating medieval texts was their search for an alternative to not only the ideas, but the literary language and associations of the rationalistic Enlightenment.[15] Heinrich Heine, A. W. Schlegel's student, describes the early German Romantic movement as:

> nothing more than the reawakening of the poetry of the Middle Ages as it had manifested itself in medieval songs, pictorial art and architecture, art and life. This poetry had emerged from Christianity; it was a passion-flower sprung from the blood of Christ.[16]

"Romantisch" literally meant having qualities of the late medieval romance. It is not the modern, empirical portrayal of a truly historical Middle Ages we will find in Jena Circle fiction. Nor is it the "emergence of the modern concept of literature . . . bequeathed by Kant to his successors" which Werner Hamacher sees in Lacque–Labarthe and Nancy's *The Literary Absolute*.[17] Primarily represented in Jena Circle fiction is a critical imitation of the late medieval romance: its themes, its structures, its literary language, its idealistic and sometimes mystical Catholicism, and its cultural values as seen by the Jena Circle in medieval texts, comprehended, and incorporated into their own fiction. It is precisely the presence of the medieval romance's structural elements and language, as opposed to simple borrowing of plots and characters, which argues against charges that the Jena Circle relied on contemporary foreign summaries of the medieval material for their knowledge.

One illustration of Arthur among the German Romantics is to be found in *Heinrich von Ofterdingen* by Friedrich von Hardenberg (known as Novalis). Novalis began his work on this unfinished romance in 1799 while he was at Artern. The legendary Heinrich of Ofterdingen (or Afterdingen), appears in the *Wartburgkrieg* fragments which were probably written in Thuringia in about 1250 and eventually were connected with the Bavarian Lohengrin story.[18] The Thuringian element of the legend is short and describes only a contest of poets. Ofterdingen supported the Duke of Austria in a legendary contest of singers held at Wartburg in 1207. His competitors, listed on the side of the Landgrave of Thuringia, were no less than Walter von der Vogelweide, Reinhart von Zweten, Wolfram von Eschenbach, Heinrich the Virtuous Scribe, and Biterolf. He lost, but invoked the Landgräfin Sophia's protection to have the minstrel Klingsohr brought in from Hungary to put Wolfram through his paces. Eschenbach came out victorious. The fate of Ofterdingen is not addressed.

It is Novalis' borrowing of the figure Klingsohr (Klingsor) which Kimpel lists as a tangentially Arthurian element in Novalis' *Heinrich*.[19] Novalis' Klingsohr is a poet of the South who serves as Heinrich's mentor and tells him the *Märchen* which is at the center of the larger romance.

Critics quickly point out that the medieval Thuringian story of the contest of poets has little to with Novalis' *Heinrich*, beyond supplying him with the figure of the poet Klingsohr and of Ofterdingen's patroness, Sophie, Countess of Thuringia, since the thirteenth–century story begins *after* Ofterdingen has become a poet, while Novalis presents the hero's unchronicled poetic development. The usual response at this point is to turn to Goethe's influence on Novalis, beginning with the notion that Klingsohr represents Goethe, and that Heinrich's meeting him in the South connects the Klingsohr–Goethe figure to neo–classicism — leaving the medieval abruptly behind as mere window dressing.[20]

Scholars have only occasionally asked about other medieval sources or influences on Novalis' *Heinrich*. Acknowledged, but insufficiently explored, is Tieck's comparison of Novalis to Dante, especially in Novalis' rendering of the figure Sophie, whom Tieck sees as functioning much like Dante's Beatrice.[21] There exists a second possible connection to Dante in that the action of "Klingsohr's *Märchen*," the tale within a tale at the center of *Heinrich*, places its action on earth, in the inferno, in a strange purgatory called "the moon world" and finally in heaven.[22]

Such medieval connections have, however, been greatly minimized with the general conclusion that similarities to anything medieval are purely superficial. Gudrun Horton, summarizing the work of Richard Samuel and others, argues that *Heinrich* demonstrates a "modern consciousness" rather than being "truly Catholic in a medieval sense."[23]

I suspect that there are many more medieval connections to be made in examining Novalis' *Heinrich*, including a debt to the medieval *Romance of the Rose* and to Chrétien's *Erec et Enide*. Certainly there is one neglected figure in the "Klingsohr's *Märchen*" of Novalis' *Heinrich von Ofterdingen*. That figure is King Arthur.

In his widely–used English translation of *Heinrich von Ofterdingen*, Palmer Hilty summarizes "Klingsohr's *Märchen*":

> [I]t symbolically portrays the struggle between eighteenth–century Rationalism and the Romantic reaction . . . [T]he sun may be taken as the symbol of the Enlightenment, the scribe and his fellow conspirators as the arch spirit of Rationalism, perhaps as "the petrifying and petrified reason." Ginnistan is imagination, Fable a metonymy for poetry, Sophie wisdom, Freya the spirit of peace, and Eros of course love. This struggle between cold, calculating reason and poetic spontaneity is given a cosmic setting and decked out with all kinds of symbols and figures.

In the fairy tale, the father and mother (on earth) have a child, Eros; and Ginnistan, who is the daughter of the moon and represents phantasy, has a child, Fable, sired by the father. Ginnistan, or phantasy, nourishes both Eros and Fable. These two go forth on wanderings, Eros to be symbolically enchanted by Circe, Fable to be confronted by questions of the Sphinx. The wanderings of Eros are a sort of pilgrimage and purification, presenting a symbolic fall and salvation of man.

The cosmological events in this fairy tale take place so that Eros may be refined into real love, Fable turned into true poesy, and so that Sophie (wisdom) may be eternally wedded to Arcturus (who apparently is Saturn or Time) and become the priestess of the heart forever.[24]

The only figure whom Hilty seems to have uncertainty in identifying is "Arcturus," his translation of the original German "Arctur." Hilty equates Arctur with "Saturn or Time" to eventually be wedded with wisdom. The difficulty with this identification, apart from the error of suggesting that Arctur and Sophie will be wedded in the future — they are already married and have been separated against their will — is that at the end of the *Märchen,* one of Fable's final acts is to abolish time so that eternal spring again reigns.

Friedrich Hiebel summarizes the essential tale somewhat differently:

Sophia, doomed to separation from her divine spouse, seeks ultimately to be reunited with Arcturus forever. To bring about the return of the Golden Age, Eros must be redeemed from the Realm of the Moon to awaken Freya, daughter of the gods; Fable must vanquish the Scribe, the Underworld, and the Parcae, before she can sing her paean of praise to heavenly Sophia. Thus the tale tells how Eros became the power of pure love and Fable develops the force of divine poetry, in order that Sophia, reunited with Arcturus, may become the everlasting priestess of the heart .[25]

Hiebel divides the characters he finds in the tale into six categories: "names from the most diverse elements of Greek mythology (Eros, the Parcae, Perseus, the Sphinx), from Nordic–Germanic legend (Freya), from Arabian sources (Ginnistan), from astronomy (Arcturus, Moon)—or they are given general names like Fable, Mother, Father, Scribe, and lastly, in wholly individual fashion, Sophia." [26] For Hiebel, Arcturus is a figure from astronomy. "The realm of Arcturus, to the North, where sleeps the Princess Freya, awaiting her awakener, is," he says, "the spiritual world, the Paradiso, the home of Sophia, who after a period of separation is reunited with her consort Arcturus."[27] In his more detailed description of the beginning of the tale in the "Realm of Arcturus," Hiebel explains:

> Arcturus holds sway to the north of the world. (In astronomy, Arcturus is a star in the constellation Boötes, near the Big Dipper and the Pole Star. North is the region of midnight, traditionally looked upon by mystics as the realm of pure spirituality.) Here it becomes "night," hidden from the eyes of man. But the King exclaims prophetically: "Iron, hurl thou thy sword into the world, that they may learn where dwells peace." Peace is Freya, the Princess, awaiting her awakener. From her womb the world shall be kindled anew. Night shall fade, the ice melt, the Iron Age give way to the Golden Age.

> But for this to happen, Eros and Fable must travel their paths, to suffer inner change and purification. This the story images tell us in the symbolic language of sin and redemption .[28]

With minor deviations, Hiebel's analysis of Novalis' Arctur is
to be found in most of the later criticism. Marianne Thalmann
uses the Arcturus identification in her effort to show the standard
fairy tale pattern in all of Novalis' *Märchen*; in this case Arcturus,
as a star among stars, shows how the "land of the fairy–tale king
has taken on cosmic proportions."[29] Bruce Haywood's interpretation of Arctur is also in basic agreement with the Hiebel reading,
though Haywood has more to say on the identity of Arcturus and
makes more of the identification.[30]
     The identification of Arctur with the star Arcturus rests par-
tially on a similarity observed by F. J. Obenauer between the
pattern of stars in the sky and one description of Arctur as wearing
a Northern crown and holding the scales in his right hand, a lily in
his left, with an eagle and a lion at his feet.[31] Haywood also points
to an example from Novalis' *Geistliche Lieder,* in which a polar
region is transformed into an exotic land, to argue that the blooming of polar regions is one of Novalis' favorite metaphors. He
notes, however, that this is "one of the rare uses of nontraditional
imagery in the cycle" [of *Geistliche Lieder*].[32] Haywood's conclusions about Arctur and his realm, greatly distilled, are that
Arctur is both the star Arcturus and "the guiding spirit of the
universe, a spirit that finds delight in harmony and order." He has
some powers, but "it is suggested that certain unalterable laws
function independently of Arcturus." His realm is both "the
region of the North Pole" and "the realm of the stars" which is also
"heaven" or the "Platonic realm of ideas." This realm is also the
realm of cosmic laws, natural forces and basic elements; it is of the
earth, but apart from it — that part of nature which is concealed
from man.[33]
     Heinz Ritter points to the relationship between the Klingsohr
tale and the larger *Heinrich*. The Arctur of the tale corresponds
to Kaiser Friedrich in the rest of *Heinrich,* and the *Sinnbild* for
both figures is the "Geist des Lebens" (spirit of life).[34]
     As diverse as the readings of Novalis' *Heinrich von Ofterdingen*
are, there seems to be agreement with the notion that Arctur is the

star Arcturus, though precisely what Arcturus represents is a cause of minor disagreement.

Despite the astrological evidence, there are difficulties with this identification of Arctur with the star Arcturus. The most glaring problem is that it ignores the most commonly known association of the star of Arcturus with either the entire Great Bear constellation or, at least, with the tail of the bear. For Novalis to have picked as a central symbol in his tale simply a bright star in the North but to have ignored the most common associations of that star seems puzzling.

The other two objections to the simple identification of Arctur with the star Arcturus are of two kinds: 1) what this identification fails to account for; and 2) the unlikelihood of Novalis having ascribed to this association sufficient importance. In the first category are questions surrounding the "old hero" or "Iron." He is the first character we meet in the tale, the guardian of Freya and loyal servant to King Arctur. Both his shield and his magical sword are important appendages which move the action along. King Arctur's order to throw the sword "into the world, so they may learn where Peace (Freya) lies" begins Poetry's (Fable's) quest to reunite Arctus with his queen and restore the Golden Age. Haywood's attempt at explaining him is inadequate, especially given the otherwise tight framework of astronomical allusions.

Why is the somewhat unusual figure of Arcturus — recalling Haywood's term, "a rare use of nontraditional imagery" — frequently referred to in the tale as only "the king" or "monarch"? Certainly the introduction of an entirely new mythological figure from astrology would profit from the rhetorical underscore of being addressed by his name. How do we come to terms with the original home of Novalis' beloved Sophie, the figure of pure wisdom, as the North Pole? Or, if we assume that Arcturus actually resides in heaven or the realm of Platonic ideals, did Novalis really expect us to comprehend that this eternal realm had recently undergone a transformation in the thrall of Rationalism, or that it

would again be transfigured and improved by the action below? If
the star charts mirror Novalis' pictures of Arthur with his crown,
scales, eagle, and lion, whence the lily in his left hand with which
he touches Fable? In the second category of objections is, primarily, would
Novalis have put at the poetic center of his romance, as consort of
his beloved Sophie, simply a star of the North, albeit an important
one? Would he attribute to his star or the frozen polar region
which constitutes its realm the attributes of peace, Christian
unification, and love, to be juxtaposed to a world of warfare and
disunity brought about by Rationalism at the expense of mystery
and the enslavement of an altar?

Since the astronomical evidence is present in "Klingsohr's
Märchen," the association with Arcturus cannot be dismissed.
Neither, I believe, can it stand alone. The Jena Circle's interest in
and knowledge of the Matter of Britain and Arthuriana provides a
likely answer: the conflation of King Arthur and the star, Arcturus,
in the figure of "König Arctur."

There are at least three precedents of conflating King Arthur
and the star Arcturus, any one of which Novalis might have directly or indirectly known. The first is the case of Gildas' *De Excidio
Britanniae*. Both Richard Barber and Geoffrey Ashe have discussed this case. Gildas, in his reproach of five sixth–century kings
of Wales and southwest Britain, reproaches King Cuneglasus with
the phrase "thou bear, rider of many, and driver of the chariot of
the bear's den."[35] Barber discusses an article which suggests that
this reference to "the bear" is an attempt by Gildas to castigate
Cuneglasus for his association with Arthur without mentioning
Arthur's name. Barber notes that the appellation bear would be a
play on Arcturus, the star in the constellation Ursa Major, a
phrase which occurs in the Latin poet Claudian which Gildas
probably knew. Barber points out, however, that this identification is "pure conjecture" and depends "on the assumption that
Gildas was deliberately suppressing Arthur's name." [36]

Geoffrey Ashe points out, however, that Gildas "is oddly reluctant to name names in general, before his own contemporaries."[37] Since the only fifth century Briton Gildas mentions by name is Ambrosius, there is the possibility that he left out Arthur's name for a variety of possible reasons, both clerical and personal. Whether Gildas was alluding to Arthur or not in his allusion to Arcturus cannot be proven. It is, however, likely that much later readers of Gildas assumed the reference was to Arthur because of Caradoc of Llancarfan's 1130 work which suggests that Gildas and Arthur knew each other and that the unsympathetically portrayed Arthur was often forgiven and aided by the saintly Gildas. Ashe points out that Gildas's omission of Arthur from *De Excidio* "paradoxically became part of the story."[38]

Barber offers two other instances of Arthur and Arcturus as interrelated terms. The first appears in Ailred of Rievaulx's *The Mirror of Charity*. Barber says that Ailred of Rievaulx: "tells how a novice at his monastery (in northeast Yorkshire) was never moved by pious stories, although he had wept over tales which the common folk recited about some Arthur (Arcturus) or other before he had entered the monastery."[39]

A second instance occurs in the work of Ben Jonson. Barber explains: "Ben Jonson, writing masques for James' elder son, Prince Henry, introduced Arthurian themes. In *Prince Henry's Barriers* of 1612, devised as the framework for a tournament, Arthur appears in the guise of the star Arcturus to give his blessing to the proceedings." This occurrence is set during a period in which "the folklore of Arthur was turned to political ends."[40] Both English and Scottish monarchs tried to tie their political futures to the return of Arthur.

Given Ritter's argument that Novalis intends to link the König Arctur of "Klingsohr's *Märchen*" with Kaiser Friedrich of history in the larger *Heinrich of Ofterdingen*, Ben Jonson's model for conflating the star and the legendary King Arthur of the Nine Worthies would have special appeal.

Does this technique of conflation fit what we know of Novalis' poetic language? The critics disagree on precisely how to characterize Novalis' language. Haywood, for example, after explaining that figures in the "Klingsohr's *Märchen*" are derived from a hodge–podge of astrology, science, alchemical allegory, and Böhme, concludes:

> Many of the figures of the tale have more than one symbolic function. What their real significance is can be deduced only from the sphere of reference in which they move—the "*Märchen*" itself. In that there is no fixed system of symbols this tale is not pure allegory. It is rather a symbolic—and often humorous—action which hints at hidden meaning without presenting this meaning in consistently developed metaphor.[41]

Hiebel, on the other hand, starts from a phrase Goethe used to explain his own work as containing language which "intertwines images, ideas, and concepts." This Hiebel applies to Novalis' "Klingsohr's *Märchen*" :

> Concepts are expressed in allegory. Allegory personifies the concept. Here alone it is proper to inquire into intellectual meaning. Ideas are encompassed by symbols. They are the expression of a process, as function. Images, finally, are the real element of the tale as such. They are myths of free imagination. We must focus on their metamorphosis, asking what it is that becomes disenchanted, deciphered, redeemed—or, in the language of Novalis, 'unveiled.'[42]

Neither of these characterizations seems as accurate as that of Heinrich Heine:

> Classical art had only to represent the finite, and its figures could be identical with the idea of the artist. Romantic art had to represent or rather suggest the infinite and pure spiritual relationships, and it had

recourse to a system of traditional symbols or rather to the parabolic [figurative/allegorical].

Heine points to the Jena Circle's "discovery" of the features of the late medieval poet's "literary vocabulary" in his summary of the difference between "plastische" art in its classical and romantic manifestations:

> It is different in romantic art; there the wanderings of a knight also have an esoteric meaning, they perhaps signify the wanderings of life as a whole; the dragon that is defeated is the sin; the almond tree which the hero so comfortingly smells from afar that is the trinity, God the Father, God the Son, and God the Holy Ghost, which are at the same time one, just as the nut, fiber and seed are the same almond. When Homer describes the armor of a hero, it is nothing more than good armor which is worth so and so many oxen; but when a medieval monk describes the robes of the mother of God in his poem, one can count on it that he is thinking of this robe as so many different virtues, that a special meaning is hidden under this holy covering of Mary's unspotted virginity, which also, because her son is the almond seed, will quite reasonably be praised as the almond bloom. That is the character of medieval poetry, which we call the romantic.[42]

How, given the language and literary conventions of the Enlightenment, especially as they manifested themselves in North Germany, does Novalis begin to express romantic vision when each crucial word for mental and spiritual faculties has been tainted by the spirit of excessive rationalism, every literary reference to standard mythology associated with some standard truism in the *Aufklärung* world view? His answer to this crisis of literary language was to imitate and integrate the language and system of thought which he found in the Christian works of the late Middle Ages, works which the closely knit Jena Circle read, translated, and edited.

But development of a new poetic vocabulary, unfamiliar or indecipherable for his audience, was also not an unproblematic course, as Friedrich Schlegel acknowledges in his own call for a new mythology free of Enlightenment connotations. The appropriation and creative metamorphosis of late medieval literary conventions are thus modified by Novalis's awareness that his audience is not used to reading the Book of Nature. He can't be subtle, nor can he assume any of the systematized connections that modern medievalists take for granted. We can't, then, be too hard on Novalis for occasionally straying from his late medieval models to borrow an Arabic personification of imagination from Wieland. The overall pattern of his work and his literary language is nonetheless based on late medieval models.

Ludwig Tieck's comparison of Novalis to Dante suggests that there are similarities between Beatrice and Sophie and perhaps additional similarities of poetic representation which may help us decide whether Novalis would have been likely to conflate Arcturus and Arthur. To borrow the traditional symbol system which Heine suggests the Jena Circle employs, would, according to Erich Auerbach, involve the poet in a combination of allegorical and figural language: "Most of the allegories we find in literature or art represent a virtue (e. g., wisdom), or a passion (jealousy), an institution (justice), or at most a very general synthesis of historical phenomena (peace, the fatherland) — never a definite event in its full historicity."[44] Auerbach hypothesises that the *figura* is usually employed by the medieval poet in treating medieval content (concrete events and persons) and Christian themes, whereas the allegorical is usually used for pagan/ancient content and more secular themes.

The *figura* is also to be distinguished from the symbol:

What actually makes the two forms completely different is that figural prophecy relates to an interpretation of history — indeed it is by nature a textual interpretation — while the symbol is a direct interpretation of life and originally no doubt for the most part, of nature. Thus figural

interpretation is a product of late cultures, far more in-
direct, complex, and charged with history than the symbol
or myth.[45]

The figural thus lacks the symbolic's "Ur" quality.
This analysis of how the allegorical and figural work goes far
to explain how Novalis' *Märchen* works. Most of the characters in
the tale are allegorical representations of qualities which are easy
to identify because the name he chooses is simply identified with
the qualities it represents (Freya, the Sphinx, the Parcae) or he
adds adequate description to make this one-to-one correspondence clear (the scribe = rationalism at its worst; Fable =
poetry, to be distinguished from the petrified wisdom of the
scribe). It is significant that the proper names which Novalis uses
in these one-to-one correspondences are pagan, either Greek or
Nordic. Eros is a bit more complicated since his development
within the tale suggests both the *caritas* and *cupiditas* kinds of love,
but, whether the source is Greek or medieval, the point here is that
he represents unequivocally these two kinds of love. Novalis' figure for the imagination seems to be usurped from Wieland's exotic
Arabic figure, perhaps to make her more like "Fantasie" than an
Enlightenment version of imagination.[46] She is the nurse of Eros
and the child of the moon, but she is distinct from both poetry and
true wisdom.

The two troubling figural figures are Sophie and Arctur, both
of whom, according to Auerbach's formula, would be more likely
to suggest medieval (or perhaps romantic?) content and Christian
themes. Sophie has two antecedents in what for Novalis would
have been history: Sophie the patron of the legendary medieval
poet, Heinrich von Ofterdingen, and Sofie von Kühn his personal
Beatrice, the fiancee who died in her youth, who remains his
personal muse and apparently the vehicle for Novalis' mystical
experience by her graveside. Sophie is, we are told in "Klingsohr's
Märchen," "the everlasting priestess of the heart," a form of true
wisdom to be distinguished from the petrified reason of the scribe.
She is associated with a marvelous vessel which tests the truth or

eternal quality of the written word. She is further associated with an altar and at one point gives the kneeling Eros and Ginnistan benediction and water from her marvelous vessel to take on their journey through the dreamy world of the moon. Sophie is the consort of King Arctur, longing to be reunited with him in a return of the Golden Age. Death, time, the Fates, the evil of the scribe, and the amorous adventures of an Eros, distracted from his quest and purification process, impede this reunification.

For Novalis, the Golden Age is not a pagan period. In *Christianity or Europe,* he describes his vision of a medieval Golden Age: "Those were beautiful, glorious times, in which Europe was one Christian land, in which one Christendom occupied this humanly constituted continent. One great common interest united the remotest provinces of this broad spiritual kingdom."[47] Sophie thus expresses a Christian content in the *Märchen.* She is both the real Sofie of Novalis' religious awakening and the historical Sophie who was the patroness and protector of the poet Heinrich von Ofterdingen. But more, she is a figuration or incarnation of revelation.

King Arctur works in a very similar way. He is not a clear allegorical figure as the confusion of the critics regarding his meaning suggests. The association with the star Arcturus is insufficient in itself to allow us to make the nearly effortless one–to–one correspondence we have made with other characters in the tale. Arcturus' also having a strong association with the bear presents an additional impediment to relying on the reader to make an uncoached easy a = b equation. Novalis' usual clues for the allegorical equation are missing here. Arctur stands apart from the rest of the cast of "Klingsohr's *Märchen"* in the same way Sophie does. But reading Arctur as a conflation of King Arthur and the star Arcturus, as a *figura,* with more than one association and a clear association in history, leads to a far more coherent tale.

Viewing Arctur as King Arthur nicely resolves several problems in the *Märchen.* To see the frozen Northern realm as a kind of suspended animation, in which the spirit of the great king dwells waiting for his ultimate return to a Golden Age of eternal spring, not only generally fits into the Arthurian tradition, but also solves the problem of the realm in the story. It is much easier to conceive of Arthur having essentially been exiled from his former home with Sophie, than to see the eternally frozen realm of Arcturus as the original home of true wisdom. References in the tale to Arctur's conferring with the court seem less contrived. The presence of the old hero and the prominence of both the magic shield and the powerful sword, which serves to link the spirit of the king with the material world, below fall into place. The lily in Arctur's left hand associates him with the tears of Eve as she left Paradise, with Christianity, and with purity and virtue. Nor are the royal symbols of the crown, lion and eagle incongruous with the representation of the famous king.

King Arthur is much more than a great medieval king to be associated with a glorious Christian past and perhaps linked to King Friedrich. For this alone Novalis might have picked a Barbarossa or a Charlemagne. Arctur is married to Novalis' muse, to eternal wisdom, to Sophie. It is King Arthur who gives little Fable the instrument of her art, the lyre, and guides her on her quest to restore the Golden Age. Just as important, it is poetry, the heroic artist, which serves King Arthur, which recognizes the nature of the quest and battles the worst of the material world to free him from the prison of time and death, to reunite the king with his beloved consort, to wed his daughter, Peace, and the spirit of true love. It is poetry in King Arthur's service which restores the Golden Age.

Indiana University of Pennsylvania

NOTES

[1]Richard Kimpel, "German Arthurian Literature (Modern)," in *The Arthurian Encyclopedia*, ed. Norris Lacy (New York, 1986), 222. Hereafter cited as Kimpel.

[2]Richard Barber, *King Arthur: Hero and Legend,* 3rd rev. ed. (1961; Woodbridge, 1986), 171.

[3]See for example F. W. Stokoe's *German Influence in the English Romantic Period* or, as recently as 1965, Josef Körner's *Nibelungenfor schungen der deutschen Romantik* which defends throughout the notion that all German romantic studies of medieval literature descend from Herder's interest in origins and pre–Christian *Germanentum*. To stand the genetic fallacy on its head, Körner further assumes that any romantic translation of medieval literature was motivated by the interests of those nineteenth–century philologists whose origins he seeks to trace.

[4]The Hoffmann Athurian material, too long to include here, will be the subject of another article.

[5]Janet E. Goebel, "The *Frühromantik* as a Critical Imitation of the Late Medieval Romance," Diss. Nebraska U at Lincoln, 1986. See also Janet E. Goebel, "Medieval History and Medievalism: the Case for the Reconstructionists," in *Selected Papers on Medievalism*, 2 (Indiana, 1988). Although W. D. Robson–Scott (*The Literary Background of the Gothic Revival in Germany,* 1965) has argued that Wackenroder was anti–Gothic and that the early Jena Circle interest in the fifteenth century is not really "medieval," we must keep in mind that definite dates to distinguish the late medieval from the early renaissance were not yet fixed.

[6]Even Oskar Walzel's *German Romanticism* (1932) throws clarity on this point. The best discussion is to be found, however, in Gudrun S. Horton's "Die Entstehung des Mittelalterbildes in der deutsche Frühromantik, Wackenroder, Tieck, Novalis, und die Brüder Schlegel," Diss. U of Washington at Seattle, 1973.

[8]Gerhard Kozielek, *Mittelalterrezeption: zur Aufnahme altdeutscher in der Romantik* (Tübingen, 1977), 29.

[9]A. W. Schlegel, *Sämmtliche Werke*, 10.27. All translations from the German are my own except where otherwise indicated.

[10]Ludwig Tieck, "Brief an F. Fromann," in *Ludwig Tieck: Erinnerungen aus dem Leben des Dichters nach dessen mündlichen und schriftlichen Mitteilungen,* ed. R. Köpke (Darmstadt, 1970).

[11] See Kozielek, 26.

[12]Ludwig Tieck, "Vorrede zu *Minnelieder aus dem Schwäbischen Zeitalter: neubearbeitet und herausgegeben von Ludwig Tieck*" (Berlin, 1803; rpt. in *Mittelalterrezeption: zur Aufnahme altdeutscher Literatur in der Romantik,* ed. Gerhard Kozielek, 1977), 47.

[13]Tieck, 48.

[14]Kozielek, 23.

[15]See Goebel, *Frühromantik.* That this method of focusing primarily on the aesthetic qualities of medieval literature could result, despite charges of "poor scholarship," is apparent in A. W. Schlegel's 1803 suspicion that *Ossian* was not an authentic medieval work. See A. W. Schlegel's "Deutsche Ritter Mythologie" in *Vorlesungen über schöne Literatur und Kunst,* (Heilbronn, 1884).

[16]Heinrich Heine, "Die Romantische Schule" *Heines Sämtliche Werke,* ed. Manfred Windfuhr 8/1 (Düsseldorf, 1979), 131.

[17]Philippe Lacque-Labarthe and Jean-Luc Nancy, *The Literary Absolute: The Theory of Literature in German Romanticism,* trans. Philip Barnard and Cheryl Lester (1978; Albany, 1988).

[18]See Karl Otto Brogsitter, *Artusepik* (Stuttgart, 1965), 117.

[19]Kimpel, 224.

² ⁰Heinz Ritter, *Der Unbekannte Novalis: Friedrich von Hardenberg im Spiegel seiner Dichtung* (Göttingen, 1967), 219-20, cites Hiebel and Kluckhohn as holding this view of Goethe as Klingsohr, but maintains that Goethe cannot be the source of the figure given the antagonism which Novalis felt toward Goethe and his poetry at the time he was composing this work. Ritter, in his highly biographical mode of analysis, maintains that the figure must be the father of Novalis' second fiancée, Mr. Charpentier.

²¹*Novalis Schriften*, ed. Paul Kluckhohn and Richard Samuel, (Stuttgart, 1960), 4. 558.

²²See Friedrich Hiebel, *Novalis: German Poet — European Thinker — Christian Mystic* (Chapel Hill, 1953), 60.

²³Horton, 91-92.

²⁴Palmer Hilty, "Introduction" in Novalis' *Henry of Ofteridngen*, trans. Palmer Hilty (New York, 1964), 7-8.

²⁵Hiebel, 61.

²⁶Heibel, 59.

²⁷Hiebel, 60.

²⁸Hiebel, 61.

²⁹Marianne Thalmann, *The Romantic Fairy Tale: Seeds of Surrealism*, trans. Mary Corcoran (Ann Arbor, 1964), 25-6.

³⁰Bruce Haywood, *Novalis: The Veil of Imagery* (S'-Gravenhage, 1959), 91.

³¹F. J. Obenauer *Hölderin-Novalis* (Jena, 1925), 252, quoted in Haywood, 114.

³²Haywood, 81.

³³Haywood, 115-16.

³⁴Ritter, 208.

³⁵Gildas, *De Excidio*, ed. and trans. Hugh Williams (1899), 72-3.

[36]Richard Barber, *The Figure of Arthur* (London, 1972), 50. Referring to Alan Orr Anderson and Marjorie Anderson in *Zeitschrift für Celtische Philologie,* 1928, 405-6.

[37]Geoffrey Ashe, "Gildas" in the *Arthurian Encyclopedia*, ed. Norris Lacy, (New York, 1986), 234.

[38]Ashe, 235.

[39]Barber, *Hero and Legend*, 23. See Ailred of Rievaulx, *The Mirror of Charity,* trans. Geoffrey Webb and Adrian Walker (London, 1962).

[40]Barber, *Hero and Legend*, 13.

[41]Haywood, 112.

[42]Hiebel, 59.

[43]Heine, 131.

[44]Erich Auerbach, *Literary Language and Its Public in Late Latin Antiquity and in the Middle Ages*, trans. Ralph Manheim, (New York, 1965), 53-4.

[45]Auerbach, 57.

[46]Fantasie in the sense of *Imaginatif, vis imaginativa,* or *vis phantastica* in the neoplatonic tradition of ancient rhetoric in which Maimonides, Albertus Magnus, Langland, or Dante would have used it: An internal sense which creates pictures or images normally by combining them without any stimulation from the external senses and having a higher rather than a lower role as transmitter of knowledge. Imagination in the sense of a vehicle of divine assurance and truth, as related to prophecy and certainly as the source of dreams. See Bloomfield's *Piers*, 170-74.

[47]Novalis, *Die Christenheit oder Europa* in *Novalis Schriften,* 3. 507.

Sir Frederic Madden
and Arthurian Scholarship

Gretchen P. Ackerman

It is fashionable to chronicle the virtues of the Victorian age, virtues relating to high energy fructifying into solid achievement in such diverse fields as empire–building and three–volume novels, consistent extension of the franchise, technological revolutions in transportation and manufacturing. Among these achievements we should remember one other especially close to our own concerns, the emergence of modern scholarship in the field of Old and Middle English studies, scholarship from which we still reap benefits. This scholarship consists of the discovery, re–discovery, and dissemination of texts from the period 700–1500. Since the time of Walter Scott until the time of Walter Skeat, we can see steady progress in the fixing of canons — Chaucer did not write "The Flower and the Leaf" — and the editing of texts, with glossaries that ultimately provided materials for Old and Middle English dictionaries. One of the earlier contributors to this forward–looking movement was the Reverend Sharon Turner, whose *History of the Anglo–Saxons* attempted among other things to give a chronological account of King Arthur's life. A young man from Portsmouth newly established in London read Turner's recently published book in 1824, and found that "the attempt to trace King Arthur's life with precision" was somehow unconvincing.[1] This was Frederick Madden (1801–1873), destined to become the leading Arthurian scholar of his age.

Madden is the true godfather of the great poem in B. L. MS Cotton Nero A.x, having christened it *Sir Gawain and the Green Knight*, and making it the central showpiece in his *Gawayne* anthology of 1839. At least equally impressive is his edition of Layamon's *Brut*, published in 1847 after nearly two decades of exhausting textual labor. Madden's work on the *Brut* was undertaken in the evenings, after he had completed his routine as an officer of the British Museum. We should also remember his fine article on *Sir Tristrem* (1833), which acknowledges Sir Walter Scott's pioneer work on this poem and, at the same time, calls for a more rigorous scholarly method which would help to illuminate this curious northern contribution to the Tristan legend.[2]

Volume, variety, and above all quality might be three words which describe Madden's achievement as a medievalist, and which explain the admiration he still commands today. Renewed interest in his personal journals, covering his daily activities over a period of more than fifty years, gives him special status as a privileged, London–based observer of the mid–Victorian scene. Living in the midst of London's artistic and intellectual life, Madden encountered many of the new movements of the age; he usually responded with an indignant Toryism which was a state of mind rather than a fixed political creed. For example, he was blind to the beauties of Tennyson's poetry, not excluding the *Idylls*, going so far as to say that the poet's admirers were victims of delusion. He was even more negative about pre–Raphaelite "horrors" in painting, which he viewed at the time of their first exhibitions. We can safely say that the neo–Gothic revival in mid–nineteenth century England did not elicit from him even minimal sympathy, let alone a sensed identity of interest.[3]

In this essay we will look chiefly at Madden the editor, whom we honor for effecting the recovery of two great parts of the Arthurian corpus, *Sir Gawain and the Green Knight* (hereafter *GGK*) and the *Brut*. We should concede at the outset that he never tries to provide the sophisticated esthetic criticism which is now commonplace in discussions of *GGK*. What is more, the term "Arthurian" to describe his own special field of scholarly endeavor was apparently not used in his time.[4] If, however, we look ahead from the generation of Skeat and Sweet which followed Madden's to the late 1890's and the early work of Jessie Weston, Arthurianism is suddenly with us in recognizable form. The reinforcement of myth and folklore, provided by the burgeoning science of anthropology, created approaches to the Arthurian legend demonstrated in our own century by Roger Loomis and his followers. Some of Madden's limitations are matter of chronology, some of temperament. There is one ingredient of scholarship, however, which would have made him enviable in any age, and that is serendipitous luck, which enabled him to discover on the shelves of the Bodleian library the seemingly lost romance of *Havelok the Dane*, an edition of which became his first major publication. An even greater event was his discovery of a hitherto unrecognized poem in MS Cotton Nero A.x, which was to become the focal point for his *Gawayne* anthology.

The pattern of his career would be a model for a young scholar even today. During the 1820's, he familiarized himself with the manuscripts of the Cotton collection and improved his command of classical and vernacular languages. He paid particular attention to Cotton Caligula A.ii, developing an affection for Wace and Layamon which would bear later fruit. As the decade of the 1820's closed, he won his position as Assistant Keeper of Manuscripts in the British Museum and saw the publication of his *Havelock* (1828). As early as 1825, Henry Petrie, his superior officer at the Museum, encouraged him to begin work on Layamon with a view to editing the *Brut*. As we have seen, this project would take nearly twenty years to complete.

Madden's personal life offered complications in the year 1830, when he lost his young wife and newborn son, losses he did not take lightly. Work was his panacea, as he undertook to edit the romance of *William and the Werewolf*, at the request of Lord Cawdor, and at the same time accepted the commission of editing the *Brut* when it was offered to him by the Society of Antiquaries.

At a time of personal tragedy and professional fulfillment, Madden had already found his special claim to fame. Thanks to the Diary entry for 9 July, 1829, we know that this was the day when he looked carefully at Cotton Nero A.x and discovered "The very curious romance of Gawayn and the Green Knight."[5] As a diligent reader of Warton's *History of English Poetry,* which had been edited by Richard Price in 1824, Madden realized that Price, too, had come upon this work, attributing it to Huchown of the Awle Ryle and giving it an approximate date in the mid–thirteenth century. Always a man of scrupulous honor where scholarship was concerned, Madden wrote to Price, who was already suffering from the dropsy which was to cause his death in 1833 and no longer interested in editorial labors of the sort that his poem would demand. The *Gawayne* anthology of 1839 pays appropriate tribute to Price as the first reader of record to note the existence of *GGK*.[6]

Price and Madden had been linked in the past by their common interest in the romance of *Sir Tristrem*, edited by Sir Walter Scott as early as 1804. As men of a younger generation, they had more austere standards of scholarship than Sir Walter, and read his edition with a mixture of admiration for his pioneering zeal and regret that dictionaries and glossaries were not available to make the apparatus attached to the poem more valuable. With *GGK* as a new motif in his life, Madden remembered Scott as someone most assuredly interested in early northern poetry, one who might well help with publication plans. Scott responded not only with a positive letter, but with a visit to the British Museum in 1831, a visit which Madden records in his diary with an abundance of memorable detail:

> ...it is impossible to convey by the pencil, an idea of the uncouthness of his appearance and figure. Hair almost white, large gray unexpressive eyes — red–sandy complexion and straggling whiskers — slow and thick manner of speaking — and broad Scotch accent — his figure equally gauche — square built — limping very much, so as to elevate the right shoulder considerably above the left, and using for support an immense, thick stick; draped in checkered black and white trousers, and dark square cut coat. Such is the greatest literary man of the age! (Diary, 6 October, 1831)

This informal portrait of Scott would be valuable under any circumstances, but especially when we remember that it depicts him in the last year of his life.

Even in age and illness, Scott took a proprietary interest in the "new" Gawain poem, which Madden and he both regarded as "Scotch."[7] Scott suggested that the poem in MS Cotton Nero A.x should be printed with two other northern Gawain poems, *The Awntyrs of Arthure* and *Golagros and Gawane*. It was Madden himself who decided to improve on Scott's suggestion by including all the Gawain poems known to him as well.

A modern reader may wonder why, with a prize like *GGK* in one's grasp, an editor would decide to range far afield to find other, inferior poems with the same hero. The answer lies in a new concept of editorial responsibility, of which Madden was the supreme exemplar. He was determined to improve on the earlier generation of medieval scholars, who were content with "Selections," "Specimens," and "Remains." These were men like Bishop Percy, the younger Thomas Warton, George Ellis, David Laing, H. H. Weber, even Walter Scott himself. Madden was to offer complete manuscript transcriptions of eleven Gawain poems, enriched by commentaries, notes, and glossaries which would prove invaluable to later scholars. What is more, he sensed that he was dealing with a coherent body of material, since none of the English Gawain poems shows any obvious or even plausible indebtedness to a French original.

Robert W. Ackerman has told the story of each text as Madden eventually secured it for his great *Gawayne* book.[8] Persistence, prescience, and prophetic powers were the qualities Madden had to call upon, first of all in his quest for the Percy Folio MS, which in 1831 was the property of Mrs. Samuel Isted of Ecton Hall, Northamptonshire, the late Bishop's elder daughter. Madden travelled by coach to Ecton Hall and was greeted cordially but with some reserve. Mrs. Isted reminded him that the manuscript was the special possession of the Percy family, and its contents would not be automatically available even to selfless scholars.

When Madden expressed interest in the ballad of the "The Grene Knight," she became more cooperative, offering him her father's transcript of that poem and allowing him to collate the Percy version with the manuscript itself.

Five years later, when in need of the remaining Gawain poems in the Folio, Madden received colder treatment from the new heir, Ambrose Isted. He would be permitted to consult the manuscript *in situ*, but only if accompanied by an agent appointed by the family. By this time Madden was Assistant Keeper of Manuscripts at the British Museum and could not accept these humiliating terms. As it happened, the agent designated by the Isteds was a colleague of Madden's in the Society of Antiquaries, George Baker. Baker was an able copyist, who rendered excellent versions of "The Turke and Gowin," The Carle of Carlile," and "King Arthur and King Cornwall." The happy few who have read the Madden Diary *in toto* will know that Bishop Percy's descendants continued to play a role in Madden's life that was vexatious rather than benevolent. The story of the Percy Folio and its fortunes in the nineteenth century is worth telling by someone who finds the story of Victorian scholarship a stirring one.[9]

An obstacle of a different kind separated Madden from another text, "The Weddynge of Sir Gawen and Dame Ragnell," incorrectly identified in Warton's *History of English Poetry* as a Tanner manuscript (455 Bibl. Bodl.). Exercising that special, radar–like gift which had brought the *Havelok* romance into his hands over ten years earlier, Madden discovered the "Weddynge" poem in another manuscript, Rawlinson C. 86, barely in time to include it in his anthology, where it appeared without the scholarly apparatus provided for the other poems.[10]

Although a modern reader senses the lack of a critical synthesis in the introduction to *GGK*, Madden does occasionally reveal his awareness of the poem's merit. For example, he calls the author a man of superior education, birth, and "poetical talent" (301–02). Inevitably Madden discerns the two major motifs of the beheading and the temptation; he perceives that "the author may have mingled together narratives for the purpose of rendering his own more attractive" (*Gawayne*, 307). His notes are particularly rich and helpful when he comments on the hunting scenes; here he wonders if the romance of *Sir Tristrem* was a source, "but whether this be so or not, the present poem has greatly the superiority, both in the extent of the details and the more graphic character given them" (*Gawayne*, 321).

Madden's contemporaries were most immediately appreciative of his Glossary, which raised the standards of all subsequent editors of medieval texts, in an age when even so basic an aid as the *Oxford English Dictionary* lay far in the future. John Robson's *Three Metrical Romances* ("The Anters of Arther," "Sir Amadace," "The Avowynge of King Arther") were published by the Camden Society in 1842. In his Introduction Robson says:

> If the publication has any value, it is in great measure owing to his [Madden's] suggestions, and the Glossary is, in its most important parts, a literal copy of his most excellent one to *Sir Gawayne*.[11]

Madden's vision of the Arthurian corpus was never narrowly limited to philological matters, whatever his expertise in that field. His first love affair with the Arthurian legend came from his youthful readings in MS Cotton Caligula A.ix, where he discovered Layamon's *Brut*. He always admired Layamon for both substance and style: "a glorious old fellow," he said more than once.[12] Again, his special genius for discovering and rediscovering manuscripts came into play. Early in the course of a long career, in which the restoration of damaged Cottonian manuscripts was a major motif, he helped unearth and restore leaves from Cotton Otho C. xiii, which offered a later text of Layamon.[13] The three–volume *Brut*, published by the Society of Antiquaries in 1847, consisted of the text — over 30,000 half–lines — with literal translation, notes, and glossary. From the moment of its appearance it was hailed as a masterpiece of nineteenth–century scholarship, even to our own day, when G. L. Brooke and R. F. Leslie brought out their own edition of Layamon in 1961. Their preface begins with a tribute to Madden:

> The footnotes...include a collation with Madden's text, since the manuscript is often difficult to read and Madden is in general so accurate that his readings deserve to be recorded.[14]

Although published eight years after the *Gawayne* anthology, the *Brut* was a project that Madden worked on jointly along with *GGK*. Even when the *Gawayne* had seen publication, Madden could say in 1843, "Every week day, to say nothing of Sundays, am I occupied at my desk from ten to twelve hours" (Diary, 31 December, 1843). Monumental as a work of scholarship, the *Brut* also represents a high point in the Victorian printer's art. Physically, the three volumes are more attractive than the *Gawayne* anthology, possibly because of the more artful use of printed marginalia and the variety of type fonts employed.

Ten years before the publication of the *Brut*, Madden's personal life had taken a happy turn. The year of Victoria's accession — 1837 — also saw Madden's elevation to the post of Keeper of Manuscripts, which, with his five–year–old knighthood, made a second marriage possible. This marriage was successful from the first, and produced four children, three boys and a girl. Madden was not fanciful enough to give his children Arthurian names, though his youngest son, born in 1850, received the second name of Wycliffe, to commemorate the publication of the Wycliffite Bible in that year. Madden had found the long labors on the collating of Biblical texts unusually exhausting, and far less congenial than the comparable work he had done on the *Gawayne* and Layamon.[15]

During his married life Madden made three trips to the Continent with his wife. On the second of these, in 1857, he examined a manuscript of Geoffrey of Monmouth's *Historia Regum Anglorum* at its home in the public library at Berne, Switzerland. Since Madden's vision of the Arthurian corpus quite properly recognized Geoffrey's work as the great treasure house drawn on by Wace, Layamon, and ultimately the *Gawain*–poet, it is enlightening to see what he says and how he works when writing a modest scholarly article for the *Archæological Journal*.[16] The Berne text is remarkable, he says, because of its altered dedication; no longer is the dedicatee Robert, Earl of Gloucester, "natural son of Henry I" (299), but King Stephen himself, who ultimately became an active enemy to Robert. Since Geoffrey was genuinely indebted to the Earl of Gloucester, who had encouraged the composition of the *Historia*, Geoffrey provides a "supplementary dedication" to Robert which the Berne text reveals. Madden is fascinated by this matter of the double dedication, and argues with abundant evidence for the dating of Geoffrey's *Historia*, "...which must have been commenced before the death of Henry I and completed before the commencement of 1136 and the end of 1138" (310). After 1136, Earl Robert responded to Stephen's hostile actions towards him by siding with Matilda's party, so that this year seems to Madden to belong to the Berne manuscript. Always the paleographer, Madden confesses to having examined many copies of Geoffrey's *Historia* in England, but none as early as this Swiss specimen. He is typically knowledgeable in commenting on the two twelfth–century hands in which the work is written.

His opening comments show an unusually expansive Madden as he describes Geoffrey's seminal power in generating the Arthurian corpus:

The fame of the work itself as the fountain–head of legendary British history and the source of —

what resounds
In fable or romance of Uther's son,
Begirt with British and Armoric knights —

as well as its being the original to which we are indebted for the writings of Wace, Layamon, Robert of Gloucester (the rhyming historian), Robert of Brunne, and many more, — not to mention its influence on the historical

literature of England up to the seventeenth century,—
would combine, not without reason, to claim for it an
unusual degree of interest (299–300).

Here Madden jauntily quotes from Book I of *Paradise Lost*, in a
passage which more clearly than any other I know of from his pen,
indicates his awareness of the Arthurian heritage as he saw it. The
Gawain–poet receives no special mention here, nor does Malory,
whom he had studied well in both the Wynkyn de Worde version
of 1498 and the Robert Southey edition of 1817, which he quoted
frequently in the preface to his 1839 anthology. In that same
preface Madden had pointed out a possible later Gawain in
Spenser's Sir Calidore.[17] In this article of 1858, he suggests a
cutoff point for the Arthurian legend itself in the seventeenth
century. He wrote this article one year before the publication of
the first four Tennysonian *Idylls*. Given his expressed distaste for
the Laureate's poetry, he would not have regarded this event as a
new lease on life for the Arthurian epic.[18]

If Madden could know of the scholarship and criticism inspired by *GGK* which has come into being during the one hundred
and five years since his death, he would probably feel that the
world of Swift's Laputan Academy had become a reality.[19] And yet
Madden would have rejoiced in the discovery of new Celtic sources for the poem, just as he would have enjoyed speculations about
the green man in English folklore.[20] Within a normal lifespan, he
lived to help true scholarship emerge to supplant the world of the
gentleman–antiquary into which he had been born, and for which
he had had a youthful affinity. Just as antiquarianism became
scholarship within his lifetime, partially as a result of his own
contributions, so did folklore become anthropology. It may be the
anthropological dimension which separates modern Arthurians
from great Victorian pioneers like Madden. One might shape an
argument, asserting that Victorian England as a whole was waiting
for that special revelation which only *The Golden Bough* could
bestow. Significantly enough, 1890 was the year in which that work
was first published, thereby enriching literary criticism with sun

gods and rain dances, wasteland and fertility symbols. If the historical Arthur did indeed shrink to a Roman or a Celtic resistance leader, a Hereward the Wake in his own historical context, the mythological Arthur waxed strong under the power of a new dispensation. Madden's death date — 1873 — precluded any awareness of this coming change. In that year, however, the New Shakespeare Society was founded, having been preceded by the Ballad Society in 1869, the Chaucer Society, established by Furnivall in 1868, and the Early English Text Society (1863), to which Madden paid dues as a charter member. We should remember, too, that Hales and Furnivall published their four–volume edition of the Percy Folio Manuscript in 1867–68. Can we not say that these scholarly activities were latter–day outgrowths from the highly productive decade of the 1830s, which had brought to birth such major works as John M. Kemble's *Beowulf* (1833–37), the Bosworth–Toller *Anglo–Saxon Dictionary* (1838), and Madden's *Gawayne* anthology of 1839, which introduced *GGK* to a world of readers who have never allowed it to be forgotten?

Walpole, New Hampshire

NOTES

[1] Frederic Madden, Diary, 43 vols., Bodleian MSS English history, c. 140-82. 31 March 1824. Subsequent reference to Diary will cite dates in text.

[2] F[rederic] M[adden], [Remarks on the Glossary to Sir Walter Scott's *Sir Tristrem*], *Gentleman's Magazine*, new series 103 (October 1833), 307-12.

[3] Robert W. Ackerman and Gretchen P. Ackerman, *Sir Frederic Madden: A Biographical Sketch and Bibliography* (New York, 1979), 23, 34.

[4]*A Supplement to the Oxford English Dictionary* (Oxford, 1972), 128. The first reference, to the "Arthurian cycle," occurs in 1869, just four years before Madden's death.

[5]Robert W. Ackerman, "Madden's Gawain Anthology," *Medieval Studies in Honor of Lillian Herlands Hornstein*, ed. Jess B. Bessinger, Jr. and Robert R. Raymo (New York, 1976), 6.

[6]Sir Frederic Madden, K. H., *Syr Gawayne, A Collection of Ancient Romance–Poems, by Scotish [sic]and English Authors, Relating to that Celebrated Knight of the Round Table* (London, 1839), 300.

[7]Ackerman, "Madden's Gawain Anthology," 8.

[8]See Note 5.

[9]Ackerman, "Madden's Gawain Anthology," 13-14.

[10]Ackerman, "Madden's Gawain Anthology," 17, Note 23.

[11]John Robson, *Three Early English Metrical Romances, with an Introduction and Glossary* (London, 1842), Introduction, xxxvi.

[12]Ackerman, "Madden's Gawain Anthology," 7.

[13]Ackerman and Ackerman, *Sir Frederic Madden,* 23.

[14]G. L. Brook and R. F. Leslie, *Layamon's Brut,* 1, *EETS* 250 (London, 1961), x.

[15]Ackerman and Ackerman, *Sir Frederic Madden,* 19.

[16][Frederic] Madden, "The *Historia Britonum* of Geoffrey of Monmouth," *The Archaeological Journal* 15 (1858), 299-312.

[17]Sir Frederic Madden, ed., *Syr Gawayne*, Introduction, xli.

[18]Ackerman and Ackerman, *Sir Frederic Madden,* 34.

[19]For a still timely summary of critical approaches to the poem, see Morton W. Bloomfield, "*Sir Gawain and the Green Knight*: An Appraisal," *PMLA* 76 (1961), 7-19.

[20]For a work of scholarship which Madden would have comprehended and admired, see G. L. Kittredge, *A Study of Sir Gawain and the Green Knight* (Cambridge, 1916.)

Tennyson's Urban Arthurians: Victorian Audiences and the "City Built to Music"

Linda K. Hughes

Tennyson's *Idylls of the King* (1859-1885) inspires two principal responses among late twentieth-century commentators. Insofar as it is praised, the poem is often valued for its lambent, diaphanous, self-referring language that embodies a skeptical, even nihilistic meditation on civilization and its constructs.[1] Insofar as the poem is disparaged, it is faulted for pallid characterization, priggish didacticism, and the egregious expression of imperialism by Victoria's poet laureate. Victorian readers might have understood the latter; a few in Tennyson's time also objected to didacticism or weak dramatic skills, and many understood the connection between Tennyson's poem and England's prestige. But if some would have recognized twentieth-century blame of the *Idylls*, most would have been confounded by the praise.

Victorians who entered into the poem might be said to have inhabited a different Camelot from that praised by twentieth-century audiences, to whom the city is more notable (like the Cheshire Cat) for disappearing than enduring. Victorian reviews of the poem indicate that most of Tennyson's first readers approached Camelot as a city filled with lively human beings and a king who inspired hope.[2] The contrast between Victorian and twentieth–century response suggests not merely that each age tends to interpret a literary work through its own preoccupations, but that Tennyson's first audiences responded to cues no longer recognizable to many readers.

One of these cues was a very different publishing format from that generally encountered in the late twentieth century. The Victorian reading situation and predominant Victorian interpretations of the *Idylls* are, I think, connected phenomena. In "Gareth and Lynette," before Merlin announces to Gareth and his

companions that Camelot is a "city . . . built / To music, therefore
never built at all, / And therefore built for ever," the poem describes how the city is perceived by the three men who approach
it:

> At times the summit of the high city flashed;
> At times the spires and turrets half-way down
> Pricked through the mist; at times the great gate shone
> Only, that opened on the field below:
> Anon, the whole fair city had disappeared.
> (189-93)[3]

The same pattern might be said to have characterized Victorian
glimpses of Camelot. Tennyson's original audiences did not view a
complete, sequential poem in a single volume. Instead they
encountered the poem a part at a time over some four decades,
even viewing idylls out of the order of the completed poem's
chronology. What many considered the "summit" of the *Idylls*,
"Morte d'Arthur," appeared in Tennyson's 1842 volume of *Poems*
and later formed the core of "The Passing of Arthur" in 1869. An
Arthurian work pitched at a less exalted, more earthly tone
("spires and turrets half–way down") appeared in 1859, when
Tennyson first gave the name *Idylls of the King* to a set of four
poems named after as many women: "Enid," "Vivien," "Elaine,"
"Guinevere." Ten years later (in a volume dated 1870 but issued in
December 1869) he published "The Coming of Arthur," "The
Holy Grail," "Pelleas and Ettarre," and "The Passing of Arthur."
In 1871 a single, detached idyll, "The Last Tournament," "shone /
Only" in the December issue of *Contemporary Review*; it was then
reprinted in 1872 alongside the newly–published "Gareth and
Lynette." Finally, in 1885, "Balin and Balan" appeared in *Tiresias
and Other Poems*.

   Thus, from 1842 to 1885 Victorian readers caught only
glimpses of the completed poem we now know, and in between
publication dates "the whole fair city . . . disappeared." But if

Camelot disappeared at intervals, it also returned in subsequent installments;[4] rather than tracing a path of irrevocable decline and destruction, the Victorian *Idylls* first presented Camelot at an end (in "Morte d'Arthur"), then later showed the city in its days of freshness and glory (first in "Enid," then in "The Coming of Arthur," then in "Gareth and Lynette") as well as in its subsequent decline.

Fully to understand Victorian perspectives on the *Idylls*, then, we need to restore the context in which Tennyson's audience first encountered the poem. Especially from 1842 to 1869, parts–issuance helped insure the popularity of the *Idylls* by establishing the humanity of the characters and accessible themes. In this light, Victorians' ability to inhabit a more congenial Camelot than is true for twentieth–century readers is less a naive exercise in fantasy than a plausible outcome of Tennyson's artistic design and his poem's publication schedule.

Had Tennyson chosen to publish his "Morte d'Arthur" as a free–standing poem in 1842, it might have been seen as "The Lady of Shalott," "Sir Galahad," or "Sir Lancelot and Queen Guinevere" were, as related Arthurian works but each separate, single, gesturing toward no larger whole. After completing the "Morte," however, Tennyson wrote "The Epic," which framed "Morte d'Arthur" in the 1842 *Poems*. This frame identified the inset poem as the eleventh (and lone surviving) book of an epic written, then burned by the poet Everard Hall. "The Epic" suggests not only the themes embedded in the "Morte" (the passing of civilizations, the decay of faith, the search for new leaders to replace the fallen) but also a model of response for readers. Initially, in the first section of "The Epic," Arthur is identified with a defunct tradition by Hall; as Arthur has been nearly erased by time, so his story has been all but burnt by the poet. The "Morte" itself presents Arthur as a grand but dying king, still a great leader but one passing from view. The concluding section of "The Epic," however, reverses this movement toward erasure and enacts Arthur's revival and return as the unnamed narrator internalizes the

story he has heard, and dreams of Arthur "come again" as "a
modern gentleman / Of stateliest port" (296, 294-95). Moreover,
"The Epic" models a shift of Arthur from the margins of time and
place to the center of modern civilization. In the first part of "The
Epic" the story of Arthur is read aloud in a remote, rural corner
of England[5] to an audience of three; in the concluding lines Arthur
advances and is made known to a modern city: "To me, methought,
who waited with a crowd, / There came a bark that, blowing forward, bore / King Arthur" (292-94).

Tennyson had clearly planted the suggestion in readers' minds
that the rest of his epic would be forthcoming, and that Arthur's
city and the reader's own could merge. John Sterling, however,
termed "Morte d'Arthur" remote and inhuman in a review of the
1842 volume. As Tennyson told William Allingham in 1867, he
"was prevented from doing his Arthur Epic, in twelve books, by
John Sterling's Review of 'Morte d'Arthur' in the *Quarterly*."[6] But
if Tennyson desisted from his Arthuriad, he continued to reissue
his collection of poems (ten editions between 1842 and 1860),
reaching an ever–wider audience with "Morte d'Arthur" and
arousing hopes that he would write the entire epic of which the
"Morte" was a penultimate part. Thus, in 1859, when the first four
Idylls of the King appeared, the October 1859 *Westminster Review*
observed that the new volume "is regarded by most readers as in
part the fulfillment of a much older promise. . . . The manner in
which ["Morte d'Arthur"] was given forth, as a specimen or fore-
taste of a longer poem, seemed to indicate the poet's intention, as
it gave a sufficient proof of his capacity, to illustrate and recall
more of the great features of the legend to which it belonged"
(503-04). The 1842 "Morte," then, aroused hope for a return of the
subject and planted the suggestion that Camelot and the modern
city could merge.

When the 1859 volume finally appeared seventeen years after
the "Morte," the four idylls were especially suited to evoke a
popular response. Much as he had done with the pastoral elegy in
In Memoriam, Tennyson likewise took a grand form of the past—

the epic — and domesticated it in *Idylls of the King*. The *Idylls* of the King did not focus on wars, jousts, or a grand hero's lonely quests. Rather, these four poems developed love stories among eight central characters. The love stories were bound up with the fate of the kingdom, of course; what set Tennyson apart from his predecessors was his approaching the story of the kingdom through individual human beings and their relationships, rather than presenting lovers as a subsidiary interest whose fate was shaped by issues of war, governance, or the chivalric code. Tennyson's approach was both pluralistic and domestic, centering on individuals and localized narratives more than on issues of national identity and fate. One thinks in contrast of the first book of Malory's *Le Morte Darthur*. True, the instigating plot motive in Malory is Uther's sexual obsession with Igrayne (though Malory quickly shifts his focus to battles between the forces of Uther and the Duke of Cornwall). Malory also presents the actual consummation of Uther's lust and Igrayne's perplexity after learning of the duke's death at the time she had thought herself embracing her husband. But thereafter attention shifts to the series of conflicts surrounding Arthur's succession and crowning. The marriage of Arthur and Guinevere merits only two sentences in this first book, a minor digression amidst a larger focus on war.

Scholars such as Victor Kiernan[7] have emphasized the *Idylls*' link to empire and imperialism, but restoring the poem to its place in literary history, especially in its contrast with Malory, reveals a kind of democratic ethos underlying the poem. That is, many of the democratizing forces associated with the increasing prominence of cities and the middle class are also evident in the 1859 volume. Domestic details and plots, for example, would have enforced the implicit connections between middle–class readers and the characters of whom they read. In this respect Tennyson tapped elements that made the domestic novel so important in the 1840s. His characters throughout display responses that might have been seen in middle–class drawing rooms — or in novelists' portrayals of them. Enid worries about proper attire for presentation at court,

and both she and her mother yearn after the finery stolen by the
Sparrow Hawk. Gawain, the urbane, sophisticated knight, attempts to overawe what he thinks a raw country girl when he visits
Astolat: "he set himself to play upon [Elaine] / With sallying wit,
free flashes from a height / Above her, graces of the court" (LE
642-44). As the October 1859 *Bentley's Quarterly Review* asserted,
"take what he will, we may surely trust [Tennyson] to enliven it
with touches of human feeling, life, and pathos; he will certainly
bring it somehow or other within the compass of our sympathies.
He will bring his subject to *us*, not require us to go back through
all the ages to a world of legend . . ." (162). And as an instance of
this practice the reviewer added, "Those whose expectations of
this work were formed on the solemn glories of [Bulwer Lytton's]
conventional 'King Arthur,' have probably been surprised to find
how much of the interest of the first tale rests on 'a faded silk'
gown . . ." (177).

If Tennyson incorporated domestic sentiment, however, he
also tapped the forces of what Debra Mancoff terms "ethical medievalism." As she explains in the second chapter of *The Arthurian
Revival in Victorian Art* (New York: Garland, 1990), this phase of
the Arthurian revival led to the conception of legendary characters
as types whose exemplary behavior could be emulated in everyday
life. Insofar as the domesticity infusing the 1859 *Idylls* made the
characters more human and accessible, less grand and remote, the
effect was indeed to make of Arthur a "modern gentleman of
stateliest port" whose ethical imperatives to "speak no slander, no,
nor listen to it" or "To lead sweet lives in purest chastity" (G 469,
471) could be imitated by ordinary urban citizens of the mid–
nineteenth century.

The democratic ethos of the 1859 poems is even clearer in the
attention given to women. Though Tennyson also takes care to
delineate the traits of proper manhood, his attention to women is
the more original contribution to Arthurian literature. Guinevere
and Morgan le Fay are, of course, essential characters in Malory,
but, as women, exist at the margins of Malory's fictive world.

Tennyson takes what is marginal in Malory and moves it to the center of the 1859 poems, a strategy that at once underscores the increasing domestication and democratizing of his Arthuriad.[8] Each of the 1859 idylls thus opens by mentioning a female character and, in three of the four, her relation to a male character. The first four lines of "Enid" emphasize her married state, the first five lines of "Vivien" her sexual posture and bent toward manipulation ("At Merlin's feet the wily Vivien lay"). Elaine is established at the outset as a fair, lovely maiden who guards Lancelot's shield, an anticipation of her later request to serve as Lancelot's squire (LE 932-34). Queen Guinevere alone is introduced without mention of a male character, since her essential plight in this idyll is her severance from Arthur: "Queen Guinevere had fled the court, and sat / There in the holy house at Almesbury / Weeping, none with her save a little maid, / A novice" (G 1-4).

As the 16 July 1859 *Examiner* concluded of women's role in the *Idylls*, "In each of them King Arthur's knights are the adventurers, in each the King incidentally appears, as an image of pure manhood; each is inscribed with a woman's name and has a woman's heart for centre of its action" (452). Four months later the importance of woman was still being stressed in *Blackwood's Edinburgh Magazine*: "Arthur, Lancelot, and Merlin — the king, the warrior, and the sage of the poem — are represented to us, not so much in council or in action as in their dealings with, and in the effect they produce on, Guinevere, Elaine, and Vivien" (610). In the late twentieth century Tennyson's women seem most notable for conforming to egregious stereotypes, and certainly the docile Enid is a disappointing sequel to William Morris's 1858 "Defence of Guenevere." Yet within the Victorian framework Tennyson's calling his volume *Idylls of the King*, then naming each idyll after an individual woman, signalled that the idea of a "kingdom" could no longer be limited to male leaders. His four idylls insist that women are essential in the workings of the realm, that women must be inscribed in the idea of Camelot. Hence the effect of the 1859 *Idylls* was to open up, to democratize, Arthur's city.[9]

Even the form adopted by Tennyson conduced to a less pretentious and grand, more modest and democratic, framework for his Arthuriad. Unlike Bulwer Lytton in his 1848-49 epic, *King Arthur*, Tennyson abjured supernatural machinery, catalogues, overt celebration of England's manifest destiny, or a complete, coherent narrative which attempted to control interconnections among parts and subordinate all to a single, dominant point of view. Some readers were disappointed by this choice of form. Invoking the general expectation of a completed epos after "The Epic" and "Morte d'Arthur" appeared in 1842, the 16 July 1859 *Critic* commented, "This expectation . . . is destined to a still further postponement, for the volume now before us contains only four fragments of the great Arthur Epic; longer and more complicated works than 'Morte d'Arthur' it is true, yet fragments indubitably" (52). Many reviewers, whether praising or censuring Tennyson's choice of form, compared the four idylls to cabinet pictures — small, intimate views. If the term "idyll" harked back to the classical epyllion, it also suggested the vignette associated with the domestic world of Mary Russell Mitford, from whose *Our Village* Tennyson had drawn for "The Miller's Daughter" of 1842. The form of the *Idylls*, then, was deliberately less grand than Bulwer Lytton's. It was also a form which depended on readers to relate the *Idylls* to each other. Indeed, Tennyson omitted to provide so much as a preface to these poems, even though, as Kathleen Tillotson has pointed out, Arthurian legend was not yet common knowledge in 1859.[10] The same directness that led Tennyson to publish in simple green covers and open immediately with the first line of "Enid" is also manifest in his choice of form. In all these ways Tennyson brought Arthurian materials to a large reading public rather than insisting on an elite literary model accessible only to the educated few, and he also affirmed the active role of individual readers among his urban Arthurians.

Tennyson's artistic choices helped determine not only his audience's response to his poem in 1859 but also the reception of later parts. The most frequent reaction to the 1859 *Idylls* was praise for the vividness and humanity of Tennyson's character-ization. The reviews published on 16 July 1859 in the *Athenaeum* and *Saturday Review* set the tone of later comments. Of Tennyson's earlier poems, even "Morte d'Arthur," the *Athenaeum* argued, "Mr. Tennyson hitherto has not dealt with the springs of human action, or displayed character analytically or dramatically" (73). But in the *Idylls*

> the human figures are still the chief attraction. The scen-ery, gorgeous or gloomy, as it may be, is glanced at, in-deed, with admiration; but we turn from it to gaze upon the human figures who move therein, — following the story of their passions, their glorious errors, their sublime vir-tues — becoming sensible of active partizanship, as we are admitted to the secrets of each, — weeping with the weeper, warming under the influences of the great of soul, and smiling, perhaps sometimes fearing, as scenes and incidents pass before us, glowing with tenderness or pas-sion, both equally under the control of the pure and refined master who wrought the magic, and lost not sight of a healthy moral. (74)

The *Saturday Review* likewise exclaimed at length on the humanity of the *Idylls* compared to Tennyson's earlier Arthurian poems, and concluded: "His fabulous knights and ladies are not only true men and women, but, sharing in the highest interests of genuine human life, they think and speak with the pregnancy of meaning which, in the creations of great writers, never interfere with dramatic propriety or illusion" (76). Perhaps less expected is the praise recorded in the 31 July 1859 *Weekly Dispatch*, since this had a more popular, less prestigious readership than the journals of the critical establishment. Tennyson, the reviewer asserted, had "clothed" ancient days "in all the colours of romance, and has imparted a human interest to incidents and events of the wildest, strangest, and most fantastical sort. His conception of the mission and character of the King is very masterly . . ." (6).

Even a year after the *Idylls'* first publication, Margaret Oliphant digressed on the *Idylls* before proceeding with a review of
poetry by Owen Meredith (pseudonym of Bulwer Lytton's son) in
the July 1860 *Blackwood's Edinburgh Magazine*. She remarked that
if the *Idylls* suddenly perished, "if even in a chance memory no
musical line lingered, and the charm of words had evaporated
from the tale — who could forget that noble Lancelot, sorrowful to
the soul for the sin he could not shake off, profoundly and sadly
faithful to the love which broke his heart? Or maiden Elaine,
lovesick for that grandest melancholy figure, dying for love of the
unattainable splendour and excellence — sweet, maidenly visionary,
longing towards the highest?" (42). Oliphant's response is especially important because it occurs at a distance from the *Idylls'*
initial publication, and suggests the degree to which the vivid characters of 1859 lingered in readers' minds.

This, in fact, is a crucial difference between Victorian and late
twentieth–century encounters with the *Idylls*. For Victorian audiences, *Idylls of the King* meant from the start a human–centered,
accessible, vivid set of stories about attractive characters. So well
entrenched did the humanity and interest of the *Idylls* become
among Tennyson's public that when the 1869 volume turned to
metaphysical themes and heavily symbolic patterns, Victorian audiences perceived these within a framework of identifiable and
lively human interest. In contrast, late twentieth–century audiences first encounter the mythic patterns of "The Coming of Arthur,"
then ("Gareth and Lynette" excepted) a narrative of unremitting
corruption and decline. Many modern and postmodern readers
accordingly see the poem as a denatured one, either because the
symbolic pattern seems so much more forceful than the characters
or tales themselves,[11] or because they see the whole point of the
Idylls being the draining of significance and vitality from all human
attempts at constructing meaning and institutions. Victorians
responded to a very different facet of Tennyson's art, seeing in the
Idylls affirmations of humanity and the individual, a framework
which remained intact as they encountered subsequent parts.

This humanity extended to Arthur, who was most frequently hailed as an attractive leader and embodiment of hope. As the October 1859 *Bentley's Quarterly Review* argued, "Guinevere" presents a very different Arthur from Malory's, whose monarch is resigned to his queen's loss but not to the demise of his table, since Tennyson's king feels the human loss of Guinevere. Moreover, the reviewer continued, "when the end comes, and the extinction of his dream, he rises to the majesty which has failed him hitherto" (189). Arthur's kingdom may come to naught, and all his plans, but as an individual he is victorious. Once again, in their original context, the *Idylls* asserted the importance of the individual in terms less apparent now. This has partly to do, of course, with a far more active Christian framework among Tennyson's first readers and reviewers. The Arthur who submitted to death as part of his attempt to elevate humanity, who forgave the spouse who had brought him great pain, and who was prophesied to return again was readily absorbed into the Christ who offered the hope of individual rather than political salvation. But two other factors intensified this pattern in Tennyson's text. This Arthur first appeared, in 1859, in the company of vivid characters whose stories exemplified the theme of the individual. And the 1859 Arthur had already been resurrected and had returned after the moving portrayal of his death in 1842. The order of publication meant that, in a literal sense, Arthur's death was surely followed by his return and triumph.

Arthur returned again in December of 1869, when *The Holy Grail and Other Poems* was issued. Several months later, writing in the *Edinburgh Review*, Margaret Oliphant remarked with some puzzlement on the shift in tone and style of this second set of idylls:

> The picture, which he has set before us in separate chapters ... will be and has been received by the mass of readers as a series of romantic tales. ... From such a point of view the volume last published, 'The Holy Grail,' has a certain confusing effect upon the mind. ... The Quest of

the Grail is evidently a chapter in some greater drama, a
fragment throwing broken light behind and before, meaning and inferring much that is not included in itself. The .
. . Coming and Passing of Arthur. . . are the beginning and
ending of a great historical–traditionary romance, a
tragedy full of the highest aims, a story of human effort
and passion surpassed by none in lofty meaning or in
melancholy certainty of fate. ("Epic" 503)

Oliphant's insistence on high symbolic form ("a great
historical–traditionary romance") and on gloom ("tragedy"
imbued with "melancholy certainty of fate") reflects the new
direction of Tennyson's Arthuriad—and also begins to anticipate
twentieth–century views.

The new idylls enacted the shift in mode from 1859 to 1869 in
several ways. The first four lines of "The Coming of Arthur" would
have echoed the format of the 1859 poems, since the lines introduce a central female character (Guinevere) and her relation to a
male character (her father): "Leodogran, the King of Cameliard, /
Had one fair daughter, and none other child; / And she was fairest
of all flesh on earth, / Guinevere, and in her his one delight."
Indeed, the whole issue of Arthur's origin and claim to kingship is
narrated only when Leodogran struggles to determine whether
Arthur is a fit mate for Guinevere. Kingship is well nigh subordinate to a marriage plot. Despite this clear link to the focus and
technique of the 1859 idylls, however, "The Coming of Arthur"
modulates into a symbolic mode implicit in the identification of
Guinevere with the fairest flesh on earth. By the end of this idyll,
after the official, formal wedding (so different from the intimate
domestic portraits of the 1859 volume), Guinevere has disappeared from view, perhaps because she is to be understood as absorbed
into Arthur's identity at this point. The idyll ends with no mention
of her: "And Arthur and his knighthood for a space / Were all one
will, and through that strength the King / . . . made a realm and
reigned" (CA 514-15, 518).

"The Holy Grail" articulates a sense of isolation and decline in its introductory verse paragraph, since it presents Percivale alone, in retreat from Camelot, and foretells his death. Ambrosius, in effect, tries to turn the idyll's story toward the subject of the 1859 idylls when he asks, " 'Tell me, what drove thee from the Table Round, / My brother? was it earthly passion crost?' " (HG 28-29). But in the world of the grail quest, kindred ties are dissolving, and the only vignettes of love between men and women occur as suppressed interludes amidst grand, heroic, lonely quests — a reversal of the 1859 idylls. The implicit eroticism infusing Galahad's interactions with Percivale's sister (HG 149-65) remains implicit, suppressed from conscious articulation; and Percivale likewise suppresses the sojourn with his lost love (HG 563-611) until late in the tale, treating it as a digression and falling away from his true quest. Arthur, like Ambrosius, emerges as a force that attempts to impede the idylls' swerve into radically spiritual or symbolic modes. He argues, in his famous closing lines, for keeping one's feet on the ground, for maintaining a human foundation interfused by spiritual vision rather than abandoning humanity in favor of transcendent, dematerialized visions:

> The King . . . is but as the hind
> To whom a space of land is given to plow.
> Who may not wander from the allotted field
> Before his work be done; but, being done,
> Let visions of the night or of the day
> Come, as they will. (HG 901, 902-7)

The knights whose stories dominate this idyll, however, follow a contrary impulse.

The next idyll reverts to the tone and style of the 1859 idylls, but now with disastrous results. As the 18 December 1869 *Graphic* remarked, " 'Pelleas and Ettarre' . . . brings us back to ordinary flesh and blood, and, dealing with the faithlessness of a fair woman, prepares us for the grand discovery of faithlessness in the story of Guinevere" (67). But if the reviewer's aligning of this new idyll with "Guinevere" is quite plausible, there are also salient differences. "Guinevere" opens with severance and disaster and closes with recognition and potential reconciliation. "Pelleas and Ettarre" opens with hope, innocence, and affection and closes with bitter disillusionment and vengeance. A hint of this plot occurs in the introductory lines, since Pelleas is introduced, not in relation to Ettarre, but in relation to Arthur's losses: "King Arthur made new knights to fill the gap / Left by the Holy Quest" (PE 1-2). The interactions of Pelleas and Ettarre, like the love relationships of the 1859 volume, indicate the state of the realm and serve as a central focus for the idyll. But in fact there is never an authentic relationship between the two at all, only the symbiosis of Ettarre's ambitions and Pelleas's illusions. Pelleas's true relation is to Arthur, and the idyll recapitulates the whole story of the realm's origin and fall; it opens on a note of plenitude, the king firmly on the throne, and ends on loss and Arthur's displacement by Modred.

By the time of "The Passing of Arthur" (the result of Tennyson's adding a new frame to the old "Morte d'Arthur"), the introductory paragraph presents only a voice existing, like Everard Hall's, after the fall of Camelot: "That story which the bold Sir Bedivere, / First made and latest left of all the knights, / Told, when the man was no more than a voice / In the white winter of his age, to those / With whom he dwelt, new faces, other minds" (PA 1-5). Here the possibility of relationship, so central in the 1859 poems, is gone, and for the first time — now that the realm has foundered — Tennyson presents a view of battle up close: "Shocks, and the splintering spear, the hard mail hewn, / Shield–breakings, and the clash of brands, the crash / Of battleaxes on shattered helms, and shrieks / After the Christ" (PA 108-111). The 1869 idylls may invoke the manner and matter of the 1859 idylls, then, but do so only to break the pattern.

The greatest difference between the two volumes, of course, is the introduction of metaphysical themes, the battle of sense and soul, of civilization and bestiality. These themes have become critical commonplaces ever since James T. Knowles (architect and friend of Tennyson) and Henry Alford, Dean of Canterbury, identified them in commentaries published in January 1870.[12] Moreover, this interpretive framework could absorb and integrate the 1859 idylls, transforming the romantic stories identified by Oliphant into the symbolic acting out of faith (exemplified by faith in a Christlike Arthur) versus doubt and sin, of spirituality versus degrading materialism. A further result was a tightening of links and connections among individual idylls. The 1869 idylls thus articulated a more conservative vision — moral imperatives sanctioned by traditional faith and hence extant social order — and assumed a more conservative form, a tightly-bound single poem more closely approximating the epic.

This framework was affirmed by reviews across the political and intellectual spectrum. Knowles and Alford expressed the views of the intellectual and social elite, but their interpretations of the *Idylls* were shared by the more popular journals. The 25 December 1869 *Illustrated London News* suggested that a more appropriate title for the *Idylls* might be " 'The Round Table of King Arthur; or, The Royal College of Virtue,' " since "The six idylls of the Round Table are intended to show ... the process of corruption and dissolution of that Royal College of Virtue ... by the scandalous intrigue of Queen Guinevere with Sir Lancelot of the Lake" (654). The 26 February 1870 *Chambers's Journal*, similarly, argued that "The Coming of Arthur" depicted "the infusion of the higher and immortal principle into the lower nature of man, the rebellion of the flesh against the spirit, the commencement of the struggle of which the whole poem constitutes the history and the development" (139). Review after review applauded the overarching design of the *Idylls*, which most now took to be complete. The 23 December 1869 *Times* proclaimed the completed *Idylls* "unequalled in its great, finished, and happy design since the time of Milton" (4). The 2 January 1870 *Sunday Times* hailed "the completeness which is now given to the Arthurian legends Mr. Tennyson has collected. Beautiful as they are, the *Idylls of the King* were but so many separate poems with no very apparent link of connection. In the later volume, the link is supplied, and the poem, as it appears, according to Mr. Tennyson's arrangement, is a work of completed and consummated beauty" (7). As Margaret Oliphant concluded in her April 1870 analysis in the *Edinburgh Review*, "The more it is studied the more manifest it will be that every part of it has been composed with careful reference to the leading conception, and that those individual portions which throw but broken lights when taken by themselves, become full of force and significance when considered in their relation to the rest" (537). What had been individual was now seen as subordinate to a dominant intellectual and artistic design.

Such views are common in the twentieth century as well. But when Tennyson's first audiences discovered the poem's "parabolic drift" they also kept in mind the humanity of the 1859 idylls, since they had the opportunity to read and re–read the 1859 poems during the ten–year interval between the first and second installments of the *Idylls*. Hence, even when they embraced the new allegorical pattern, they continued to perceive an underlying earthiness and vitality. The February 1870 *Victoria Magazine* liked "The Holy Grail" because it gathered "into one focus the personages to whom we have been introduced in 'Enid,' 'Vivien,' and 'Elaine,' and showing them in contrast to each other, under the influence of a strange and searching test, which brings out the inmost character of each" (376). The 23 December 1869 *Times* termed "Pelleas and Ettarre" an "exquisite novel in verse" (4). Two reviewers even worried that the poem was too earthy, the 2 January 1870 *Sunday Times* finding a single inferiority of Tennyson's to Morris's Arthurian poems because "the light, tender and opaline, Mr. Tennyson throws upon the court of Arthur and the woods around it is earthly. It lacks the mystical beauty of that which Mr. Morris bestows in many poems, as for instance, in 'The Chapel in Lyoness' " (7). H. Lawrenny, writing in the 8 January 1870 *Academy*, and faulting the poem for mannered simplicity and

self–conscious polish, also complained that Tennyson had subor-
dinated traditional elements of Arthurian legend "to a *study of
character* in which the good is not ancient, nor the evil modern."
The characters, she added, seemed to "have escaped from the
pages of a French novel" (92; emphasis added).

More characteristic attestations of the *Idylls'* human interest
came in the form of praise for Arthur's character, as in the *St.
James's Magazine*: "The 'Coming of Arthur' is the coming into
existence of no mere mythical hero of forgotten times; the 'phan-
tom king' of history becomes, in the poetry of the 'Idylls,' a man
near to us by the humanity of tenderness, truth, and generosity"
(Jan.-April 1870: 789). The 25 December 1869 *Spectator*, asserting
that the completed *Idylls* embodied "no allegories" (1533), dis-
cerned both the celebration of individualism in the 1859 volume
and the intensification of Arthur's authority in the 1869 volume,
when it remarked that Arthur "combines a strangely modern tolerance, a deep reverence for the individual nature of every one
under his rule, with that 'great authority' by virtue of which he
reigns" (1531). The majority of reviews written in response to the
1869 volume suggest that, partly as a result of Tennyson's artistic
choices, partly as a result of publication sequence, Victorian audiences had learned to read the eight idylls according to two
simultaneous interpretive strategies. Tennyson's readers retained
their sense of Camelot as a city inhabited by identifiable human
beings, yet this audience also delighted in the newly-found moral
allegory. As the 26 February 1870 *Chambers's Journal* concluded,
"Now we have the whole 'mind of the mystery,' the master–thought
which inspired the noble allegory, and it is all the more welcome
by reason of its not having been brought too obtrusively before the
reader, but kept, as all allegorical signification should be kept, in
due subordination to the literal and natural meaning" (138).

The story of the *Idylls'* reception becomes more complicated
after 1869 for several reasons. Because so many thought the *Idylls*
complete in 1869, the later additions in 1871, 1872, and 1885 were
sometimes unwelcome. These later idylls pried open what had

seemed to many an emphatically closed poem in 1869, reinjecting contingency into the poem's shape. Many readers were reluctant to relinquish what had seemed a masterly poem. Moreover, by the 1870s taste had begun to change. Robert Browning, Swinburne, and Morris began to receive increasing attention and praise, and Tennyson came to represent the old school. Reviews of the 1871 "Last Tournament" or 1872 "Gareth and Lynette" sometimes expressed weariness with the whole subject of Arthurian legend, finding it out of date. Others accepted Arthurian legend but wanted no more idylls. To the degree that attention shifted away from Tennyson's Arthuriad and toward newer fashions in poetry, it is difficult to construct a pattern of response to the last three installments of the poem. Camelot had not disappeared or dematerialized for this segment of the reading public; it had been deserted by those who found its towers and spires increasingly banal.

But for those readers whose interest and sympathies continued to be engaged by the poem, subsequent installments allowed them to develop additional interpretive strategies, to discern new layers of meaning while continuing to affirm the poem's humanity. The theme of art, frequently discussed in late twentieth–century commentaries on the *Idylls*, received virtually no attention prior to 1872, when "Gareth and Lynette" and the re–issued "Last Tournament" appeared. These two idylls included the famous "city built to music" passage in "Gareth," and the extensive attention to Tristram's "broken music" in "The Last Tournament." Moreover, the slow growth of the *Idylls*, from the 1842 "Morte" to the volume published thirty years later, gave special meaning to the lines describing the growth of a city through music. As the 2 November 1872 *Saturday Review* commented, "The three paradoxes which puzzled Gareth are to the readers of the *Idylls* both intelligible and true. The whole world of Camelot and Arthur has up to this time been in building still, because it is built to a fine and creative music, and though it was never actually built at all, it is built for ever" (569). Similarly, Richard H. Hutton asserted in the November 1872 *Macmillan's Magazine* that Tennyson "himself has

told us very finely in his newest poem, when describing the building of Arthur's great capital, —which, like Ilium, was rumoured to
have been built to a divine music, —how the highest works of the
human spirit are created" (143). The theme of poetry was now
added to those of love and moral or spiritual struggle for readers
of Tennyson's Arthuriad.

Meantime, the lasting effect of the 1859 poems continued
among sympathetic readers. The 30 October 1872 Church of England *Guardian*, in its favorable review of the most recent volume,
viewed each idyll in its newly–assigned place in terms of character
and motive. "Gareth and Lynette" it considered to have "a little of
the pert liveliness of youth about it, gay, picturesque, and brilliant,
with the true touch of romance," while, in what followed, Enid
"rides obediently along, with her sullen husband after her, and
wife, husband, and readers, as they go together by wildernesses
and perilous paths, by towns and castles, are liable from time to
time to strange surprises, but are never very far from the verge of
deep and solemn moralities" (1370). The 26 October 1872 *Spectator* saw the lineaments of allegory in "Gareth and Lynette" but
was more impressed by its realism: "All this looks a little like
allegory, but there is no allegory in the poem, beyond what allegory
there is in all real life" (1364). These two readers continued to
celebrate the humanity of character and victorious temper which
dominated reviews of the 1859 volume.

Thirteen years later, when "Balin and Balan" was unobtru-
sively inserted into *Tiresias and Other Poems* (1885), even the
youngest readers of the 1842 "Morte d'Arthur" would have grown
old. "Balin and Balan," with its theme of the *doppelgänger*, suggests a psychological approach which could be applied to other
idylls as well, so that the final installment of the *Idylls* introduced
yet another thematic layer and potential reading strategy. But by
1885 the reading public was no longer primed for more idylls, and
no reviews suggested extended interpretive modes. Still,
enthusiastic notices of the new idyll appeared in the 12 December
1885 *Spectator*, 26 December 1885 *Athenaeum*, and the April 1886

Edinburgh Review. The last is especially important because it demonstrates that, almost three decades after the 1859 volume appeared, the poem's humanity was still being affirmed:

> One of the great defects alleged against the *Idylls* is, that the characters are modern personages masquerading in ancient dress; but, from another point of view, this fault renders them contemporary teachers. The poet's object seems to have been to make Arthur sufficiently true to his age not to disturb our sense of the probable, and yet to raise him so much above it as to be, without reference to degrees of civilisation, a type for all time of chivalrous manhood.
>
> Lord Tennyson does not, like the late Lord Lytton in 'King Arthur,' recall his characters to poetic life by a copious use of the supernatural, nor does he veil his figures in the dim transparency of the Spenserian allegory, but teaches living lessons by the universality of the humanity he portrays. (488)

The Victorian city of Camelot was thus a rather more habitable place than the one favored by twentieth–century commentators. Its foundations had been set in 1859, in idylls that emphasized individuality, the importance of women and human relationships within the kingdom, and pluralistic form and interpretation. Tennyson, much like Arthur pulling "petty princedoms under him" until he "made a realm, and reigned" (CA 18-19), gradually pulled together individual idylls into a coherent artistic sequence and design that articulated a more conservative, less hopeful vision. But because of the poem's publication sequence, readers who cared for the poem seemed never to lose sight of its naturalistic core or susceptibility to optimistic symbolic patterns.

Of course, the Victorian middle class has long been linked with – and condemned for – its literalism and optimism, but middle–class responses to the *Idylls*, as indicated by reviews, have their own plausibility when restored to the original context of publication dates and reading sequence. Their responses also, I think, provide a balance to the reactions of late twentieth–century approaches. By now the assertions of the poem's amorphousness, radical skepticism, nihilism, and reflexiveness threaten to become critical cliches in turn. Such views are suited to twentieth–century culture; they are also cogent interpretations for those who begin the poem by encountering the ghostly tone and heavily symbolic patterns embedded in "The Coming of Arthur." But there is also value in restoring the poem's links to humanity, whether by recalling how nineteenth–century individuals first received the poem or by decentering the parabolic drift which threatens to overwhelm the poem's tales. To assess the poem fully we must look at the completed, sequential work Tennyson left us. But if we do so as a second step, not a first, we may more successfully remain alive to the poem's multivalent possibilities of meaning and its susceptibility to differing reading strategies. We could see the poem as a paradigm of demise *and* a pattern of hope, as a series of romantic tales *and* a symbolic design, as a collection of realized characters *and* the ghostly voices of Victorian empire.

Thus, like Gareth lopping off the head of a contrived construction of Death to find a blooming boy within, we might detach ourselves from the poem standing at the head of Tennyson's completed sequence, repeat the reading sequence of Tennyson's contemporaries in classrooms and individually, and so re–establish contact with the freshness of characterization that helped to insure the lasting fame of the poem among Tennyson's urban Arthurians.[13]

Texas Christian University

NOTES

[1]See, for example, Margaret Homans's "Tennyson and the Spaces of Life," *ELH* 46 (1979), 693-709, and John Rosenberg's *Fall of Camelot* (Cambridge, 1973) and "Tennyson and the Passing of Arthur," *VP* 25 (1987), 141-50.

[2]The reviewers represent a specialized audience, it is true, but their comments are the only readily available ones we have for establishing how the reading public responded in the main. If reviewers shaped opinion, moreover, they often reflected opinions of their readership as well. No exact count of reviews has been established, but I have read more than one hundred issued between 1859 and 1886. J. Phillip Eggers (*King Arthur's Laureate* [New York: New York U. P., 1971]) also surveys Victorian reviews (53-104), but tends to set Victorian against modern critical analyses of the *Idylls* and to find the former wanting. My interest in Victorian reviews lies in their indicating how the *Idylls* came to constitute meaning for Tennyson's first audiences. Referenced page numbers are in parentheses.

[3]Citations of Tennyson are from *The Poems of Tennyson,* 2nd ed., ed. Christopher Ricks, 3 vols. (Harlow, Essex, 1987).

[4]Kathleen Tillotson was the first to examine the installment format of Tennyson's Arthuriad in "Tennyson's Serial Poem" (in *Mid–Victorian Studies,* by Geoffrey and Kathleen Tillotson [London,1965], 80-109). Her article remains an important statement on Victorian reception of the work and Tennyson's evolving design.

[5]The references to ice skating on a pond and the narrator's description of the observance of Christmas customs as "some odd games / In some odd nooks like this" (8-9) establish the setting as a rural one.

[6]William Allingham, *A Diary,* ed. Helen Allingham and D. Radford (1907; rpt. Harmondsworth, Middlesex, 1985), 150.

[7]"Tennyson, King Arthur, and Imperialism," in *Culture, Ideology and Politics: Essays for Eric Hobsbawm,* ed. Raphael Samuel and Gareth Stedman Jones (London, 1982), 126-48.

[8]Cp. Elliot L. Gilbert's "The Female King: Tennyson's Arthurian Apocalypse," *PMLA* 98 (1983), 863-78.

[9]Bulwer Lytton's *King Arthur* again forms an interesting contrast. In the first part of the epic, the single notable female character is important only within an enclosed valley set apart from

time and space; and she dies (in the second part) when Arthur returns to the larger, "real" world.

[10]Tillotson, 82-85.

[11]See, e.g., Robert Bernard Martin, *Tennyson: The Unquiet Heart* (New York,1980), 495.

[12]As Patricia Srebrnik points out, Alford drew many points of his argument from a letter written to him by James Knowles; Knowles, in turn, had benefitted from conversations with Tennyson (*Alexander Strahan, Victorian Publisher* [Ann Arbor, MI, 1986], 111).

[13]My research on Victorian reviews of *Idylls of the King* was partly supported by a 1985 Grant–in–Aid from the American Council of Learned Societies.

An Assessment of Swinburne's Arthuriana

Rebecca Cochran

Most students of the Arthurian revival recognize the importance of Tennyson's *Idylls of the King*. Swinburne also contributed significantly to Victorian medievalism, but his Arthurian poems have failed to receive the attention they deserve. Both poets had a lasting fascination for the subject; both composed substantial works which employ the *Matter of Britain*. It is here, however, that the similarities cease.

Tennyson rewrites the entire Arthurian cycle in order to stress the importance of a strong social order with a Carlylean leader at its center. In Tennyson's Camelot, women are expected to act as moral guardians of the domestic realm, while the knights are called upon to sacrifice desire for the public good. In short, Tennyson uses the legend as a vehicle to express his moral vision — a distinctly Victorian one — and freely alters his sources to do so.

Swinburne, like Morris, selects for his poetry only his favorite Arthurian characters. He extols heroic individuals who accept the role of fate in their lives and who understand that nature's laws are more important than the social order created by the institutions of God and man. Swinburne also respects the authority of his sources in his attempt to remain faithful to the spirit of the Middle Ages. Thus, his Arthurian verse presents a version of the medieval past that stands in opposition to Tennyson's. The popularity of the *Idylls* in Victorian England stemmed from their modern tone and sentiment. The poems of Swinburne and Morris, more medieval in tone and attitude, were not appreciated because they were not understood.

Swinburne's Arthuriana divides itself into three phases: the juvenilia, composed between 1857 and 1860; his masterful *Tristram of Lyonesse* (1882); and *The Tale of Balen*, published relatively late in his career (1896). That Swinburne composed these works over a period of some four decades attests to his enduring interest in Arthurian subjects.

In order to assess his contribution to Arthurian literature, I will consider Swinburne's selection of material, his attitude towards it, and his use of sources. I will also evaluate the poems in the context of the medieval revival in Victorian Britain, with special reference to his contemporary Arthurians. Finally, I hope to suggest how these works enrich our understanding of and appreciation for Swinburne's poetic abilities. One detects thematic similarities between his Arthurian verse and his other poetry, particularly in his emphasis upon fate, his reverence for nature, and in his concept of the hero.

The youthful Swinburne composed five Arthurian poems and fragments. Of particular interest is his selection of subjects. Two of the five, "Queen Yseult" and "Joyeuse Garde," demonstrate his early fascination with the Tristram legend, even though *Tristram of Lyonesse* bears little resemblance to these early efforts. The other three compositions, "Lancelot," "King Ban," and "The Day Before the Trial" (a poem about Arthur), suggest, as David Staines observes, "that, like Morris, he was seriously considering the possibility of creating an Arthurian cycle."[1] This seems plausible in view of the fact that Swinburne fell under the spell of the Pre–Raphaelites in 1857 when he met Rossetti and Morris, who were painting Arthurian frescoes on the walls and ceiling of the Union debating hall. Like Morris, Rossetti had also planned and abandoned the idea of composing a complete Arthurian cycle.[2]

Swinburne's early verse reveals a marked Pre–Raphaelite influence and owes much to Morris' *The Defence of Guenevere and Other Poems* (1858). Both poets employ archaic diction and monosyllabic words, make use of vivid coloration, concrete detail, and synesthesia, and explore altered psychological states. However, Swinburne's youthful inexperience and his enthusiastic imitation of Morris results in poems of uneven quality.

Although "Queen Yseult" was planned in ten cantos, only six are extant. For his plot, Swinburne relies upon Scott's 1804 edition of the Middle English *Sir Tristrem*, but he embellishes his work by borrowing details from Malory. The following description of Iseult of Brittany demonstrates the Pre–Raphaelite influence:[3]

> Purple flowers, blue and red,
> On the rushes round the bed
> Strewed they for her feet to tread.
> But about the bed they set
> Large while blossoms, white and wet,
> Crowns the fairest they could get. (1. 49)

This pictorial quality, the desire to paint visual images in verse, exemplifies Swinburne's imitation of Rossetti and Morris in these early efforts.

"Queen Yseult" also demonstrates Swinburne's lack of attention to details of plot and to the development of character. For instance, he omits from his source Tristram's battle with Morhaunt, an effort to save Cornwall from heavy taxation. Tristram is victorious, but he receives a terrible wound which is healed by Iseult of Ireland. When Tristram returns to Cornwall singing her praises, Mark sends his nephew as his emissary to win Iseult's hand in marriage. Because Swinburne deletes these details, we do not know how Mark has heard of Iseult's beauty and become betrothed to her, nor do we see Tristram's heroic efforts to save Cornwall by engaging in combat with Morhaus. This neglect suggests that, in his early attempts, Swinburne focused more on style than content, in contrast to his later *Tristram of Lyonesse.*

In "Joyeuse Garde" Tristram and Iseult are reunited at Lancelot's castle. Although this episode is ultimately derived from Malory, it was probably directly inspired by Morris' painting, "How Sir Palomydes loved la Belle Iseult with exceeding great love, but how she loved not him but rather Sir Tristrem."[4] We also see the Pre–Raphaelite influence in Swinburne's use of sensual imagery; we feel the heavy noon and the flies buzzing around the peach tree (104).

More important, however, is the celebration of sexual passion that sets Swinburne apart from his fellow Victorians. He describes Iseult's sexual fulfillment:

Her eyes said 'Tristram' now, but her lips held
The joy too close for any smile or moan
To move them; she was patiently fulfilled
With a slow pleasure that slid everwise
Even into hands and feet...(1.104)

Swinburne's erotic descriptions become more explicit in Part II of his later Tristram poem, but even the above passage defies Victorian standards.

"Lancelot" is perhaps the most accomplished of these early poems. It possesses most of the Pre–Raphaelite characteristics and presents the hero's altered state of consciousness. Although it is modelled directly on Rossetti's painting, "Sir Launcelot at the Shrine of the Sanc Grael," the influence of Morris' poem, "King Arthur's Tomb," prevails. Both works occur after the Round Table's demise and dramatize Lancelot's thoughts as he rides to meet the queen. In "Lancelot" the wearied knight stops by a chapel to rest and falls into a sleep–trance that provides him with a dual vision. He first sees a vision of the Grail, but it is obfuscated by the shadowy form of Guinevere. In the remainder of the poem, the entranced knight recalls memories of his illicit love for the queen. This altered state of consciousness which dramatizes in a symbolic, distilled form the two most significant experiences in Lancelot's life — his illicit love and his quest for holiness — is a sophisticated device that Swinburne employs later in his "Sestina,"[5] where his experiment with the sleep–trance shows the poet's developing aesthetic interests.

These works should be viewed as "practice poems" for Swinburne's later, more accomplished verse, in much the same way that Tennyson's early neomedieval poems (e.g., "The Lady of Shalott," "Sir Launcelot and Queen Guinevere") served as experimental forerunners for the *Idylls*. Apparently, Swinburne did not hold these attempts in very high regard; some remain unfinished. If he had planned a complete Arthurian cycle, he probably abandoned the idea because much of the material clearly did not suit his artistic taste or his temperament. For instance, it is doubtful that a repentant Lancelot and Guinevere or a righteous Galahad would have appealed to his sensibilities. For nearly a decade, Swinburne's poetic endeavors lay elsewhere, until his disdain for Tennyson's treatment of Arthurian subjects forced him to renew his attention to Camelot or, more precisely, Cornwall.

In *A Study of Swinburne*, T. Earle Welby remarks upon Swinburne's composition of *Tristram of Lyonesse*:

> A great poem on this subject had been among his projects since his first year at Oxford; in 1869 it was now begun, the immediate impulse being intense irritation with Tennyson's latest installment of Arthurian or Albertian idylls.[6]

Why did Tennyson's "The Last Tournament" cause his rival such 'intense irritation'? A brief summary of the laureate's mistreatment of the Tristram legend provides the answer.

Tennyson employs the less flattering medieval prose tradition found in Malory, but he blackens the primary characters considerably. In the *Idylls* Tristram represents the "broken music" of Arthur's court; his story, recounted in "The Last Tournament," occurs during the "autumn" of the Round Table. He is a cynical opportunist whose loyalties change to suit his own immediate desires. Furthermore, Iseult of Ireland is a hardened, aging adultress married to Mark, an evil monarch and a coward, who stabs Tristram in the back. Swinburne's reaction to this distortion of the legend also states succinctly his own purpose in composing his *Tristram*:

> My aim was simply to present that story, not diluted and debased as it had been in our own time by other hands, but undefaced by improvement and undeformed by

transformation, as it was known to the age of Dante wherever the chronicles of romance found hearing, from Ercildoune to Florence: and not in the epic or romantic form of sustained or continuous narrative, but mainly through a succession of dramatic scenes or pictures with descriptive settings or backgrounds.[7]

His distaste for a drastic alteration of the legend also held true for his opinion of Arnold's *Tristram and Iseult* (1852). The latter had used the Tristram story in order to comment on the malaise of modern life. Arnold does not present Tristram and Iseult in the heroic love–splendor of their youth, but rather depicts them as geriatric lovers who are destroyed by "the gradual furnace of the world" — passion. They do find peace on their deathbed, however, and they are not maligned like their counterparts in Tennyson: even Mark is a kind, forgiving man. Nonetheless, Swinburne, who celebrates sexual passion in his retelling of the Tristram story, was prompted to restore the original dignity enjoyed by the medieval characters. Even his respect for Arnold did not prevent Swinburne from commenting to him:

> The legend was so radically altered in its main points by your conception and treatment of that old subject...that the field was really open to a new writer who might wish to work on the old lines.[8]

Arnold's Iseult of Brittany is his most heroic character. He expands her role considerably although, quite unforgivably, he "awards" her with the primary Victorian honor for women — motherhood. Swinburne's only significant borrowing from Arnold's Tristram poem is his expansion of Iseult of Brittany's character, but, as we shall see, he does so for very different reasons.

In his *Tristram*, Swinburne rebels against the standard Victorian modes of conduct and presents a return to the ideal world of nature; here, he is philosophically opposed to Tennyson's need for individual restraint and the dictate to channel personal desire into public works. Thus, Swinburne chooses as his primary source the poetic version of the Tristram legend — Scott's edition of *Sir Tristrem* — because all of its characters enjoy greater nobility and its plot provides a dignified end for the lovers. David Staines notes that Swinburne had read "a compilation by Francisque Michel of various Tristan legends,"[9] and the poet also relied on Malory for a few details, primarily to present his story against an Arthurian backdrop. For instance, Tristram and Iseult discuss many prominent members of Camelot (Arthur and Morgause, Lancelot and Guinevere, Balen, Merlin), and Palamede makes a brief appearance in Swinburne's poem. However, because he conceived of the legend as essentially a love story, Swinburne relies most heavily on the more romantic poetic version.

Despite his conviction to remain faithful to his medieval source, Swinburne alters some details. Like Wagner, he begins with the lovers' journey to Cornwall, thus eliminating the long history of Tristram's parentage and birth. Instead, he presents these details in abbreviated flashbacks later in his narrative. In this way, Swinburne arrives more quickly at the consumption of the love potion, which enables him to expand upon its consequences. In addition, the poet deletes several of Tristram's encounters with supernatural opponents, which he sees as largely digressive of the main plot. Swinburne thus tightens the narrative structure and renders his poem more appealing to a post–medieval audience that valued a coherent plot.

Swinburne's changes "purify" the legend and enhance its romantic plot without interfering with his professed purpose: to re-tell the original story. In his view, the medieval Tristram legend is primarily a celebration of passion. The lovers derive fortitude from their harmony with the transcendent forces of nature. If we examine Swinburne's depiction of his main characters and his conception of fate, love, nature, and change, we can understand why *Tristram of Lyonesse* is such a great contribution to Swinburne's poetic achievements and to Arthuriana.

In his "Prelude," Swinburne presents an overview of his prevalent themes. Love is the prime mover of the universe, and, in the case of Tristram and Iseult, love and fate are the same. Swinburne makes this clear when he presents parallels between the opening lines of the "Prelude," a tribute to love, and those of the final canto, a tribute to fate. Echoing Francesca's speech in Canto V of Dante's *Inferno*, Swinburne begins:

> Love, that is first and last of all things made,
> The light that has the living world for shade,
> The spirit that for temporal veil has on
> The souls of all men woven in unison,
> One fiery raiment with all lives inwrought
> And lights of sunny and starry deed and thought (4. 25).

Compare the above lines with the tribute to fate at the opening of Part IX:

> Fate, that was born ere spirit and flesh were made,
> The fire that fills man's life with light and shade;
> The power beyond all godhead which puts on
> All forms of multitudinous unison,
> A raiment of eternal change inwrought
> With shapes and hues more subtly spun than thought (4. 150).

The enemies of love and fate are the man–made concepts of God and time. The "Prelude" redefines time according to astrological months, each presided over by such heroines as Dido, Helen, Isolt, and Francesca. In Part IX, God is exposed as a vindictive product of man's imagination; he thrives on jealousy and on humankind's fear of punishment and is a would–be usurper of the true force which drives the universe – love. Swinburne here depicts heroic fate, "Trampling the head of Fear, the false high priest," that is "The Miscreation of a miscreant God" (152-53). In

Part VII, as we shall see, Iseult of Brittany invokes this vindictive deity, just as Iseult of Ireland has rejected him in Parts V and VI.

Swinburne's references to Dante in his "Prelude" are intentional. As Jerome McCann explains:

> [Swinburne] brilliantly reinterprets Dante's vision by reassigning all the values.... For Swinburne, Dante's distinctions between heaven and hell no longer matter because judgment is rendered now in aesthetic rather than ethical terms.[10]

Thus, love reigns supreme in the universe, and those who submit to it unconditionally achieve heroism and fame. They no longer need fear punishment, time, and change. Furthermore, true lovers acknowledge the working of inexorable fate (love) in their lives and accept its appropriateness. Those who give all for love also win the sympathy of future generations and gain immortality: they are resurrected when their stories are transmitted through the songs of poet–lovers (e.g. Dante, Swinburne) throughout the ages.

The "Prelude" also introduces, through its extensive use of oxymoronic phrases and paradoxes, another major theme: everything in the universe is dependent on and nourished by its complementary opposite. For instance, Swinburne glorifies the "body spiritual," asserts that love is "flesh upon the spirit of man," lauds the "changeless change of seasons," and refers to "space out of space and timeless time" (25, 27, 29). Because this interdependency is cyclical — one thing must die so that its opposite may live — change does and does not exist. Swinburne makes special use of seasonal and diurnal rhythms to illustrate this unalterable but edifying pattern in nature.

Tristram and Iseult are heroic precisely because they submit to the operation of fate/love in their lives. They recognize that, by doing so, they are in harmony with nature, God's child, which serves as a manifestation of this universal law (love). While they cannot anticipate their particular fate, they know intuitively that it governs their lives.

Although they are innocent before they drain the cup, Swinburne's lovers are predisposed to accept the end that fate has foreordained for them. This is made clear from the sympathy they express for Arthur and Morgause, who have committed a "sinless sin" by their indulgence in blind love. Iseult remarks that God should be at least as forgiving as those He has created; Tristram, in defiance of the doom that awaits Arthur, predicts that the king will be remembered, not for his illicit liaison with his half–sister, but for his extraordinary assembly of knights.

Just before they consume the potion, Tristram sings to Iseult. His lyrics reveal his understanding of fate and change, as they are manifest in the rhythms of the natural world:

> Love, is it morning risen or night deceased
> That makes the mirth of this triumphant east?
>   Is it bliss given or bitterness put by
> That makes most glad men's hearts at love's high feast?
>   Grief smiles, joy weeps, that day should live and die (50).

"Your song is hard to read," Iseult complains, so Tristram sings one that reveals the parallel influence of fate and change in the lives of human beings. As he does so, he unwittingly comments upon their own future passion and common fate:

> Art thou not I as I thy love am thou?
> So let all things pass from us; we are now,
>   For all that was and will be, who knows why?
> And all that is and is not, who knows how?
>   Who knows? God knows why day should live and die (52).

Tristram's submission to fate and change is clear. At the song's conclusion, Iseult is so thrilled by the knight's description of love's bonding power that she yearns for it to enter her life. Ironically, at the end of Part I, the two consume the love potion, "And their four

lips became one burning mouth" (57). Tristram's unwitting
prophecy is fulfilled.

In Part II, "The Queen's Pleasance," Iseult and Mark marry,
but soon after, Palamede abducts Iseult, who is, in turn, rescued
by Tristram. The lovers then enjoy a summer interlude in the
forest. Once again, Tristram's musical compositions instruct
Iseult. He expresses his trust in love and fate and his defiance of
time and death:

> And each bright song upon his lips that came,
> Mocking the powers of change and death by name,
> Blasphemed their bitter godhead, and defied
> Time...
> . . . .
> For well he wist all subtle ways of song,
> And in his soul the secret eye was strong
> That burns in meditation.... (67-68)

At this point, Iseult fears the future, evinced by the fact that "she
/ Drank lightly deep of his philosophy" (68). It is not until the
lovers' second meeting in Part VI, "Joyous Gard," that she
completely comprehends the lesson her preceptor has derived
from his direct observations of nature.

Once the lovers part, Swinburne presents in detail Tristram's
"meditations," as he contemplates his love: "We have loved and
slain each other, and love yet" (73). He acknowledges that their
love will end in their death, but he understands the appropriateness of fate:

> How should the law that knows not soon or late,
> For whom no time nor space is – how should fate,
> That is not good nor evil, wise nor mad,
> Nor just nor unjust, neither glad nor sad –
> . . . .
> How should it turn from its great way to give

Man that must die a clearer space to live? (78)

Tristram sees that what matters is not the length of one's life but its quality, and he understands that he must overcome his fear of death. By doing so, he will be in harmony with the transcendent forces of nature and will obey the universal law of love.

In Part IV, "The Maiden Marriage," Tristram weds Iseult of Brittany, but his remorse prevents him from consummating the marriage. "Iseult at Tintagel" (Part V) depicts Mark's unhappy wife as she struggles to accept her fated love for Tristram. Burdened with the fear that a vindictive God will punish Tristram with eternal damnation, she attempts to renounce her adultery, but her efforts are unsuccessful. Her dilemma remains unresolved until, while reunited with Tristram in the next section, she benefits from his philosophy and from her contact with the didactic power of nature.

During the lovers' stay at Joyous Gard, Iseult at last resigns herself to fate. She loses her fear of divine retribution and understands that love leads one through death to peace, a main theme of the "Prelude." Tristram expounds upon: "Death that bears life, and change that brings forth / seed / Of life to death and death to life indeed" (116). He then continues: "Ah, that when love shall laugh no more nor weep / We, too, might hear that song and sleep!" (116). We then see Iseult's agreement:

'Yea,' said Iseult, 'some joy it were to be
Lost in the sun's light and the all–girdling sea,
Mixed with the winds and woodlands, and to bear
Part in the large life of the quickening air,
And the sweet earth's, our mother...' (116-17)

And part VI concludes with her affirmation of her love. She tells Tristram: "dying I may praise God who gave me thee, / Let hap what will thereafter" (120).

In Part VII, "The Wife's Vigil," Swinburne depicts, in a masterful dramatic monologue, Iseult of Brittany's hateful supplication to a wrathful God, the one her namesake had feared and addressed her unsuccessful prayer to in Part V. Tristram's wife prays that God will make her His instrument of revenge so that she may enjoy the satisfaction of knowing the lovers are suffering in Hell. Swinburne places this episode after Joyous Gard to show the futility of placing one's faith in a deity who thrives on hate and fear. For Tristram and Iseult of Ireland no longer fear divine retribution; they have gained the strength to face death bravely. Thus, Iseult of Brittany's curse is innocuous.

Part VIII, "The Last Pilgrimage," includes some of Swinburne's finest verse. Here, after he and Iseult have been parted once again, Tristram experiences communion with the true God, Love, when he swims in the sea and enjoys a rejuvenation of life. This revitalizing contact with elemental nature prepares him for the battle that will leave him mortally wounded. Swinburne employs an abundance of musical images to emphasize Tristram's complete harmony with the natural world. The knight awakens to "the wind's clarion and the water's chime" (142) but, we are told, this joy transcends mere sensual delight:

> . . . . and his mind
> Was rapt abroad beyond man's meaner kind
> And pierced with love of all things and with mirth
> Moved to make one with heaven and heavenlike earth
> And with the light live water (143).

Swinburne emphasizes that this mystical fusion results in the hero's rebirth, his return to the childlike pleasure in all living things. Tristram's "soul...waxed whole / As a young child's with rapture of the hour" (142), and the poet heralds him as "Child of heroic earth and heavenly sea, / The flower of all men" (143).

The poet also stresses the seductive aspect of the sea and Tristram's joyful response to it by infusing this passage with words like "rapture," "gladness," "mirth," and "delight." Furthermore, Swinburne introduces a parallel between Tristram's draining of the cup in Part I—which had signalled his submission to fate—and his orgiastic mingling with the sea here, which prefigures his passage through death to peace. After he consumes the love potion in Part I, Tristram feels "heart–stung with a serpentine desire" (56); in this section, as his lips touch the sea, the knight is "Heart–stung with exultation of desire" (144). Tristram's communion with the sea culminates in a climactic moment: "till each glad limb / became / A note of rapture in the tune of life, / Live music mild and keen as sleep and strife" (144).

In order to link this scene with Part I, Swinburne introduces one more parallel. Just before the lovers drink the potion, the poet comments that Tristram: "saw her [Iseult's] clear face lighten on his face / Unwittingly, with unenamoured eyes, / For the last time" (55). Here, after his swim, Tristram looks upon the morning "Unwittingly, with unpresageful eyes, / For the last time" (146). Although they are innocent of any specific knowledge of their fate, Tristram and Iseult submit to its unalterable course. Because Tristram feels in harmony with nature, he can, like "the brief blossoms of the sea...Dance yet before the tempest's tune, and die" (146). He is ready to meet the death that fate has foreordained for him that day.

In the final section, "The Sailing of the Swan," the moribund Tristram wishes only to see Iseult of Ireland before he dies. As he reviews his life, the hero feels no anxiety about his impending death. He addresses the God that Iseult of Brittany has enlisted for her revenge: "Lord, now do all thou wilt with me...For that thou gavest me living yesterday / I bless thee though thou curse me" (160-61). Although Iseult of Brittany obstructs the final reunion of the lovers when she lies to Tristram about the color of the sail, thus bringing about her husband's death before the other Iseult arrives, she cannot deny them their peaceful union after death.

Swinburne's poem concludes with the lovers' burial by a forgiving King Mark, who has learned the circumstances of their
passion. The poet follows his source here, but he introduces one
change: the bodies of Tristram and Iseult are claimed by the sea
which at last unites them. The sea, an important maternal force
and image of eternity in much of Swinburne's poetry, acts here as
a great comforter and protector.

Tristram of Lyonesse is unique among Victorian versions because in it Swinburne remains faithful to the spirit of the legend,
but also infuses it with his most powerful philosophical expression.
The story of fated love suited his artistic purpose very well. Swinburne carefully leaves undisturbed the main elements of the
medieval poetic tradition, but still improves upon it with his poetic
genius. Its structure, Swinburne's rendering of the story by use of
"a succession of dramatic scenes" in a natural setting, also contributes to the poem's medieval spirit. As Oliver Elton points out:
"Tristram is a true romance, where the conception of time is
abolished altogether...the active world is a far–off murmur, not
suffered to intrude otherwise."[11] And Swinburne himself recognized the degree to which he had patterned his poem on medieval
models. Responding to an objection in *Saturday Review*, July 1882,
that Tristram's soliloquy in Part III violates the medieval spirit, he
asserts:

> There is surely nothing more incongruous or anachronistic
> than in the lecture of Theseus [in Chaucer's "Knight's
> Tale"] after the obsequies of Arcite. Both heroes belong
> to the same impossible age of an imaginary world: and
> each has an equal right, should it so please his chronicler,
> to reason in the pauses of action and philosophize in the
> intervals of adventure. After all, the active men of the
> actual age of chivalry were not all of them muscular
> machines for martial or pacific exercise of their physical
> functions or abilities.[12]

This defense of his method in *Tristram* suggests the degree to which Swinburne had familiarized himself with medieval romance, and the lengths to which he went to preserve the essential spirit of the legend.

Swinburne returned once more to the world of Camelot when he composed the *Tale of Balen* in 1896. Again, his distaste for Tennyson's *Idylls*, coupled with his attraction for fated characters, prompted him to write:

> And I think it has not been found unfit to give something of the dignity as well as facility to a narrative which recasts in modern English verse one of the noblest and loveliest old English legends. There is no episode in the cycle of Arthurian romance more genuinely Homeric in its sublime simplicity of submission to the masterdom of fate than that which I have reproduced rather than recast in "The Tale of Balen."[13]

Thus, in *Balen* Swinburne shows the same respect for his medieval source — in this case, Malory — as he had in his *Tristram*. We witness his effort to restore Balen to his original heroic dignity, which had suffered a severe blow in Tennyson's "Balin and Balan," where Balin is depicted as "the savage" whose base, aggressive nature is contrasted with Balan's more reasonable one. Thematically, Balen mirrors Tristram even though it does not center on sexual passion. In both works, Swinburne presents a hero who courageously accepts his fate, and who derives strength from his harmony with nature.

Swinburne observes not only the spirit but the letter of his source. As David Staines observes, the poet frequently reproduces Malory's exact words.[14] However, as I have argued elsewhere, Swinburne was too innovative to resist the impulse to improve upon his source when its spirit could be preserved.[15]

Swinburne restructures the opening of the Balin episode in Malory in order to tell the story chronologically. He also deletes those prophecies of Merlin which are irrelevant to Balen's story

and which Malory uses as linking devices to episodes recounted
much later in his narrative. For instance, Merlin's prediction of the
Quest and of his own entrapment is omitted. In this way, Swinburne tightens the structure and presents a self–contained tale that
heightens its tragic sublimity by accenting the inevitable chain of
events.

In addition, the poet expands upon the incestuous liaison between Arthur and Morgause; he introduces it as a sub–plot to
underscore the power of fate. In Part II, Swinburne devotes three
stanzas to a description of Morgause's prescience of the doom that
haunts her. She exchanges glances with Arthur and, we are told:
"One in blood and one in sin / Their hearts caught fire of pain
within / And knew no goal for them to win / But death that guer-
dons guilt" (178).

In another episode Swinburne also features Morgause. Part V
includes Arthur's lavish burial of Morgause's rebellious husband,
Lot. Here again, the two share the terrible knowledge of their
unwitting incest. Morgause looks upon their son, Mordred "as a
seer that sees, / Anguish of terror bent her knees / And caught her
shuddering breath" (207). Arthur also senses this: "and all his
spirit's might / Withered within him" (208). Mordred alone is
"lightened with fire" as he generates "a sense of death in birth"
(208). The only Victorian uninhibited enough to include the incestuous love, Swinburne uses it to parallel Balen's plight. He, too,
unknowingly brings down upon himself the curse that will cul-
minate in his unfortunate end. Balen, however, knows no fear.
From the beginning, Swinburne stresses the hero's acceptance of
fate; he shows Balen's wild abandon in the knight's exchange with
the damsel who brings him the sword adventure. After he has
pulled the sword from the scabbard, she warns Balen to return it,
but he refuses. She replies: "God bids not thee believe / Truth"
(181). Balen's undaunted attitude is: "What chance God sends,
that chance I take" (180). He is committed to act out his destiny.

This acceptance of fate, along with his connection with nature,
gives Balen the courage to achieve great feats of bravery with his

twin, Balan. However, fate has foreordained that Balen's good intentions will produce only a series of hapless slayings and will end in the unwitting fratricide of Balen and Balen. According to Swinburne, however, Balen is still heroic because of his courage in the face of adversity. Despite the malevolent fate that ruthlessly pursues him, Balen stoically accepts the consequences of his actions. Before he dies, Balen's life flashes before him and Swinburne comments:

> So, dying not as a coward that dies
> And dares not look in death's dim eyes
> Straight as the stars on seas and skies
> When moon and sun recoil and rise,
> He looked on life and death, and slept (4. 245).

As in his *Tristram*, Swinburne structures his *Balen* according to the seasonal and diurnal patterns of nature. He uses these cyclical rhythms to show that life should not be measured by its length, but by its quality. To illustrate that Balen's short life is complete, Swinburne opens each section of the poem with an epic simile that mirrors Balen's fortunes.

Part I begins with spring, as the youthful knight rides to Camelot, hoping to win fame. Parts II through V recount the summer of Balen's life. He gains glory with the sword adventure, performs a series of heroic feats on Arthur's behalf, and at last wins the fame he has sought. However, he also slays the Lady of the Lake, which triggers the series of events that leads to his doom. In Part VI, the autumn of the year, the hero suffers the murders of two knights in his protective custody, strikes the Dolorous Stroke, and is cursed by three kingdoms. Part VII represents the winter of Balen's life. He meets more misfortune when Garnysshe of the Mount — a knight whom Balen tries to help — slays his beloved and her lover, then commits suicide. Before he does so, Garnysshe reproaches Balen, who has only tried to aid him. Finally, Balen and

Balan commit the unwitting mutual fratricide, discovering each other's identity only at the moment of death.

Because Balen accepts his fate with stoic resolve, he will enjoy the fame of Tristram and Iseult who, by virtue of their transgression, are immortalized in art. Merlin's eulogy of the brothers, which concludes the poem, expresses this:

> This is the tale that memory writes
> Of men whose names like stars shall stand,
> Balen and Balan, sure of hand,
> Two brethren of Northumberland,
> In life and death good knights (246).

In *The Tale of Balen* Swinburne restores the hero's dignity and imparts some of the "sublime simplicity" he had hoped to achieve in his retelling of the legend. His selection of Tristram and Balen—two of the most fated figures in medieval romance and the two whom Tennyson alters for the worse—illustrates Swinburne's concept of the hero as one who accepts his destiny with courage and acts in accord with nature.

More than his contemporaries, Swinburne remains faithful to the medieval spirit of his sources while infusing his Arthurian poems with his most profound philosophical statements. In addition, these works share with much of his other verse the thematic preoccupation with fate, the reverence for nature, and the glorification of the individual who defies the stifling constraints of a humanly conceived, vindictive deity. As in his non–Arthurian poetry, these works reveal the influence of classical tragedy; they also contain some of Swinburne's experimental aesthetic devices, such as his use of the sleep–trance and his fondness for paradox. Because his interest in the Arthurian legend was a lasting one, these poems offer much to the student of Swinburne. They also serve as a fine contribution to the *Matter of Britain* and deserve careful consideration from Arthurians.

Kearney State College

NOTES

[1]David Staines, "Swinburne's Arthurian Poetry and Its Medieval Sources," *Studia Neophilogica* 50 (1978), 56.

[2]In 1858 Rossetti planned five Arthurian poems that never reached fruition. However, in the "Notes" to his edition of Rossetti's *Works*, William Michael Rossetti comments that all but one of these topics appeared in his paintings.

[3]All quotations are from *The Complete Works of Algernon Charles Swinburne*, eds. Sir Edmund Gosse and Thomas James Wise (London, 1925).

[4]Morris' painting depicts Tristram among the sunflowers. Swinburne relied on several Pre-Raphaelite paintings for his early compositions.

[5]Jerome McCann, *Swinburne: An Experiment in Criticism* (Chicago, 1972). McCann discusses the poet's employment of the sleep–trance and his view of the "secret light" in "Sestina" and elsewhere, but his remarks also shed light on this device as Swinburne uses it in "Lancelot." McCann's comments on this subject may be found on 177-82.

[6]T. Earle Welby, *A Study of Swinburne* (1926; rpt., New York, 1969), 151.

[7]Algernon Charles Swinburne, "Dedicatory Epistle," rpt in *Swinburne Replies*. ed. Clyde Kenneth Hyder (Syracuse, 1966), 99.

[8]Cecil Y. Lang, ed., *The Swinburne Letters* (New Haven, 1959-1962), 4, 286.

[9]"Swinburne's Arthurian Poetry," 54

[10]McCann, *An Experiment in Criticism*, 140.

[11]Oliver Elton, "Mr. Swinburne's Poems," was first published in *Modern Studies* (1907) and is rptd. in *Swinburne: The Critical Heritage*, ed. Clyde Kenneth Hyder (New York, 1970), 230

[12]Swinburne, "Dedicatory Epistle," in *Swinburne Replies*, 99-100.

[13]Swinburne, "Dedicatory Epistle," in *Swinburne Replies*, 105.

[14]Staines, "Swinburne's Arthurian Poetry," 65-68.

[15]See my article, "Swinburne's Concept of the Hero in *The Tale of Balen*," *Arthurian Interpretations* 1 (1986), 48-53.

Justice and Vindication in William Morris's "The Defence of Guenevere"

Florence Boos

William Morris was the only major Victorian poet who chose medieval settings for most of his poetry, a choice which often contributed to dismissals of his work as "escapist."[1] Some critics granted partial dispensation from this epithet to the dramatic monologues of *The Defence of Guenevere* (1858), but the conventional view of this work was reexpressed as recently as 1981 by Margaret Lourie, in her introduction to the Garland scholarly edition of *The Defence*:

> [The] *Guenevere* poems refused to confront a single moral or intellectual question of their own age or any other. So far from displaying "the powerful application of ideas to life" later recommended by Arnold, they displayed no ideas at all.[2]

Her subsequent oblique "praise" of Morris follows similar lines: "Like Yeats, Morris refused to compose the Victorian poetry of social responsibility."[3]

Such "modern(ist)" judgments of Morris seem to *accept* uncritically, rather than repudiate, the "moral" and "intellectual'" categories of his more censorious Victorian critics. A related middle view grants Morris's stark medieval projections a kind of alternate psychological realism, but waives further inquiry into their intellectual and emotional coherence. I will argue that *The Defence* does not evade controversy on its own terms, and that its powerful evocations of stress, rupture, and violence reverberate in a world of stark ethical imperatives. Morris's contemporaries found these imperatives appallingly bleak; most critics who interpret him as a precursor of the *fin-de-siècle* simply ignore them.

Similarly, I will suggest that the many narrative, chronological, and spatial dislocations of consciousness in *The Defence of Guenevere* are not signs of lapses in authorial control, but deliberate choices which witness the power of the principal characters' anxieties and the passions which overwhelm their lives. Many of these characters suffer near–dislocation and abrogation of the usual structures and boundaries of identity, but no comforting censor orders or inhibits their direct responses to a world of mingled desire and pain.

On this account, then, Morris's narrative disjunctions and symbolic juxtapositions anticipated techniques sometimes called "modern" or "postmodern" in ambiances which remain recognizably Victorian. The world of the *Defence* poems is decaying and war–torn, and it is inhabited by lonely men and suffering women who often seek consolation in edenic memories of childhood and fantasies of visionary reunion with nature in the moment of death. Amid these lost struggles, the *Defence* poems enjoin their protagonists to preserve a tenuous vision of beauty, at the risk of life, and often in defiance of certain failure and annihilation. The poems' testing of imagined identities against hostile forces reflects two tacit assumptions: that no honorable compromise with such "defences" of beauty is possible; and that it cannot take place in any sheltered or even durable "palace of art." In Morris's work, no such shelter exists. He was anti–puritan, and he deeply disliked conventional devices of didactic literature, so his presentations of this rigoristic ethic is implicit, but his reluctance to preach the obvious should not obscure his poetry's coherence, subtlety, and emotional force. Much of the density and subtlety of Morris's early work emerges in the passionate rhetorical indirection he used as a mode of expression for an unusual clarity of vision.

Critical considerations of the title poem, "The Defence of Guenevere," have responded to the principal question about it which I have raised above. Does the poem provide a coherent intellectual, moral, or artistic "defence" of Guenevere? Or is her monologue simply a painterly flourish of deviously emotional

self-revelation? What interpretations can be found for the angeli-
cally imposed "choice of cloths"? Her refusal to account for the
blood–spattered bed? Her allusion to her own weakness and
beauty? Or her threat that Launcelot will save her once gain, in
trial by combat?

One view of the poem, that of Laurence Perrine, presents it as
a rhetorical *tour de force*:

> ... But Morris no more necessarily condones Guenevere's
> conduct than Milton does Satan's when he describes the
> archfiend as a "great Commander" and as possessing
> "dauntless courage." Morris has merely taken one of
> Malory's characters in a moment of stress and brought her
> intensely alive. His task has been not to excuse or blame,
> but to vivify.[4]

Perrine bases his argument in part on a specious analogy with
Browning: ". . . there is no more reason for supposing that Morris
is justifying [his] characters than there is to believe that Browning
is defending the Duke of Ferrara or the Bishop of St. Praxed's."[5]
Perrine's point is undercut by the fact that the ironies of
Browning's early dramatic monologues usually underscore the sort
of moral judgments which, according to Perrine, Morris supposed-
ly waives. We enjoy the process of uncovering their systematic
deceptions *because* the Duke of Ferrara and Bishop of St. Praxed's
are manifestly evil — arrogant, grasping, murderous hypocrites.
Nor do they draw our sympathy by tremulous courage in the face
of public humiliation and a threatened execution at the stake.

Morris's own 1856 review of *Men and Women* also makes clear
that he preferred the poems of heroism and love ("Before,"
"After," and "Childe Roland," for example), and he conspicuously
failed to share Browning's fascination with devious hypocrisy: of
Bishop Bloughram, for example, he remarks bluntly that "for my
part I dislike him thoroughly."[6] In "The Statue and the Bust,"
Browning had carefully left questions about the morality of adultery in suspension, but criticized the cautious lovers as follows:

> . . . the sin I impute to each frustrate ghost
> Is—the unlit lamp and ungirt loin . . . .

In his review, Morris essentially agrees. He quickly passes over the sin of adultery, but expresses strong moral contempt for the hypocrisy of time–serving and "cowardly irresolution":

> Yet were the lovers none the less sinners, therefore, rather the more in that they were cowards; for in thought they indulged their love freely, and no fear of God, no hate of wrong or love of right restrained them, but only a certain cowardly irresolution.[7]

Such remarks express an early form of his lifelong belief in the moral value of "resolute" action and liberation of "frustrate ghost(s)," tempered by a personal ideal of fidelity which he never abandoned.

A somewhat different view of Morris's Guenevere emerges in Carole Silver's " 'The Defence of Guenevere': A Further Interpretation."[8] Like Perrine, Silver assumes Guenevere's moral culpability, but she argues that

> Our sympathy remains with Guenevere and her great but guilty love. The passion in whose name she has transgressed remains more important than her transgression. Guenevere's testimony, looked at in full, is to the awful power of a love that dissolves all—morality included—in it. Through this testimony we can plainly see Morris's profound grasp of illicit romantic passion.[9]

This interpretation is more faithful than Perrine's to the poem's rhetorical surge toward sympathetic identification with Guenevere, who at great psychic cost has told the truth about her single-minded love for Launcelot. The "sympathy" Silver senses is clearly present in the poem's strong identification of Guenevere with the elements of a verdant and joyous nature, in turn associated with the inherent moral worth of spontaneous and infelt love. But Silver's rhetoric offers only moderate hope that "the awful power of a love that dissolves all — morality included" — can suggest another, more comprehensive morality — one, say, that may have guided Morris himself, when he saw himself, ironically, cast as Arthur. In her 1981 book, *The Romance of William Morris,* Silver argues in more censorious fashion:

> [Guenevere] seeks to excuse her sin by suggesting its universality, and she blames it upon the moral confusion in the universe: things are not what they seem. But she still must admit that, whatever the cause, she has done wrong.[10]

> [She] intends a speech of self–vindication, but her words and actions persuade the reader of her adultery. . . . She does not yet recognize in her cruelty to her opponents, her glee at the death of Meliagraunce, and her threats to destroy her enemies and the kingdom, the signs of her moral and emotional deterioration.[11]

Other, less austere readings appear in several articles published in the 1970's. John Hollow's "William Morris and the Judgment of God,"[12] for example, correctly observes that Morris often pointed a moral in his early work that "[men] who concern themselves about God's judgments tend to take their own judgments for His. . . . For this reason, men should not concern themselves about God or his judgments. . . ."[13] (a later, more secular variant occurs at the end of "The Hill of Venus," in the blossoming of the Pope's staff). Here, Hollow argues, "Morris's Guenevere does not deny adultery, she denies Gauwaine's claim to know God's judgment of her."[14]

A more "aesthetic" vindication appears in Patrick Brantlinger's 1973 article, *"The Defence of Guenevere and Other Poems,"*[15] which suggests that Morris elevates Guenevere's sheer beauty to a moral force. Guenevere's defense, Brantlinger remarks, is part of a "dialectic between art and life" in which Guenevere expresses a higher morality based largely on aesthetic

response: "the substance of [Guenevere's] defense is largely that
she is so beautiful and love is so beautiful that she ought to be
forgiven."
  In "Guenevere's Critical Performance" (1979),[16] Jonathan F.
S. Post dismisses moral issues altogether, and construes
Guenevere as a rhetorician who, "like all of us, constructs dramas
and comes to accept these imagined creations as perhaps the only
form of truth we might ever know in this world."[17] Perhaps—yet
Browning's murderer Guido "constructs" as consummately as
Guenevere. Even Post adopts a mildly normative tone in his con-
clusion that "Guenevere's defense seems also a young author's
defense of poetry, while the most basic denial of Gauwaine and his
accusations, whatever they are, is the poet's refusal ever to let him
speak."[18]
  A deeper point emerges in Dennis Balch's 1975 "Guenevere's
Fidelity to Arthur in 'The Defence of Guenevere' and 'King
Arthur's Tomb,'" which attempts for the first time to read
Guenevere's allegory of the blue and red cloths as a coherent
representation of her situation. He too assumes her "guilt," but
remarks perceptively that Morris

> [p]erhaps . . . realized that the Arthurian legends em-
> bodied a system of values contrary to the values he himself
> was developing which would depend on the central impor-
> tance of the individual sensual experience rather than a
> denial of man's animal nature.[19]

  Aspects of several of these views seem to me right, but I would
stress the extent to which Morris was no more willing than the
author of "The Palace of Art" to accept *any* casuistry that there is
an underlying antagonism between morality and beauty, life and
art. Guenevere's beauty would be insufficient, were it not aligned
with a "truth" which it enhanced—a truth which Morris found
largely in sympathy with her victimization. For Morris, such sympathies clearly overrode any questions about conventional transgression of arbitrary sexual codes and harmonized with deeper

loyalties that guided his evolving sense of social and political morality.

Morris and his friends were of course familiar with discussions of that great Victorian codification of the double standard, the Divorce Law of 1857, which permitted men but not women to sue for divorce on grounds of adultery. Morris composed most of *The Defence* poems in 1857, and he and his rather idealistic and iconoclastic friends wished to make clear their support for a single standard of romantic and marital obligation based on affection, not legal compulsion. In keeping with this ethic, Guenevere eventually claims a right to tolerance and freedom from censorious male judgment, and she avers that she and Launcelot have both acted rightly, even heroically, in a context which is both restrictive and oppressive.

All the critics cited assume that Guenevere has in fact committed adultery, but Morris's poem actually leaves the issue in suspension, which suggests that the question of technical innocence may have been a matter of relative indifference to him. As Angela Carson and others have pointed out,[20] Malory had presented two possibly conflicting accounts of the lovers' conduct. The incident which resembles Morris's poem more closely occurs in "The Knight of the Cart" (Book XIX of "The Book of Sir Launcelot and Queen Guinevere"); in it, Malory makes clear Guinevere's innocence of the rather ludicrous charge that she has slept with one of her wounded knights, but describes with amusement the assignation between Launcelot and Guinevere which precedes Mellyagaunte's discovery of the blood–stained sheets.

On the other hand, in Book XX, "The Most Piteous Tale of the Morte Arthur Saunz Guerdon," Launcelot's assertion that she has been "trew unto my lorde Arthur"[21] is given what seems to be the author's endorsement. After the queen invites Launcelot to her bedchamber (as she does in Morris's poem), Malory's narrator becomes studiously coy: "whether they were abed other at other maner of disportis, me lyste nat thereof make no mencion, for love that tyme was not as love ys nowadayes" (821). Throughout Book

XX Launcelot also defends the queen's "honor" with apparent sincerity:

> .. my lady, quene Guenyver, ys as trew a lady unto youre person as ys ony lady lyvyng unto her lorde. . . . (837).

and he explains his regrettable abduction as follows:

> "Sir, hit was never in my thought. . . to withholde the quene frome my lorde Arthur, but . . . mesemed hit was my parte to save her lyff and put her from that daunger tyll bettir recover myght com" (842).

The apparent discrepancy between Books XVIII and XX remains unresolved, but some aspects of Morris's Guenevere may be consistent with the Guenevere of Malory's Book XX, Launcelot's faithful lover in spirit, who may or may not have remained loyal to her husband.

Malory's account of Arthur's kingdom also includes an immense range of other material which Morris simply omits, whose cumulative effect is to make Launcelot and Guinevere's affair one node of an elaborate network of social and political loyalties, disloyalties, and intrigues. Malory's Arthur and Guinevere are on fairly good terms, and Gauwaine's anger is partially provoked by Launcelot's killing of his two brothers Gareth and Gaheris—as in Icelandic sagas, deaths of Malorian kinspeople require reparation. Malory narrates a tragedy of inevitable conflict between honorable persons, who love and respect one another, and generally subordinate brief moments of sexual passion to more important considerations of friendship, political honor, or loyalty to kin.

Morris's "Defence," by contrast, ignored the personal ties between Malory's Arthur and Launcelot, suppressed Arthur's good nature, and modified Malory's account of a military caste's interlocking feuds and attachments, to recreate a tale of two lovers whose overarching attraction and pained loyalty overwhelm their lives. In Morris's poem, narrative intensity and analysis have migrated inward, to make Launcelot and Guenevere's love a consequence of alienation rather than courtly intrigue. Morris's anguished heroine seems especially remote from Malory's politically shrewd, cheerfully energetic, and self–respecting queen: Malory's Guinevere is routinely self–protective and resilient under stress; Morris' Guenevere blurts out her defense in a rush of inspired compulsion; Malory's queen is aloof and autocratic; Morris's intense and vulnerable. Confronting "such great lords," Malory's Guinevere might feel a prudent mixture of anger and apprehension; but never Guenevere's "awe and shame." Against the densely textual background of the poem's modified loyalties and passions, Morris seems to have intended his silence to suggest that the victim's technical "guilt" or "innocence" was not a significant moral issue.

Guenevere, in any case, is one of several *Defence* heroines characterized by physical vulnerability, courage in defense of passionate emotions, and vicarious identification with deeds of *prouesse* performed by their male lovers, a recurring pattern throughout Morris' early and middle writings. Morris's early poetic world is especially stark in its polarization by genres: in "The Defence" and its companion poem "King Arthur's Tomb," a stereotypically manly life of action and military self–defense drives Launcelot forth into the world, while Guenevere waits, confined in castle and nunnery, for external forces to determine her fate. His is an oppression of sustained arduous effort and repeated risk of life, hers of self–conscious constriction and inactivity.[22] The queen's defense is a great but isolated act, wrung from her in a state of acute distress. Memories of her moments in the garden with Launcelot provide some release from her burden of anxiety, but she remains essentially alone throughout the poem. As in the rest of *The Defence*, only the rarest and most exceptional moments of freedom from constraint bring happiness and love unmarred by fear.

The extreme rigidity of the poem's sexual roles also explains why so much of Guenevere's "defense" must indict her own victimization. She vindicates her passion as the mature love of a

woman in special circumstances — married at any early age, for
reasons of state, to a distinguished but neglectful spouse, she has
preserved for years a singleminded, faithful attachment to another
man whom she would have preferred to marry. A powerless
woman falsely judged by powerful men, she demands that she be
permitted to construe "duty" and "fidelity" in terms that are intelligible in the actual circumstances of her life.

When she lifts her downcast gaze and begins to accuse her
accusers, she also pleads her need to escape a life of weakness and
repression, and defends the transforming strength of her love for
Launcelot, her only human contact in a world of arbitrary
manipulation and intrigue. She avers that she has violated no
genuinely moral ideals; her offense is that her physical beauty and
love of Launcelot embody natural and creative forces which shame
the destructive malice of Gauwaine, Mellyagraunce, and, by implication, Arthur himself. Her love is both the flower and the green
fuse through which it drives. Nor is she altogether specious, as
several prior critics have assumed, in her claim that her beauty and
Launcelot's heroism attest the virtue of their cause. To defend
herself before her accusers, she has had to conquer internal voices
of uncertainty and shame, and give articulation to modes of self–
respect which are based on belief in natural human love.
Launcelot's final rescue only confirms the psychological freedom
she has already won from within.

*****

The opening passages of "The Defence" present Guenevere as
a desperate human being, constricted by her clothes, confined, and
about to be bound to the stake. Her emotions are painfully immediate; her forehead is clammy with sweat, and her face stings as
though she had been hit. Every thought and gesture is choked,
strained, and constricted ("She threw her wet hair backward from
her brow,/ Her hand close to her mouth touching her cheek"), as

"knowing now that they would have her speak," she begins her defense with a rote gesture of rhetorical deference:

> "God wot I ought to say, I have done ill,
> And pray you all forgiveness heartily!
> Because you must be right, such great lords — still. . . . (ll.
>   13-15)

She does not beg for forgiveness, however, and retains a measure of autonomy from the first. Speech steadies her, and soon prompts her to defend herself. Consider, she asks, how life would seem to you in my stead:

> "Listen, suppose your time were come to die,
> And you were quite alone and very weak;
> Yea, laid a dying. . . (ll. 16-18)
>   . . .
> Suppose a hush should come, then some one speak:
>
> " 'One of these cloths is heaven, and one is hell,
> Now choose one cloth for ever; which they be,
> I will not tell you . . . . (ll. 21-24)

In her allegory, the commanding patriarchal presence of a "great God's angel" presents the cloths, and demands that a bizarrely fateful choice be made without preparation or foreknowledge:

> "And one of these strange choosing cloths was blue,
> Wavy and long, and one cut short and red;
> No man could tell the better of the two.
>
> After a shivering half–hour, suppose you said:
> 'God help! heaven's colour, the blue,' and he said, 'hell.'
>   (ll. 30-38)

Some critics have argued that the blue cloth symbolizes her adultery with Launcelot, but I agree with Balch that it represents more plausibly her "choice" to marry Arthur, forced upon her by "great lords" for solemn reasons of duty and state ("heaven's color"). In retrospect, the vow of her arranged marriage has now become "a little word,/ Scarce ever meant at all." When Launcelot arrives, he turns her inner world "white with flame," and prompts the agonized recognition that things might have been different, a recognition that utterly transforms the premises of her emotional life.

The perverse arbitrariness and opacity of Guenevere's "choice" makes clear that it was no choice (perhaps the response to "red" would also have been "hell?"); her real point is that human emotional life ought not to be subject to arbitrary manipulation. The same outraged sense of good faith betrayed also underlies the sudden force of her thrice repeated defense:

> "Nevertheless you, O Sir Gauwaine, lie,
> Whatever may have happened through these years,
> God knows I speak truth, saying that you lie." (ll. 46-48)

For a time, at least — indeed, for most of her marriage, if not all of it — she has dutifully followed the forms of fidelity to her husband (the "blue cloth") as propriety, religion, and the angel required her to do. The results have been devastating.

As her defense gathers rhetorical force, so, suddenly does her physical presence:

> Though still she stood right up, and never shrunk,
> But spoke on bravely, glorious lady fair!
> Whatever tears her full lips may have drunk,
>
> She stood, and seemed to think, and wrung her hair,
> Spoke out at last with no more trace of shame,
> With passionate twisting of her body there: . . . (ll. 55-60).

The narrator's admiring tribute, "glorious lady fair!" is the poem's most direct authorial judgment). As Guenevere makes her life's most public declaration, she has thus shed her earlier "shame," and speaks without self–consciousness, as much for her own satisfaction as to persuade her accusers. Later in the poem (ll. 223-238), Guenevere almost comes to embody the beauty and energy of nature, a surge of elemental forces, winds, waters, and seasonal progressions:

> "Yea also at my full heart's strong command,
> See through my long throat how the words go up
>
> . . .
> . . . yea now
> This little wind is rising, . . . (ll. 228-29, 232-33).

In keeping with this near–apotheosis is an identification of her love with seasonal change: Launcelot has first appeared to her at Christmas, and summer brings surges of emotion that are literally elemental:

> "And in the Summer I grew white with flame,
> And bowed my head down—Autumn, and the sick
> Sure knowledge things would never be the same,
>
> "However often Spring might be most thick
> Of blossoms and buds, smote on me, and I grew
> Careless of most things, let the clock tick, tick
>
> "To my unhappy pulse, that beat right through
> My eager body. . . . (ll. 68-77)

The climax of her longing comes when she again meets Launcelot, in an emblematically walled palace garden, whose immurement paradoxically heightens her sense of pleasurable longing:

I was half mad. . .

        walled round every way;

I was right joyful of that wall of stone,
That shut the flowers and trees up with the sky,
And trebled all the beauty: . . . .(ll. 110-114)

In the epiphanic vision which follows, a strange interfusion
with nature almost impels her to the edge of rational control. Her
"tenderly darkened fingers" merge eerily into the light, and "join"
the variegated "yellow–spotted singers," which sing in the trees, all
"drawn upward by the sun."

"A little thing just then had made me mad;
I dared not think, as I was wont to do,
Sometimes, upon my beauty; if I had

"Held out my long hand up against the blue,
And, looking on the tenderly darken'd fingers,
Thought that by rights one ought to see quite through,

"There, see you, where the soft still light yet lingers,
Round by the edges; what should I have done,
If this had joined with yellow spotted singers,

"And startling green drawn upward by the sun?
But shouting, loosed out, see now! all my hair,
And trancedly stood watching the west wind run

. . . I lose my head e'en now in doing this. . . . (ll. 118-130)

In this altered state, Launcelot's oddly adventitious arrival
("In that garden fair came Launcelot walking. . . .") is quickly
subsumed into her epiphany. She now rejects forever the lesser-
souled Arthur, as a man of "great name and little love."

The lovers' dreamlike garden tryst is appropriately beatific, but also leaves a puzzling question: "After that day why is it Guenevere grieves?" (l. 13). One obvious answer — continued longing — would account for the return of the lines which follow, her second indignant refrain of denial:

"Nevertheless you, O Sir Gauwaine, lie,
Whatever happened on through all those years,
God knows I speak truth, saying that you lie. (ll. 142-44)

Passages such as these bear the interpretation that Guenevere and Launcelot, for the most part at least, have been "courtly" lovers, whose observance of the code's formal proprieties makes possible her repudiation of Gauwaine's charge — "Being such a lady, could I weep these tears/ If this were true?"

In any case, she now shifts to attack. She reminds Gauwaine that his mother had been beheaded on a similar charge of adultery, and warns him rather bizarrely that her slain spirit may return to haunt him, as a kind of malign variant of the speaker in "Ode to the West Wind":

. . . let me not scream out
For ever after, when the shrill winds blow

"Through half your castle–locks let me now shout
For ever after in the winter night;
When you ride out alone (ll. 158-62)

The threat only underscores once again her actual helplessness, for of course it can only be realized in another world.

In this one, more mundanely, she next reminds her accusers of Launcelot's physical *prouesse*, which has already defended her against Mellyagraunce's invasion of her bedchamber and observation of "blood upon my bed."

Whose blood then pray you? is there any law
"To make a queen say why some spots of red
Lie on her coverlet? (ll. 174-76)

Silver interprets the "spots of red" as evidence of a thwarted rape
attempt by Mellyeagrance,[23] but Elaine and English Showalter
have observed that the Victorians heavily censored any reference
to menstruation, the most obvious alternate explanation of the
"spots."[24] Morris's homely retention of this Malorian detail may
have seemed to contemporary readers more daring than ludicrous.

In any case, Guenevere gleefully recalls Mellyagraunce's fate
at the hands of her "half–armed" champion, and two brief passages then precede the poem's ecstatic conclusion. The first is a
remarkable set–piece, a climactic final evocation of her epiphanic
self–image as a powerful force of nature:

                    . . . say no rash word
Against me, being so beautiful; my eyes,
Wept all away to grey, may bring some sword

"To drown you in your blood; see my breast rise,
Like waves of purple sea, as here I stand;
And how my arms are moved in wonderful wise,

"Yea also at my full heart's strong command,
See through my long throat how the words go up
In ripples to my mouth; how in my hand

"The shadow lies like wine within a cup
Of marvellously colour'd gold; yea now
This little wind is rising, look you up,

"And wonder how the light is falling so
Within my moving tresses: will you dare,
When you have looked a little on my brow,

"To say this thing is vile? or will you care
For any plausible lies of cunning woof,
When you can see my face with no lie there

"For ever? am I not a gracious proof— (ll. 223-41)

Notice how remote are the elements of this self–portrait from conventional images of female sexual beauty. Even the more obviously erotic descriptions ("see my breast rise/ Like waves of purple sea") have an oddly impersonal intensity (not "see how I move my arms" or "how I speak," but "see how my arms are moved in wonderful wise. . . how the words go up in ripples to my mouth"). Such language suggests that she represents a generalized force of natural goodness, an alignment of id and superego curiously without ego. Her "face with no lie there/ For ever" also provides a "gracious proof" that innocence of spirit can embody itself in an appropriate outer form. This near–Keatsian assimilation of beauty to truth is obviously circular in its celebration of "beauty" as some kind of heterosexual lifeforce, but it is at least intelligible in these terms, and it also provides a kind of abstract formal design of human emotions under stress. After these lines the epiphanic vision fades, but Guenevere remains a person who has become conscious of her own dignity for the first time in the face of acute pain and likely death.

In the next passage, she recalls her last tryst with Launcelot, but refuses to repeat his parting words: "By God! I will not tell you more to–day,/ Judge any way you will—what matters it?" (ll. 277-78). Launcelot's last words, of course, may have included a promise of the rescue which follows (as they had in Malory), but her defiant reticence also expresses her claim to privacy and autonomy. She stands exposed to derision and judgment, and will hold private her last conversation with her lover, if necessary to death. Accordingly, she will contribute no more to her own defense: she can remember

> — all, all, verily,
> But just that which would save me; these things flit (ll. 281-82).

Those who view Guenevere as deceptive presumably consider this another evasion. I would rather believe that her "defence" leads naturally to this silence, a form of emancipation from her accusers; in the end their judgments do not matter to her, or to Morris, and she refuses to yield further to their compulsion.

After all this, there is admittedly something anticlimactic, if opportune, about Launcelot's subsequent arrival on a "roan charger," at "headlong speed," a kind of *equus ex machina* who quickly but abruptly concludes the physical action of the poem. Guenevere has already won her psychological independence, after which the narrative then conveniently provides a form of external confirmation — the "judgment of God." Appropriately, too, for the first time in the poem, Guenevere's physical movements now embody happiness in simple ways: "She lean'd eagerly,/ And gave a slight spring sometimes." Such small, human motions are consistent with the earlier idealized descriptions, quoted above ("... she stood right up, and never shrank/ But spake on bravely. . . "). But they are also less emblematic and more natural than the earlier apotheosis of Guenevere as the "glorious lady fair."

*****

What, then, are the grounds Morris assigns for Guenevere's "defence"? Earlier, I reviewed several alternate interpretations of its substance. Some would construe her argument as one of obliquity, cunning, and deceit, or hold that her defense, though sincere, is based largely on grounds of grand but helpless passion, and shifts and turns which tellingly reflect her need for evasion and lack of more "rational" justifications. Others have argued that the poem's principal criteria for judgment are aesthetic or rhetorical rather than moral. All these views seem to me inadequate or incomplete, for I believe Morris wished to make the stronger case that Guenevere is essentially guiltless – and that her claims are not only coherent but ultimately persuasive. Her defense's anacolutha follow a deeper logic of justice, reason and emotion, and eventually create a sense of personal and psychological liberation.

On this interpretation, Morris comes out well in the spectrum of mid–Victorian debates on the nature and role of women.[25] Apart from the Brownings, no major poets of the 1850's permitted their heroines to indict the straitened circumstances of their lives, much less align themselves rhetorically with liberating forces of nature.

To women who were obviously denied the most rudimentary forms of personal autonomy in contemporary Victorian society, a heroine who tries, however spasmodically, to break free of such constraints may have been an attractive figure. Compared with other adulterous women in English poetry of the 1850's – Bulwer-Lytton's passionately lonely but cruel Clytemnestra (*The Earl's Return and Other Poems*, 1855), or the abjectly "sinful" Guinevere of Tennyson's 1859 *Idylls* – Guenevere is also a virtual paragon of beneficent self–determination.

Clearly, though, some of the poem's tacit premises severely limit its value as an assertion of female autonomy. At her weakest, Guenevere is an idealized male projection of single–minded heterosexual passion, born, like Byron's "woman," "for love alone." In the entire poem she mentions no human ties but Launcelot, and apparently has no significant obligations besides fidelity to Arthur's "little love." Guenevere's "defence" – that she has been forced into a loveless marriage for reasons of state – takes her social and physical powerlessness for granted, and Morris clearly exaggerates her "feminine" helplessness to exacerbate the stifling intensity of her repressed emotions at the beginning of the poem. The overarching assumption of physical helplessness which underlies the poem's chivalric ethic assigns vastly different levels of responsibility to women and men. To impose *more* responsibility on women in sexual matters is bigotry, of course; but the reverse mixes compassion and empathy with kindly condescension and *noblesse oblige.*

So the evidence is sympathetic but mixed. Only in flashes at first does Guenevere speak with conviction, analytical power, or noticeable insight. But the insights do come, and at her best — during her brief quasi–transfiguration as a benign force of nature — she becomes for Morris an archetypal voice of liberation from the crippling social and sexual constraints that closed in on Victorian women like a vise. It is no accident that twelve years later the creator of Guenevere quietly but steadfastly refused to abide by Victorian social codes which almost enjoined on him the role of a Gauwaine or an Arthur.

At any rate, "The Defence of Guenevere" seems to me a genuine vindication of a limited but admirable female psyche. Her "defence" is really twofold: first, a weaker argument, that mercy is justice for those whose natural desires have been repressed; and a second, stronger one, that those who seem to require "forgiveness" may represent forces more natural and vital than those who "forgive" them. In poetry at least, the meek can inherit the earth. When Guenevere consciously identifies her passionate energies with the elements of nature and an idealized sanctity of natural emotion, her real self grows in dignity, self–respect, and strength.

Thus it seems to me that Guenevere's evocations of her past, her strange allegory of the opaquely ominous "cloths," her flashes of insight into herself and her accusers, and her triumphant repudiation of the self–blame and constriction which oppressed her are coherent and persuasive. In the end, Morris's rare combination of anti–puritanism, contempt for hypocrisy, and temperamental identification with victims of oppression helped him create one of the century's better vindications of a heroine's right of self–determination.

University of Iowa

NOTES

[1] A shift away from the "escapist" line in Morris criticism occurred with Patrick Brantlinger's "The Defence of Guenevere and Other Poems," *Victorian Newsletter* 44 (Fall 1973), 18-24.

[2] Margaret Lourie, ed., *The Defence of Guenevere and Other Poems* (New York, 1981), 22.

[3] Lourie, 22.

[4] Laurence Perrine, "William Morris' Guenevere: An Interpretation," *Philological Quarterly* 39 (1960), 241.

[5] Perrine, 241.

[6] *The Collected Works of William Morris,* ed. May Morris. 24 vols. (London, 1910-15), I:330.

[7] *Collected Works,* I: 344.

[8] Carole Silver, " 'The Defence of Grenevere': A Further Interpretation," *Studies in English Literature* 9 (1969), 695-702.

[9] Silver, 702.

[10] Silver, *The Romance of William Morris,* (Athens, Ohio, 1981), 21.

[11] Silver, *The Romance,* 24.

[12] John Hollow, "William Morris and the Judgment of God," *PMLA* 86 (1971), 446-51.

[13] Hollow, 450.

[14] Hollow, 447.

[15] Brantlinger, 20.

[16] Jonathan F. S. Post, "Guenevere's Crticial Performance," *Victorian Poetry* 17 (1979), 317-27.

[17] Post, 319.

[18] Post, 327.

[19]Dennis Balch, "Guenevere's Fidelity to Arthur in 'Defence of Guenevere' and 'King Arthur's Tomb'," *Victorian Poetry* 13 (1975), 70.

[20]Angela Carson, *Philological Quarterly* 42 (1963), 113-34; Silver, " 'The Defence of Guenevere'," 695-96; David Staines, "William Morris' Treatment of His Medieval Sources in *The Defence of Guenevere*," *Studies in Philology* 70 (1973), 439-64.

[21]Eugène Vinaver, *The Works of Sir Thomas Malory* (London, 1962), 848. Page numbers in text are from this edition.

[22]Please see my "Sexual Polarization in *The Defence of Guenevere*," in *Browning Institute Studies*, vol. 13 (1985), 181-200.

[23]Silver,*The Romance*, 20.

[24]"Victorian Women and Menstruation," in Martha Vicinus, ed., *Suffer and Be Still: Women in the Victorian Age* (Bloomington, Indiana, 1972), 38-44.

[25]Post correctly observes that Guenevere's eristic fluency is unusual in itself: "Tennyson's submissive Guenevere [sic] or his repeatedly hushed Enid are more faithful to the original conception of women in romance, if somewhat less interesting as characters, than Morris's Queen" (318).

King Mark in Wagner's *Tristan und Isolde*

Henry Hall Peyton III

In 1854 Richard Wagner wrote to Franz Liszt about a new idea for a music–drama, an operatic version of the legend of Tristan and Isolde. It was to be "a simple work," but a "most full–blooded musical conception."[1] Again, in an 1856 letter to Liszt, Wagner wrote of "a simple work such as *Tristan*."[2] The completed work was to be on a moderate scale, which Wagner thought would make it easier to perform.[3] Thus, Wagner informed Liszt about the inception of the composition of a music–drama which has been called "one of the supreme achievements of mankind."[4] From Wagner's comments, particularly the repeated use of the word "simple," one would expect a work of modest proportions and meager significance. Yet, in his Norton Lectures at Harvard in 1972, Leonard Bernstein viewed *Tristan* as a highly sophisticated and complex musical composition, speaking of its ambiguity exploited "in all three of the linguistic modes. . . . ."[5] In fact, Bernstein, who devoted much attention to an analysis of the Prelude, found it fascinating in development and intricate in composition to the degree that there is question as to whether the beginning section is written in the key of A minor or in no key at all. Bernstein concluded that "*Tristan* is the crisis work of the nineteenth century."[6]

Bernstein's analysis of the chromatic ambiguity of the music of this "crisis work" emphatically denies the claim of the composer that he was writing a "simple" work, for the Prelude to *Tristan* introduces a concept of musical time different from that of any previous composition. As Bernstein puts it:

> And this is what gives *Tristan* its true semantic quality—quite apart from the obvious semantic facts of the text, of Wagner's own poetry; of chivalry and magic potions and betrayal; and apart from leitmotivs signifying desire or death. I am speaking of musical semantics as we

have come to know it, as the sum of phonological and
syntactical transformations, producing a highly poetic
metaphorical language. And in this sense *Tristan* is
supreme: it is one long series of infinitely slow
transformations, metaphor upon metaphor, from the
mysterious first phrase through to the climactic heights of
passion or of transfiguration, right to the end.[7]

Considering the extremely complicated musical structure of
Tristan und Isolde, why did Wagner repeatedly refer to it as
simple? The answer to this question must rest within the context
of Wagner's narrative. As a source of information about Wagner's
artistic development, Cosima Wagner's *Diaries* tell of the
composer's interest in *Tristan*. In an entry dated Sunday, March 6,
1870, Cosima recorded that Richard wished to leave the dreadful-
ness of the *Ring* to write *Tristan und Isolde* which was to be,
according to him, a love scene.[8] Cosima wrote that Richard
thought of the work "as an Italian opera, that is to say, to be sung
by Italian singers—and in Rio de Janeiro."[9] Saturday, March 12,
1870, Cosima's entry told that in the evening Richard read to her
from Gottfried von Strassburg's *Tristan und Isolde*.[10] Another
reading followed on Monday, March 14, when it became eminently
apparent how different Richard's version of the Tristan legend was
from that of Gottfried von Strassburg.[11]

To find out what Wagner meant by "simple" with regard to his
music–drama, one must abandon any attempt to unravel the complicated musical structure of the work in favor of a study of his
prime literary source, the *Tristan* of Gottfried von Strassburg,
along with allusion to a few of the other medieval versions of the
legend; for Bernstein's "infinitely slow transformations" of the
music underscore the "simple" transformations of Wagner's major
characters from their medieval counterparts to the opera stage of
the nineteenth century.

Because Wagner worked within the restrictions of the musical
theatre, he had, first of all, to simplify the narrative by limiting the
cast of characters to a few key roles. Obviously, he had to have a

Tristan and an Isolde as the two chief figures of the music–drama, although a number of other possible roles could be pared. Aside from Brangaene, whose role might conceivably have been absorbed into that of Isolde, the one absolutely and imperatively obvious necessity was the character of King Mark without whom there could be no *Tristan und Isolde*. A love triangle has never been a duet even in a comic opera by Donizetti,[12] and Wagner was, by his own admission, writing a work whose theme was love. King Mark is then the pivotal character in the music–drama, for Wagner clearly understood that it was King Mark who propelled the action from first to last in Gottfried's version of the legend; yet Wagner's King Mark is significantly different from Gottfried's. Considering the fact that Wagner's music–drama is a modern equivalent of the oral tradition in literature, it is pertinent to ask how Wagner transformed Gottfried's King Mark into an operatic metaphorical abstraction. How was Wagner's Mark simplified? How does Wagner's king, whether on stage or off, control the fate of the two lovers and introduce earthly reality when ethereal perfection would be preferred?

To comprehend Wagner's highly original, "simple" characterization, one must look briefly at the works of Thomas, Béroul, and Eilhart von Oberg, before examining the characterization of Mark in Wagner's source, the *Tristan* of Gottfried von Strassburg.[13] Most significantly, however, only when one compares Wagner's King Mark with the carefully developed, boldly stated King Mark of Malory's *Morte Darthur,* can one assess the aesthetic success of Wagner's characterization; for Malory's distinctly different view of Mark, certainly no less valid than Wagner's, best shows contrast with the character whom Wagner later drew. A brief study of a few prominent versions of the legend of Tristan before Wagner enables one to define the simplicity of Wagner's artistry and permits one to understand his King Mark as embodiment of universal morality, a sympathetic monarch so very different from the evil monarch of Malory or the debased kings of earlier medieval versions.

By the twelfth century the story of Tristan and Isolde had been greatly altered from the prehistoric original, and thereafter followed two main lines of development, depending, because of the oral tradition involved, on the audience to which the work was presented.[14] The two chief lines for the narrative to follow were that of a rather disdainful author who emphasized the beguiling of Mark and his resultant savagery, or that of a courtly writer who presented influences which contributed to the decay of the honor of Tristan.[15]

According to Jill Mann, "the growth and increasing elaboration of Arthurian material in the Middle Ages, from individual stories such as those told by Chrétien de Troyes to complex narrative groupings such as the Vulgate Cycle, is often explained as due to a desire for elucidation of what was in the early stories left baffling or unexplained."[16] The character of King Mark was explained and developed by each medieval author in a way which supported the central theme or point of emphasis as he perceived it. Gottfried von Strassburg (c. 1210) was acquainted with the work of Thomas of Britain (c. 1170), as well as the version of Eilhart von Oberg (c. 1170), and possibly that of Béroul (c. 1190) (36). The extant fragments of Eilhart suggest that his treatment was designed to show how a knight succumbed to a sensual passion over which he had no control. Because Gottfried followed the version of Thomas, however, he emphasized Tristan's love for Isolde rather than the honor of Tristan which was prominent in the work of Eilhart.[17]

Neither Thomas nor Béroul chose for the role of Mark the stock figure of the cuckold or the cruel tyrant which he became in later versions.[18] Although Thomas's Mark is not so frequently the object of Tristan and Isolde's deception, and Béroul's Mark is, at times, quick to anger, at least when the situation demands it, in both Thomas and Béroul, Mark remains apart from the usual role of jealous husband.[19] Thomas places emphasis on the loyalty of Tristan, while Béroul has more social comment. In Béroul the three barons frequently influence Mark's actions on a social or moral level, but they fail to influence his emotions. The lovers' behavior is offensive to Mark's honor. If he neglects to avenge the wrong done to him, he opens himself to ridicule in that he shows himself to be unworthy as king.[20]

During the lifetime of Gottfried von Strassburg and for quite some time thereafter, the love affair was considered not only sinful but also destructive (36). Isolde's passion drags Tristan down from a position of great esteem to that of a conniving adulterer who betrays his uncle's trust in him. Within this scheme of things, Mark is seen to be mean and cruel, but without enough fortitude to defend himself against injustice. Both continuators of Gottfried— Ulrich von Türheim (1230–35) and Heinrich von Freiberg (c. 1290) — support this view of Mark (36). Eilhart's version, as well as that of most other early writers except Thomas and Gottfried, gives numerous examples of the lovers' ability to deceive Mark. Eilhart appears to be chiefly interested in the principle of loyalty and understanding between uncle and nephew, while Thomas and Gottfried emphasize a study of the moral conflict within the minds of the chief characters. The character of Mark in both Thomas and Gottfried derives from his reactions to the tricks which the lovers play on him and on his reaction to these. Mark's court appears to be what Gottfried saw as normal in time of peace; its chief characteristics are deception, cowardice, envy, and indecision (158–64).

Because Mark's court reflects the moral fibre of its leader, the base values of the court underscore his inadequacies. In Gottfried's version, Mark eventually evolves as the embodiment of hatred. Just as Gottfried's Mark mirrors the values of the court, the attitude of the nobles towards the love affair between Tristan and Isolde is based on envy and hatred. In Gottfried, Mark's personality is complicated by a mixture of jealousy and his admiration for his nephew's intellectual and artistic accomplishments and by his affection for the young man. Tristan's heroism encourages Mark's admiration of his nephew.[21]

An unusual feature of Mark's personality in Gottfried's poem is that he has all the outward characteristics of a middle–aged man—in both speech and action—yet Gottfried suggests that he was most probably quite young. Like Chaucer's Pandarus, he is ready with wise sayings and awkward advice, and he treats Tristan in a protective, parental way. Even when he adopts the role of Tristan's father, Mark is torn between his sexual jealousy of Isolde and his affection for his nephew. The age of Mark as rival of Tristan would make him a generation removed from his role as uncle of the young hero (98–99). Only when he is reminded that Tristan deprives him of Isolde does he allow himself to be consumed by envy and hatred.

Gottfried's Mark represents a type of love which is not degrading or reprehensible within itself, but which is earthly, imperfect, in that it is based entirely on sexual attraction and physical beauty. The object of Mark's affection for Isolde is pleasure, a view supported by members of his court. Early in the poem Gottfried affirms the right of the court to have its own ideas, but views the court's value system as inadequate. And yet, paradoxically, Tristan and Isolde can enjoy true love only when the restraints of society are removed, and these restraints are represented by King Mark, as leader of the courtly society (99).

Despite his position as leader, Mark has few admirable accomplishments as has, for example, King Arthur. Mark has no noble past to look to, nor does he have a distinguished system of values by which he governs. By a strange system of circumstances, it is Tristan, not Mark, whose brilliant artistic and heroic achievements are the shining excellencies of the court. The speeches which Gottfried gives him are notable for underscoring his glaring lack of noble character. Except for the speech in which he banishes the lovers from the court, his utterances, though few, reveal the poverty of his moral and intellectual character (158).

Gottfried von Strassburg's King Mark is, then, a monarch of few words and few thoughts. He is a man obsessed by raw physical attraction but without sensitivity or subtlety. When he speaks, he indulges in repetition, a device by which Gottfried emphasizes Mark's lack of perception. Although he has the opportunity to rise to the occasion and overcome the mean–minded influence of the court, Mark falls victim to envy, suspicion, and hatred (212–15). King Mark in Malory's *Morte Darthur* differs from the Mark of Gottfried in ways closely associated with the emphasis of each author. While Gottfried's interest lay within the scope of the courtly traditions of love and honor, Malory created a world of adventure.[22] He respected the deeds and values of his heroes and showed a remarkable lack of interest in psychological analysis of a character's mental and emotional outlook. Motivation, consistency, and broad typical traits replace minor personal peculiarities.[23] Malory appears to have altered his source material in several ways which enabled him to create a more consistent, simplified view of the character of King Mark. In Eilhart and Béroul, the effect of the love potion had been limited, the resultant effect necessarily being the degradation of Mark's character. French prose versions of *Tristan*, by establishing an early beginning for the love affair, had placed emphasis on the degraded characters of Mark and his barons, thus diminishing the possibility of an attack on Tristram's honor.

Malory took the French prose tradition one step farther. He adopted a rather matter of fact introduction of the affair between the two lovers early in *The Book of Sir Tristram de Lyones*:

> And therefore sir Tramtryste kyste grete love to La Beale Isode, for she was at that tyme the fayrest lady and maydyn of the worlde. And there Tramtryste lerned hir to harpe and she began to have a grete fantasy unto hym.[24]

And just as terse is Malory's introduction of Mark's initial disaffection for Tristram, based upon the preference of Sir Seguarides's wife for Tristram rather than for Mark (244). The jealousy of King Mark originally comes about because he and Tristram both loved the wife of Sir Seguarides and not because of their love for Isode. When Tristram does not live up to the expectations of Sir Seguarides's wife, she chooses Sir Bleoberys, who then delivers her to her husband. The lady tells King Mark about the battle between Tristram and Bleoberys, after which "kynge Marke caste all the wayes that he myght to dystroy sir Trystrames, and than imagened in hymselff to sende sir Trystramys into Irelonde for La Beale Isode. For sir Trystramys had so preysed her for hir beaute and hir goodnesse that kynge Marke seyde he wolde wedde hir. . ." (251). Ironically, Mark's desire to destroy Tristram precipitates an action most detrimental to all three of the chief characters.

Although Mark has already determined to bring about Tristram's death, the first mention of the love potion in Malory comes when Isode is preparing to go to Cornwall to become Mark's wife. Her mother gives directions that Isode and Mark shall drink the preparation on their wedding day so that they will love each other for the rest of their lives. Tristram and Isode happen upon the gold flagon containing the love potion quite by accident and assume that Brangwaine and Governaile have been hiding it as a private supply of wine. The discovery is made by Tristram, who says, "Madame Isode, here is a draught of good wyne that dame Brangwayne, your maydyn, and Governayle, my servaunte, hath kepte for hemselff" (258). Amid considerable laughter and merriment, they drink deeply of the wine, which they find unusually sweet and good.

> But by that drynke was in their bodyes they loved aythir other so well that never hir love departed, for well nother for woo. And thus hit happed fyrst, the love betwyxte sir Trystrames and La Beale Isode, the whyche love never departed dayes of their lyff. (258)

After the arrival in Cornwall and the marriage of Isode and King Mark, Malory repeats that "evir, as the Frenshe booke seyth, sir Trystrames and La Beale Isode loved ever togedyrs" (263).

When Tristram sets forth to visit the court of King Arthur, Isode instructs him to tell Queen Guinevere that there are but four lovers, Sir Lancelot and Queen Guinevere, and Sir Tristram and Queen Isode. Malory's reiteration of the permanence of the love of Tristram and Isode might conceivably have created a sympathetic attitude toward King Mark; but after the early episode with Sir Seguarides's wife and Mark's real reason for sending Tristram to Ireland to bring Isode to Cornwall, it is impossible to see the king as anything but odious.

The treachery of Mark's court is further developed when Tristram's cousin, Sir Andret, conceals himself to spy on the lovers. Sir Andret sees Tristram and Isode talking at the window and promptly tells the king. When Mark confronts Tristram and takes sword in hand to strike him, Tristram is saved by his near proximity to Mark. Tristram avoids the blow and disarms the king. Mark reacts violently: "Where ar my knyghtes and my men? I charge you, sle this traytowre!" (267). Later at night Sir Andret's treacherous watch pays off again when he and twelve knights burst in upon Tristram and Isode in bed together. The nude Tristram is bound and kept until day when Andret brings him before Mark and some of his barons to be judged. After the episode of Tristram in the forest, Mark voices his regret that Tristram has recovered and calls together his barons to pronounce a death verdict for Tristram (270–71).

In the section specifically devoted to Mark in Book 2, the king's hostility causes him to chase Tristram out of Cornwall. And once again Malory attributes Mark's hatred to jealousy of the love between his nephew and the queen. More to the point is a kind of jealousy based upon Mark's envy of Tristram's prowess in combat and his artistic and moral achievements. For when Mark hears of the brilliant reputation which Tristram has made for himself in England, not only is Mark grieved but he reacts, sending men to spy on Tristram. (Isode also sends spies to keep an eye on her great love [353].) The report that Tristram surpasses all but Sir Lancelot is good news for Isode, but causes Mark much heaviness. In disguise, Mark, taking with him Sir Bersules and Sir Amant, along with two squires, travels to England to kill Tristram. When the group stops a knight to learn the way to King Arthur's court, Mark enquires if the knight has heard of Sir Tristram and learns that he is highly respected as a fearless and honorable knight of the Round Table (353).

Mark is incensed when he hears of Tristram's prominent position at Arthur's court and for the first time confesses to his men that the true reason for the journey is to destroy Tristram by any means available, no matter how treacherous. He has tricked them into being a party to his infamous scheme. Sir Bersules calls the king's plan shameful and emphatically declines to participate in any action leading to the death of Sir Tristram. Mark also learns that Bersules will, if the king persists, desert him and offer service to Sir Tristram. Mark denounces Bersules as traitor and cruelly murders him. Sir Amant and the squires reprimand the king for his treacherous action and declare that they will no longer serve him. In addition, they will see that King Arthur hears of this foul deed. The furious Mark then sets upon Amant and would have killed him had not the knight and the two squires held him off. Vowing to defend himself of the accusation of treason, Mark demands that the men conceal his identity before King Arthur. Amant agrees to participate in this deception (354).

Stopping at a fountain, Mark encounters Sir Lamerok de Gales who identifies the king as Cornish because of his dialect. With his thoughts turning to Cornwall, Sir Lamerok is reminded of King Mark, whom he describes as shameful, an enemy of all good knights, a false coward, a jealous husband. Mark continues his deception and declines comment. Shortly thereafter, when Mark's identity becomes known, Sir Lamerok and Sir Dinadan regret that they are in his company. Sir Dinadan makes it emphatically clear that the only reason that he will continue to lead Mark to Arthur is that he has promised to do so, and as a man of honor he must make good his promise (354–57).

Up to this point, Malory has shown King Mark to be treacherous, a liar, a horrible murderer, and a fearful coward. Through trickery, Mark is made to believe that Sir Dagonet, King Arthur's fool, is Sir Lancelot. After the cowardly Mark runs through the forest to avoid combat with Dagonet, Arthur's court looks upon King Mark as an object of scorn. Lancelot calls him "recreaunte kynge and knyght" (364–65). King Arthur informs him that he is both welcome and unwelcome, the latter in that Mark is said to be a killer of Arthur's knights. When Mark promises to make amends, Malory cautions that although the Cornish king is fair of speech, underneath there is falsehood. One day King Arthur requests that King Mark be a good lord to Sir Tristram and take him to Cornwall to see his friends. Despite Mark's sacred promise to do as Arthur asks, Malory states that the Cornish king later put Sir Tristram in prison and planned to slay him (375).

The ultimate in offensive behavior of this depraved and degraded king comes when he sends for the wounded Sir Tristram to defend Tintagel against Sir Elyas, for Mark knows that only Tristram can save the castle. The king, whose hatred of and plots against Tristram are repeatedly the subject of this section of the *Morte Darthur,* faces the realization of his own worthlessness when his fortress is challenged. Only Tristram, the knight of whom Mark is jealous, not so much because of Isode's love for Tristram, but through the king's own perverse view of Tristram's chivalrous nature, can defend Mark's castle. (384–88).

Whatever Malory's source, he establishes and maintains consistently a straightforward account of the base and evil nature of King Mark. Though not derived from the King Mark of Gottfried von Strassburg, Malory's Mark takes Gottfried's characterization to an extreme. Instead of Gottfried's rather subtle degradation of Mark's character, Malory builds his case early in *The Book of Sir Tristram de Lyones* and reiterates the theme of treachery until, in *The Book of Sir Launcelot and Queen Guinevere,* he reports that Mark slew Sir Tristram as he played the harp before Isode (666).

In a radical departure from the Germanic, French, and English medieval traditions, Richard Wagner shows Mark to be an honorable, noble, wise monarch, a personification of moral justice. Just as in the case of the medieval versions of the legend, Wagner's portrayal stems directly from his choice of theme for the music–drama *Tristan und Isolde* – the tragic nature of immortal love and how it is closely intertwined with the death–wish.[25] "Wagner...immediately saw that the essence of the legend was profoundly tragic and should not be obscured by incidentals...."[26] Earlier Wagner was cited as referring to *Tristan* as a love scene. The romantic, ideal love which Tristan and Isolde share cannot exist in the real world for their love is too abstract, too spiritual. In all three acts of the music–drama, it is King Mark who forces the intrusion of earth–bound reality upon the unreality of ethereal love. In the first act, he is not even physically present; yet when the ship is about to land in Cornwall, mention of the name of King Mark strikes a note of inevitable doom for the immortal love of Tristan and Isolde, a love which has just effloresced through the drinking of the magic love potion.

Like Gottfried, Wagner gives Mark little to say. As previously noted, he does not appear at all in the first act. In Act 2, Mark's monologue, after Melot leads him to discover the lovers together, builds to greater heights the dignity of the speech of Gottfried's King Mark when he banishes Tristan and Isolde, the only time when Gottfried gives stature to his indecisive king. And at the end of Act 3, Wagner's Mark has a few short lines in which he comments on the nature of the tragedy, the deaths of the lovers, and the misery and regret which he feels.

The Act 1 narrative of Isolde about Tristan's slaying of Morholt and her healing of Tristan concludes with a curse upon the treachery by which she has been entrapped into the journey to Cornwall to become Mark's wife. She calls for death to Tristan and to herself. There is not even a slight suggestion that it is Mark, not Tristan, who is to blame for her predicament. In fact, in Act 1, mention of Mark's name serves no dramatic purpose except to remind the lovers of the ship's impending arrival in Cornwall and of Isolde's becoming his queen. From the infrequent citations of Mark's name in the first act, one must conclude that he is guiltless, noble, respected, and honorable. As a literary device, he is the personification of intense suspense, the precursor of the inevitability of disaster.

The Act 2 love duet is brought to an abrupt conclusion by Mark's sudden appearance; he is not acting on his own but is led to the spot by the treacherous Melot. Here there would be reason to liken Wagner to Gottfried, where the court reflects the values of its sovereign, were it not for the fact that Mark's monologue is filled with lofty ideals of justice and affection. About this scene, Wagner wrote to Cosima that King Mark is "that upholder of the moral world order and, thus, harbinger of death."[27] Mark mentions Tristan's base betrayal and treachery. He says that Tristan, the defender of all honor and virtue, has lost both of these noble ideals. Mark asks for what reason was Tristan's unblemished record of service, honor, might, and greatness, if the end result was to be Mark's shame. The king then reminds Tristan that it was he who threatened to leave the court if he were not allowed to support the will of the people by going to Ireland to bring Isolde to Mark: Tristan's idea, not Mark's! The king continues as he alludes first to Isolde and then to Tristan:

One whom my longing never emboldened me to approach, whom my desire renounced, awe–struck, who, so splendid, fair and exalted, could not but delight my soul, despite foes and dangers, a queenly bride you brought me hither. Now that through such a possession you had made my heart more sensitive to pain than before, why, wretched man, have you now wounded me so sore, where most tender, soft and open I could be struck, with never a hope that I could ever be healed? There, with your weapon's torturing poison that scorches and destroys my senses and brain, that denies me faith in my friend, that fills my trusting heart with suspicion, so that now stealthily, in the darkness of night, I must lurk and creep up on my friend and achieve the fall of my honour? Why must I suffer this hell that no heaven can restore? Why this dishonour for which no misery can atone? Who will make known to the world the inscrutable, deep, secret cause?[28]

Mark's mood displays confusion, incomprehensibility, dejection, disappointment, and horror. Only a true paragon of virtue could react with sensitivity and outraged justice to the scene before him as Mark does. Of course, he as yet knows nothing of the magic love potion.

Arriving in Brittany just after Isolde, toward the end of the third and last act, he finds Tristan dead and Isolde at the point of death. Mark has learned the reason for the fatal, immortal attraction of the two and has come to offer Isolde to Tristan in marriage. He speaks of his happiness at finding his friend free from guilt. The final treachery of Tristan is his death before receiving Mark's forgiveness. Isolde's Transfiguration, Wagner's term for what is usually called the *Liebestod*, completes the translation of the character of King Mark into the language of earthly justice, nobility, honor, and morality — countless spheres from the plane of immortal, spiritual, and ideal love. Gregor–Dellin wrote of "the sweetly mysterious susurrations of *Tristan*."[29] The "simple," moral metaphor personified by Wagner's King Mark, while completely denying the base nature of his medieval ancestors, is, at the end of the music–drama, subsumed into the ethereal, whispering softness of Tristan and Isolde's "highest love."[30]

Wagner, therefore, altered the legend of Tristan and Isolde from a medieval tale of adventure and intrigue, or, at times, of a knight's loss of honor, into a simple allegory of ideal love. The timelessness of the attraction between the two lovers, reflected in the timelessness of the music's chromatic metaphors, defies social, moral, and aesthetic considerations. Like his medieval predecessors, Wagner allowed his theme to dictate the structure of his work. He found an indispensable component of his narrative in the person of King Mark — not the depraved king of Gottfried von Strassburg, and certainly not the evil villain of Malory. Wagner did, however, find in Gottfried the germ of a new idea about Mark. To allow his central theme of immortal love to ascend to the heights where he believed it should be, Wagner had to have a frame of reference, and he saw in Gottfried's Mark, perhaps in the dignity of his speech when he banished Tristan and Isolde, the inhibiting force of moral reality.

In Chaucer's *House of Fame*, the high flying author reminds the reader of Boethius's caution that:

A thought may flee so hye,
Wyth fetheres of Philosophye,
To passen everych element;
And whan he hath so fer ywent,
Than may be seen, behynde hys bak,
Cloude....[31]

Setting aside the context in which Chaucer wrote, when one is immersed in Wagner's *Tristan und Isolde*, it is imperative to consider the admonition of Boethius, for Wagner came alarmingly, disquietingly close to soaring too high in his romantic pursuit of ethereal love. His philosophic and aesthetic dicta threaten the normal order of earth–human relationships. Wagner needed a realistic, uncomplicated character to remind his audience, at least by way of contrast, of the temporal order of earthly morality. To fill this need, Richard Wagner transformed Gottfried's spineless monarch, who had become Malory's regal ogre, into *Tristan und Isolde*'s "simple," noble King Mark.

Memphis State University

N O T E S

[1] Francis Hueffer, trans., *Correspondence of Wagner and Liszt*, Vol. 2 (New York, 1969), 54.

[2] Hueffer, 174.

[3] Hueffer, 206.

[4] Erik Smith, "About this Recording," 27 in Richard Wagner, *Tristan und Isolde*, with Peter Hofmann and Hildegard Behrens, the Bavarian Radio Symphony Orchestra, conducted by Leonard Bernstein, Philips 7654 091, 1982.

[5]Leonard Bernstein, *The Unanswered Question. Six Talks at Harvard* (Cambridge, MA, 1976), 231.

[6]Bernstein, 233.

[7]Bernstein, 237.

[8]Martin Gregor–Dellin and Dietrich Mack, eds., *Cosima Wagner's Diaries*, Vol. 1 1869–1877, trans. Geoffrey Skelton (New York, 1978), 197.

[9]*Diaries,* 197.

[10]*Diaries,* 199.

[11]*Diaries,* 199.

[12]In the first act of Gaetano Donizetti's *L'elisir d'amore*, the heroine, Adina, sings of "La storia di Tristano"; hence, the title of Donizetti's *opera buffa.*

[13]See the edition of Friedrich Ranke, *Gottfried von Strassburg, Tristan,* ed. Gottfried Weber (Darmstadt, 1967). For origins of the Tristan legend, see Gertrude Schoepperle, *Tristan and Isolt: A Study of the Sources of the Romance,* 2 vols., 2nd ed. (New York, 1960). See also Sigmund Eisner, *The Tristan Legend: A Study in Sources* (Evanston, IL, 1969).

[14]See Eli Sobel, *The Tristan Romance in the Meisterlieder of Hans Sachs* (Berkeley, 1963), 223–24. Wagner obviously knew the six *Meisterlieder* of Sachs, who became the chief character of *Die Meistersinger von Nürnberg,* written soon after the completion of *Tristan.* In the third act of *Meistersinger,* Sachs mentions to Eva that he has read of Tristan and Isolde's dark story and the fate of poor King Mark. The orchestral accompaniment to Sachs's comment is a musical quotation from the *Tristan* Prelude. The mastersongs of the sixteenth–century Sachs contribute nothing to the development of Mark's character.

[15]See W. T. H. Jackson, *The Anatomy of Love: The "Tristan" of Gottfried von Strassburg* (New York, 1971), 34–35. Further

references to Jackson's book will be indicated by page numbers in the text.

[16]Jill Mann, " 'Taking the Adventure': Malory and the *Suite du Merlin*," in Toshiyuki Takamiya and Derek Brewer, eds., *Aspects of Malory* (Totowa, NJ, 1981), 71.

[17]Thomas C. Rumble, "The Tale of Tristram," in R. M. Lumiansky, ed., *Malory's Originality: A Critical Study of "Le Morte Darthur"* (Baltimore, 1964),123–26.

[18]See Alberto Varvaro, *Béroul's Romance of Tristran,*" trans. John C. Barnes (New York, 1972), 87–89, for a discussion of Béroul's characterization of Mark.

[19]Varvaro, 90.

[20]See Rumble, 139–40.

[21]Varvaro, 107–08.

[22]See Eugène Vinaver, *Malory* (Oxford, 1929), 29–42 for discussion of Malory's narrative technique. See also Maureen Fries, "Indiscreet Objects of Desire: Malory's 'Tristram' and the Necessity of Deceit" in *Studies in Malory,* ed. James W. Spisak (Kalamazoo, 1985), 87–108 for an enlightening study of Malory's Tristram.

[23]Robert H. Wilson, *Characterization in Malory: A Comparison with his Sources* (Chicago, 1934), 120–21.

[24]Malory, *Works*, ed. Eugène Vinaver, 2nd ed. (Oxford, 1977), 238–39. Further references to this source will be indicated by page numbers in the text.

[25]Guy de Pourtales, *Richard Wagner: The Story of An Artist,* trans. Lewis May (New York, 1932), 218–29.

[26]Martin Gregor–Dellin, *Richard Wagner His Life, His Work, His Century*, trans. J. Maxwell Brownjohn (New York, 1983), 258.

[27]June 17, 1874, cited in Gregor–Dellin, *Richard Wagner,* 283.

[28]Wagner, *Tristan und Isolde*, trans. Lionel Salter, 151–52.

[29] Gregor–Dellin, *Richard Wagner*, 447.

[30] Wagner, *Tristan und Isolde*, 113. The final words of Isolde's
Transfiguration are:

> In dem wogenden Schwall,
> in dem tonenden Schall
> in des Welt–Atems
> wehendem All—
> ertrinken
> versinken—
> unbewusst
> höchste Lust!

[31] Larry D. Benson, ed., *The Riverside Chaucer*, 3rd ed.
(Boston, 1987), 359, ll. 973–78.

The Illustration Of Arthurian Romance

Muriel Whitaker

Romance is, by definition, an unrealistic genre. Consequently, many illustrators of Arthurian romance have endeavoured to evoke the fairy tale atmosphere of an artificial world consisting largely of castles and perilous forests inhabited by kings and queens, knights and ladies, monsters, fées and hermits. It is a world in which absolute virtue consists of loyalty to one's God, king, fellow knight, and lady, a loyalty proven through chivalric adventure. The illustrator determines which of these absolutes will dominate his pictorial representation. Inevitably, his perception is influenced by the values of his society, his medium, the intended audience, and his personal attitude to the material. In a period of eight centuries the results have been multifarious.[1]

Originally, manuscript illumination had been a monastic art. By the thirteenth century, when secular texts such as the *Chanson de Roland*, the *Roman de la Rose*, the legends of Troy and of King Alexander, and the Arthurian material became popular, book production had shifted to lay workshops where the labour was shared among a number of specialists – parchmenters, ink–makers, scribes, rubricators, illuminators, bookbinders – under a master's direction. The same layout and the same moduli were used for secular as for religious texts. One of the most important embellishments of Bibles and psalters, the historiated initial, was adapted to Arthurian romance, appearing in what may be the oldest illustrated prose *Lancelot* manuscript, Rennes 255 (ca. 1220).[2] Alternatively, a square or rectangular miniature might be set in one or two columns of text, sometimes with rubrication to indicate the subject. This is the format of such fine *Lancelot* manuscripts as London, B. L. Add. MS 10292–94 (Fig.1), and Royal 14E iii; Manchester, Rylands Library, MS fr. 1, and New York, Pierpont Morgan Library, MS 805, all produced between 1316 and 1330.

German ateliers like that of Meister Hesse in Strassburg favoured
full–page illuminations with three or four panels in tiers, as in
Munich, Bayerische Staatsbibliothek, cgm 19, Wolfram von
Eschenbach's *Parzival* (ca. 1230) and cgm 51, Gottfried von
Strassburg's *Tristan* (ca. 1236). Though this treatment allows for
narrative continuity, it causes a decisive separation of illustration
from text.

A distinguishing feature of Gothic manuscripts is the outer
border which not only frames text, historiated initials, and miniatures but is integrated with them by means of leafy arabesques and
pinnacles. A tension develops between the serious, controlled illustrations of text and the fantastic, comic, and often satiric figures
in the borders. Another feature of Gothic style before 1340 is the
use of a few large figures disposed in a frontal, linear manner
before *fonds d'or* or painted backgrounds patterned with rinceaux,
tessellation and diapering.

Since craftsmen in the lay ateliers of Northern France relied
on the pattern books used to illustrate Bibles and psalters, it is not
surprising to find that the innumerable combat scenes in the
thirteenth–century romance manuscripts resemble miniatures
from the Book of Kings, that Arthur's feast at Camelot duplicates
a Marriage at Cana or a Last Supper model, and that the *Estoire
del Saint Graal* and *Queste del Saint Graal* adventures utilise the
iconography of the Fall and the Redemption. Textual indications
are often ignored. For example, in Paris, B. N. MS fr. 342, *Histoire
du Roi Artu,* 1274, Galahad appears in a magenta or a blue surcoat
and grey helmet, despite the author's symbolic use of white and
red. The most glaring discrepancy concerns the Round Table
which, until the fifteenth century, is seldom depicted as round.

Initially heraldic forms and colours were used for aesthetic
effect rather than as a consistent method of identifying knights
who were otherwise indistinguishable from one another. However,
by 1320 the most important characters had fairly consistent
blazons[3]: Arthur two or three crowns on a red or blue field;
Galahad, silver (white) with a red cross *(argent a la croix de gules)*;

Lancelot, *argent, three bends gules* in B. L. Add. 10293–4 and Royal 14 E. iii (a reference to his great strength which equalled that of three men) but in Oxford, Bodl. Douce MS 215 and Manchester, Rylands MS fr. 1 he carries the imaginary arms *argent, two hearts gules* in reference to his role as paramount lover. Gawain's arms, *argent a Canton gules*, are probably canting arms, punning on Lot, the name of his father and lot, a section.

In the high period of French illustration (ca. 1274–1330), "le génie féminin" effects a refinement of manners and a change of motivation from the political to the social. Both literature and art portray "the mannerly ease and comfort of the social life of a cultured class."[4] The miniaturist creates a courtly ambience by means of gold leaf backgrounds, golden crosses, swords and goblets, and elegant Gothic castles with lapis lazuli roofs, pink or pale blue walls, orange battlements, beige drawbridges over streams in which several kinds of fish appear, and tower windows from which ladies watch knights engaged in jousting, dragon slaying, or crossing a sword bridge. Interior scenes depict within an architectural frame an elegantly elongated Guenevere holding a little dog, loving couples in canopied beds, naked except for their crowns, and the hospitable rituals of a Pentecostal feast. When the knight–errant rides through the forest (indicated by two or three stylised trees and rabbits emerging from their holes), he encounters such obvious signs of adventure as hunting horns, upright spears, pavilions of striped silk, a white stag with a golden chain about his neck, mysterious damsels waiting by a fountain, and the decapitated corpse of a lady. In a group of manuscripts possibly executed at the same Picard workshop,[5] the fairytale atmosphere is enhanced by the appearance of pink, blue, mauve and orange horses, while in the Morgan *Lancelot* there are even blue and pink tree trunks.

In *La Queste* illuminations, the Christian supernatural is e-voked by the mysterious, self–propelling Ship of Solomon with its golden crown on a green cushion, its enormous sword and its symbolic spindles of white, green and red or by the enormous candelabrum that marks the appearance of the Grail as Lancelot, made insensitive by sin, dozes outside the Perilous Chapel. God's hand is omnipresent, saving the righteous from various dangers but striking down the disobedient with a pillar of flames. Realistic details suggest that some illustrators strove to make the romance world credible by injecting imagery from ordinary life. The illustrator of Bonn, Universitätsbibliothek MS 526, *Lancelot*, Northern France, 1286 depicts a blood–letting with tourniquet and supporting stick when Perceval's sister gives her blood to save the bespelled lady. Fourteenth–century building practices are the subject of Royal MS 14 E. iii, fol. 85r where a stonemason hacks a block into shape, another sets a finished block in place, a third climbs to the top of a precarious ladder and a fourth, holding a trowel, listens to the king's instructions. The fruit in a basket on Guenevere's banquet table is correctly coloured to indicate apples and pears (Rylands MS fr. 1, fol. 223r). A variety of contemporary weapons is used in the attack on the Joyous Gard—a scaling ladder, a mangonel, arquebuses, swords, spears, and even a large rock which a defender is about to drop on an enemy (B.L. Add. MS 10294, fol. 81v). But this is essentially an unrealistic world where characters express emotion through a limited range of stylised gestures, and where the sweet and youthful faces seem impervious to the passage of time.

Since French ateliers had a monopoly of illuminated Arthurian manuscripts before 1340, relatively few have survived from other countries. The Munich *Parzival* retains only two folios, illustrating books twelve to fifteen of what should have been a complete narrative programme. The Munich *Tristan* illuminations (ca. 1300), eighty–four paintings on fifteen leaves, are of varying quality, since several illuminators were involved. The best, such as the court scene, (fol. 7r) which depicts musicians, dancers, and gracefully disposed spectators or the climactic dragon–killing sequence, present a lively and elegant society, but other scenes such as Mark's discovery of the grotto (fol. 90r) are meagerly drawn, the characters awkwardly disposed and socially diminished by the artists' incompetence.

Thanks to Norman knights and Breton minstrels, the Arthurian legends were known in Italy by the eleventh century.[6] The Normans' conquest of Apulia, Calabria and Sicily, which they controlled from 1030 to 1250, and the subsequent Angevin rule that began in 1260 attracted French scribes and artists to Italian courts. Neapolitan ateliers were particularly productive, providing such extant prose *Tristan* manuscripts as B.N. MS fr. 760, ca. 1300 and B.L. Harley MS 4389, 1290–1320. The scenes are highly conventional, with only the inscribed names enabling the viewer to identify characters. Scriptoria also flourished in Lombardy, where such works as Prose *Tristan,* B.N. MS fr. 12599, and an *Estoire–Merlin,* Bodl. Douce MS 178, show in their clean cut, round faces, their statuesque bodies and their orange–blue–brown colour scheme the influence of Byzantine illumination. The outstanding product of Italian workshops before 1340 is a *Tristan,* B.N. MS fr. 755, 1320–40. Probably commissioned by the Visconti of Milan, its large illuminations, occupying the lower part of one or two pages, depict expansive tournament scenes, cavalcades of pleasure–seeking courtiers, and lovely ladies watching the male activities from balconies and castle courtyards. The figures in brilliantly coloured costumes have the weight and volume which characterise the new Giottesque style.

Throughout the medieval period English manuscripts focus on the "historical" King Arthur rather than on the lovers of courtly romance. An illustrated manuscript of Peter Langtoft's *Chronicle of England,* B.L. Royal MS 20 A. ii, ca. 1307–27, is decorated with lively tinted drawings. The best known shows a youthful King Arthur with the Virgin and Child on his shield and at his feet thirty shields signifying his territories (fol.4r). B.L. Egerton MS 3028, *Chronique D'Angleterre,* mid–fourteenth century, is an abridged version of Wace's *Brut.* Most folios are adorned with a half–page square miniature of great specificity in relation to the text though the execution is rather crude. The Arthurian section (fols. 24–53) includes depictions of tricky Hengist preparing to kill the bull, Merlin building Stonehenge, Arthur's coronation and a marvellously vivid evocation of the heavy–browed, hairy–eared, lolling–tongued giant of Saint–Michel.

In the mid–fourteenth century a France ravaged by the Black Death and the early disasters of the Hundred Years War was no longer a congenial place for book–production. When a revival occurred about 1380, the business was dominated by the taste and acquisitiveness of aristocratic patrons like Jean, Duke of Berry, and his brothers Charles V, Louis of Anjou and Philip the Bold, Duke of Burgundy, as well as by their bibliophile relatives, the Visconti and the Armagnacs, *inter alia*. Patronage affected subject and style in several ways for the princely consumers wanted to be personally identified with their possessions. Personal coats of arms appeared not only in manuscript borders but even as the blazons of literary knights. Illuminations no longer focus on courtly love and the service of ladies and oppressed knights. Rather, the manuscripts depict such princely entertainments as fighting, tourneying, hunting with hawks and hounds, playing games of chess or cards, and forming cavalcades to ride into the country where the noble males could feast in a leafy arbour as they listen to lutanists. The women are reduced to passive spectators. To accommodate these representations of noble life, long prose romances were preferred: *Palamède, Guiron le Courtois, Meliadorus, Perceforest,* the French Prose *Tristan* and such combinations of *Tristan, Lancelot,* and *Queste* materials as *La Tauola Ritonda*.

Contributing significantly to the realistic effect was the rediscovery of perspective. Instead of the constriction imposed by architectural frames, flat patterned backgrounds and the frontal images needed for the action, there is now the opening out of a composed landscape. Winding rivers, green hills, leafy groves, blue skies lightening at the horizon as aerial perspective requires, and the towers and spires of distant cities provide a locale for outdoor adventure, while interiors, historically accurate in their vaulting, furniture, and diamond window panes, enclose groups of people placed at varying distances from the viewer. A fine example of the new style is the Oxford *Guiron le Courtois,* (Bodleian, Douce MS 383), a late fifteenth century Flemish manuscript. Prominence is given to the art of costume. In the *Guiron* and another Flemish manuscript, the *St. Alban's Chronicle* (London, Lambeth Palace Library MS 6, ca. 1470 [Fig. 2]), the artists carefully reproduce contemporary dress with plumed acorn hats, long velvet gowns slashed to reveal loose–sleeved shirts, and doublets so short that the wearers look like monkeys. The ladies' low cut gowns of black, scarlet, and blue, the gold chains worn as necklaces, and the steeple headdresses convey the elegance of International Gothic; however, the static roles of the women and the infrequency with which they are depicted indicate that "le génie féminin" is no longer the dominant inspiration.

Even as the painters were achieving a high degree of realism, technological changes in book production brought about a change in the illustrators' mode. Block books with illustration and text cut on the same block began to appear on the continent about 1430 as a cheap substitute for illuminated manuscripts. By mid–century Johann Gutenberg's perfecting of movable type, which made it possible to produce large numbers of books in a short time, necessitated a kind of illustration that could be reproduced with equal facility. Since a design drawn on the surface of a block of wood and then cut away could be set, inked and printed at the same time as the text, woodcuts replaced paintings as the most common form of illustration. For a time illumination and printing proceeded side by side. The leading Parisian book manufacturer, Antoine Vérard, who established his business in 1485, printed deluxe copies on pages of vellum, then had them illuminated by hand. However, his *Tristan* (1494), *Lancelot* (1494), and *Merlin* (1498) all were furnished with large woodcuts.

William Caxton, who set up the first English press in 1476, was not particularly interested in illustration; only nineteen of his hundred extant books have woodcuts, and the group does not include Malory's *Morte Darthur* (1485). However, when his successor,

Wynkyn de Worde, reissued the *Morte* in 1498, it was enlivened by
twenty–one woodcuts, each occupying the top half of a folio page.[7]
At least two illustrators were involved. The designs of the lesser
artist are derivative, based most likely on continental manuscripts.
The joust between Arthur and Tristram (Bk X), for example,
seems to be a simplified version of such a miniature as that in a
fifteenth–century *Tristan* BN MS fr. 99 fol. 561 r. The second artist,
whom Edward Hodnett calls the Arthur–cutter, is much more
lively and original. In most cases he takes his subject from the titles
which Caxton attached to each book. The cut in Book I shows on
the right, an elongated King Uther embracing Igraine in front of a
crenellated castle, and on the left the Duke of Cornwall hastily
riding away, his wife mounted behind him, as the diving black
birds, this artist's signature, fill the sky above (Fig. 3). The
elaborately composed scene for Bk. VIII shows two gentlewomen
attending to the new–born Tristram in the forest. On the ground
lies his mother, dead, as the arms crossed at the wrist indicate. The
two groves of stylised trees show a variety of texture, and the
designer has also worked in a rock, a plateau, three plants, a
steepled church, an oriental tower and the blackbirds.

Put off by the skewed faces that in most of the woodcuts reveal
the cutter's lack of skill, critics have dismissed the illustrations as
crude, bizarre, and clumsy. Yet if one looks beyond the technical
infelicity, one is struck by the genuine attempt at realism. In fact,
the Arthur–cutter seems particularly concerned to replace the
romantic atmosphere of medieval manuscripts with an impression
of the contemporary world. The supernatural, both Celtic and
Christian, is generally ignored, and although Perceval's aunt in a
nun's habit appears in Bk XIV and a monk in Bk XV, the overall
impression is secular and monarchical. This interpretation is understandable, if we recall that the Tudors claimed descent from an
historical King Arthur, and that the successful conqueror who had
defeated the Roman Emperor might serve as a model for the
Tudor imperialists.

Contemporaneity is conveyed by the cannon of Bk XXI, the fluted armour of Bk XVI, and the sallets worn by Gawain (Bk XVI), Lancelot (Bk XIX) and the archers (Bk XXI). The elegant court dress of the Gothic manuscripts gives way to the late fifteenth– century "bulky look" with its deliberate untidiness, denoted by wrinkled hose, shaggy hats, fluffy shoulder–length hair and short, wide doublets. Mordred, Balin, Galahad, La Cote Male Taille, Gareth's supporters and Lancelot all wear the stubby shoes which had replaced elongated, pointed footwear in the 1480's. The ladies' headdresses have changed from Gothic steeples to long hoods, split vertically so that the pieces can fall before and behind the shoulders.

De Worde's Malory was republished in 1529, using seventeen of the original blocks, now rather wormeaten. For the remaining books the printer substituted blocks that he had already used with other texts. In 1557 another London printer, William Copland, brought out *The Story of Kyng Arthur, and also of his noble and Valiante Knyghtes of the Round Table,* with de Worde's text and many of his illustrations. There are some peculiarly irrelevant substitutions; for example, Bk XV, originally prefaced by a two–stage cut showing Lancelot talking to a monk near a chapel, now shows a knight sleeping in an enclosed garden. Wynkyn de Worde had used this cut in 1520 to illustrate Christopher Goodwyn's poem, "The Chaunces of a Dolorous Lover."

The last illustrated Tudor Malory was Thomas East's *The Story of Kynge Arthur and also of his Knyghtes of the Rounde Table* (1585). Based on Copland's text, it is carelessly executed with little regard for consistency of size and style. Some of the 1498 designs have been recut, gaining in realism of facial expression and treatment of perspective, but losing the dramatic intensity of the originals. As a concession to the militant Protestantism of Elizabethan England, visual references to Catholicism have entirely disappeared. Even the de Worde cut of a fashionably dressed Perceval talking to an anchoress (his aunt) has given way to a picture of a knight and his squire being greeted by several ladies in Tudor court dresses with low necklines and draped skirts, costumes quite inappropriate to the Grail Quest setting.

After the Tudors, Puritanism and rationalism determined that the Arthurian material would suffer a long period of neglect. Not until the nineteenth century did the figure of the knight again become an embodiment of physical, social, moral, and spiritual idealism. Unlike the anonymous early illustrators of Arthurian romance, nineteenth– and twentieth–century artists are individuals with expressed views about the relationship of illustration to text. In addition, they have at their disposal a wider range of technical processes, as well as a sense of historical perspective.

An important contributor to the revival of interest in the Arthurian Legend was Alfred, Lord Tennyson whose *Poems*, published by Edward Moxon in 1842, included "The Lady of Shalott," "Sir Launcelot and Queen Guinevere," "Sir Galahad," and "Morte d'Arthur." Early in 1855 Moxon called on Rossetti, wanting him to contribute some wood engraving designs for a new edition of the *Poems* (1857).[8] Rossetti was probably the first Arthurian illustrator to record his view of the artist's relationship to his text.:

> [I] fancy I shall try the 'Vision of Sin' and 'Palace of Art', etc.—those where one can allegorize on one's own hook on the subject of the poem, without killing for oneself and everyone a distinct idea of the poet's. This I fancy, is *always* the upshot of illustrated editions—Tennyson, Allingham, or any one—unless where the poetry is so absolutely narrative as in the old ballads, for instance.

Rossetti contributed drawings for "The Palace of Art," "Mariana in the South," "Sir Galahad" and "The Lady of Shalott." For the latter, Holman Hunt had already undertaken a drawing which George Layard later praised for its depiction of "an exquisite woman yearning for what she cannot tell, impatient of what she hardly knows, less than half conscious of the possibilities of her womanhood."[9] The lady's hair was so excessively billowy that Tennyson complained, "My dear Hunt...I never said that the young woman's hair was flying all over the shop," to which Hunt replied, "No, but you never said it wasn't." Half a century later he claimed that he had intended the Lady of Shalott to be "the evident impersonator of a soul entrusted with an artistic gift destined to bring about a great end, who, failing in constancy, is overwhelmed by the ruin of her life's ideal." The flying hair conveyed "the idea of the threatened fatality by reversing the ordinary peace of the room and of the lady herself." The design consists of a series of ovals — the loom with its unfinished tapestry; the mirror in which are reflected the river, the grainfields and the passing knight; and a plaque of the crucified Christ.

Daniel Maclise provided two "Morte d'Arthur" drawings, one showing Arthur receiving Excalibur from the lake spirit's hand, and the other showing a swan–prowed ship with Arthur reclining in the arms of a plump and youthful Morgan le Fay. The images of dragon–crested helmet, water–lilies, chain mail, highly ornamented sword, carved prow, and full moon partly hidden by clouds exemplify the combination of medieval and contemporary motifs that characterises much Victorian medievalism.

Nowadays, the *Moxon Tennyson* derives its chief interest from the Rossetti pictures. The three Arthurian drawings display the crowded space and frontal positioning (which give a sense of confinement), the symbolic images and attention to texture found in Rossetti's paintings. The Maid of Astolat lies on her barge, enclosed by roof and candles, in a patterned dress and a jewelled cloak (fig. 4). Her face in the shadows, she is peripheral while it is Lancelot, unnaturally enlarged and elaborately costumed, who occupies most of the picture plane. The hero's expression of rapt contemplation is repeated in "Sir Galahad at the Ruined Chapel" when the Grail knight scoops up holy water in the symbol–studded refuge. The design which best reveals Rossetti's capacity for expanding or contradicting his text (a practice which Layard regarded as unethical) accompanies lines from "the Palace of Art":

Or mythic Uther's deeply–wounded son
In some fair space or sloping greens
Lay, dozing in the vale of Avalon,
And watch'd by weeping queens.

In the foreground and occupying most of the picture space, to
the virtual exclusion of the hero, are nine women wearing differentiated crowns and Elizabeth Siddal expressions. They almost hide
the recumbent king who has been carried to the Celtic Otherworld, as Geoffrey of Monmouth described. Gleeson White, writing in 1897, considered these Tennyson illustrations "the genesis
of the modern movement."

Tennyson's most important Arthurian work, *The Idylls of the
King* (1859), attracted the services of a notable illustrator. The
Alsatian Gustave Doré (1832–1883), provided thirty–six drawings
to be reproduced as steel engravings in folio editions of *Elaine*
(1866), *Vivien* (1866), *Guinevere* (1866) and *Enid* (1867). Doré's
strength is his ability to create a landscape imbued with the wild-
ness and strangeness appropriate to romance. While Tennyson's
idea of wilderness came from Cornwall and Wales, the artist derived his from the more rugged scenery of the Vosges and Savoy
where he found the castle–topped crags that became his signature.
Doré can effectively evoke an emotional relationship between
character and setting, as in "The Remorse of Lancelot" (*Elaine*, ill.
9) where the grey waters of the Thames, the misty atmosphere and
the wind–blown reeds create a feeling of desolation (Fig. 5). He
can also use setting to provide a sense of momentous occasion as
in "The King's Farewell" (*Guinevere*, ill.9) where the Romanesque
architecture, intrusive shrubbery and dark shadows emphasize the
Queen's degradation. But the immensity of towering cliffs and
dark forests dwarfs the humans, making them seem inconsequen-
tial.

Tennyson's central interest, the personalities of the women
who represent "The True and the False," is of little concern to
Doré. Vivien, appearing in only four scenes and individualized in

only one, "Vivien and Merlin Repose," is a plump, lazy–looking houri. She fails to project the impression of "Sense at war with Soul" that Rossetti, Sandys, and Beardsley convey in their depictions of femmes fatales. And in Guinevere's most dramatically emotional encounters – "The Parting," "The Dawn of Love," and "the King's Farewell" – we are shown only her back. The four idylls do not provide opportunities for the caricature, grotesquerie, and sublimity that are Doré's forte. Moreover, they present moral situations with which the artist could not or would not deal. And the fact the Doré did not understand English must have been an insuperable barrier to accurate realization of text.

Tennyson was so disappointed with the Doré illustrations that, in 1874, he approached his Isle of Wight neighbour, the pioneer photographer Julia Margaret Cameron,[10] with the request, "Will you think it a trouble to illustrate my *Idylls* for me?" She replied, "Now *you* know, Alfred that *I* know that it is immortality to me to be bound up with you." Her elderly husband made an excellent Merlin, a soulful–looking porter at Yarmouth pier was the model for Arthur, while visiting girls and even passing tourists posed in other roles. *Illustrations to the Idylls of the King and Other Poems* was published in two albums (1874–5). A miniature edition was also prepared for gift presentation to her friends (1875–9).

The limitations of her photographic technique, the soft focus which blurred outlines and deepened shadows, produced a romantic atmosphere appropriate to her approach which was emotional rather than narrative. The obviously home–made appearance of helmets, swords, and nuns' habits in "Sir Galahad and 'The Pale Nun,' " "King Arthur," and "The Little Novice and the Queen in 'the Holy House at Almesbury,' " together with the fixed expressions (betokening weary hours of posing) are unintentionally comic. But in the best, such as "The Parting of Sir Lancelot and Queen Guinevere," she achieves her stated objective, "a picture with as much power and pathos as one can bring into a photograph consistently with what I think the great principle of high art, reserve and composure expressive of subdued passion."

One effect of the *Idylls'* popularity was the renewed interest in Malory's *Morte Darthur*, especially in illustrated abridgements suitable for young readers. Adventures illustrating the virtues of courage, purity, honesty and sportsmanship were emphasised while the unfortunate adulteries were removed. In a Preface to *The Story of King Arthur and his Knights of the Round Table* (1862), Sir James Knowles asserts that, in adapting the *Morte Darthur* for boys, he is following the rule laid down in *The Idylls of the King.* He has "suppressed and modified where changed manners and morals have made it absolutely necessary to do so for the preservation of a lofty and original ideal." When an American edition of Knowles's classic was published in 1923, it contained an "artist's note" in which Louis Rhead explained that his task had involved "the necessity for careful research and study of the habits of life, the dress, armour, weapons, and domestic architecture and design of the 6th century." Having asserted the historical authenticity of his own style (derived from the Book of Kells!), he attacks the inaccuracy of others: "Of the seventeen most important illustrated editions of the Arthur story produced here and abroad in the last fifty years, every one of the artists has chosen to depict Arthur and his knights in the costume and with the mail armour of the 14th, 15th, 16th and even 17th centuries."

Determining an appropriate period for the Arthurian legends was, indeed, a major problem. Malory's temporal inconsistencies—Roman Wars, thirteenth–century armour, fifteenth–century cannon, and a Grail quest that begins four hundred and fifty–four years after the Crucifixion—might go unnoticed by the average reader. But the Victorian illustrator was catering to an audience that had become familiar with images of British history not only through Sir Walter Scott's historical romances but also through the paintings of "artist antiquarians" like Richard Bonington, Benjamin West and George Cattermole. If medieval authenticity were sought, the illustrator could consult Joseph Strutt's *A Complete View of the Dress and Habits of the People of England* (1796–9) or Joseph Nash's *The Mansions of England in the Olden*

Time (1839–49), *inter alia*. Arms and armour were displayed at the Tower of London and in commercial collections such as those at the Gothic Hall in Pall Mall and the Egyptian Hall, Piccadilly. However, most Arthurian illustrators were content with a vague medievalism evoked by means of Romanesque or Gothic Architecture; furnishings both ecclesiastical and domestic of the kind designed by Pugin, Burges, and the Morris Company; armour that combined chain mail and bits of plate with colourful surcoats, mantles, and plumes; and for the ladies, free–flowing gowns of indeterminate period.

The predominant influence on Arthurian illustration during the past century has not been antiquarianism but Pre–Raphaelitism. Even the juvenile editions evoke the spell of beauty tinged with strangeness that for Matthew Arnold was the essence of the Celtic imagination. The beauty is that of romantic landscapes recreated with botanical accuracy, of jewel–like colours and ingenious patterning in costume and furnishings, and of enigmatic women whose value as lovers seems to depend on their sensuality. The Pre–Raphaelite woman has luxuriant hair, brooding eyes, white skin, full lips and an air of pathos or of disdainful reserve.

Howard Pyle (1853–1911), whose Arthurian adaptations for American audiences have never lost their popularity, exemplifies the combination of masculine morality and realistic intention with a fondness for the feminine and the decorated. In the foreword to *The Story of King Arthur and his Knights* (1903) he explains, as Caxton had done, the moral value of the tales:

> For when in pursuing this history, I have come to consider the high nobility of spirit that moved these excellent men to act as they did, I have felt that they have afforded such a perfect example of courage and humility that anyone might do exceedingly well to follow after their manner of behavior in such measure as he is able to do.... King Arthur was the most honourable, gentle knight who ever lived in all the world.

Pyle, the author, concentrates on chivalric adventure; Pyle, the illustrator, prefers to depict in head pieces, tail pieces, and full page illustrations almond–eyed ladies with long, black tresses, heavy jewellery and japonesque gowns (fig.6); swords so weighted with ornament that they could never have been used in battle; and chairs decorated with full–breasted sphinxes. The result is a strange glamour unlikely to be found in the Brandywine River Valley or in any historical period.

Pyle's pupil, N.C. Wyeth, inherited his master's belief that imagination was more important than technical training in the creation of a picture. The artist must physically and mentally project himself into the subject to produce a sense of reality. Wyeth's experience as a hard–working farm boy gave him, in his words, "a vivid appreciation of the part the body plays in action." In paintings for an American edition of Sidney Lanier's *The Boy's King Arthur* (1917), one senses the muscle strain of the jousting knights and their horses, despite the camouflage of ornamented medieval costumes and caparisons.

The Pre–Raphaelite version of the Middle Ages, with tapestries, church furnishings, stained glass windows, and antique "pointed" woodwork — "everywhere device and symbolism" as William Burges remarked — permeates the most extensive cycle of Arthurian paintings to have been produced since printed books replaced manuscripts. The Medici Society's four–volume edition of Malory's *Morte Darthur* (London, 1910–11) was accompanied by Sir William Russell Flint's forty–eight watercolours. Flint subverts Malory's conception by focusing on the female characters and the claustrophobic castle life. His choice of subjects seems determined by the opportunity each affords to depict ladies in various degrees of nakedness; the artist is noted both for his landscapes and his breastscapes. Standing in the mouth of a cave, Merlin seems startled by his last sight of a crowned Nimue, boldly flaunting her pink–nippled breasts and naked torso, an ironical reminder of his fatal weakness. A naked Elaine, released from the boiling bath, conveys that combination of purity and eroticism which Edward

Burne–Jones also mastered. However, when Flint applies the same mode of female portraiture to Perceval's saintly sister, he is guilty of bad taste and of insensitivity to the Grail Quest's significance.

Flint's Arthurian world opulently displays the mannerly ease and comfort which characterize medieval courtly romance. The characters, gorgeously dressed in burnt orange, sea–green, rose and creamy white, recline on the battlements to watch the jousters far below, relax on the lakeshore listening to a harpist, or dally in a rose garden. They do not devote much energy to martial activities. These watercolours, though self–indulgent, are indubitably charming. The *Burlington Magazine*'s art critic, Roger Fry, however, described them as "the romantic clap–trap of a provincial theatre. Woodcut, whether plain or coloured, is the only possible accompaniment to such type."

Fry's allusion to woodcut suggests another aspect of the Pre–Raphaelite interest in decoration, one exemplified by the Kelmscott Press, which William Morris established in 1891. His purpose was to produce books which would be as beautiful as the earliest printed books had been. The fifteenth–century books of Schoeffer, Mentelin and Caxton were his models because all the visual elements — type, illustration, border, page layout, paper and bindings — were harmonised into a unity. Though Morris and his artist friend, Burne–Jones, did not produce many illustrated books, their example restored wood–engraving as a mode of decorative illustration.[11]

The most immediate response to the Kelmscott books came from the publisher J.M. Dent and the "weird" young man he hired in 1892 to illustrate the *Morte Darthur* in a woodcut style that could be cheaply reproduced by a photo–mechanical method rather than from hand–engraved blocks. At the time of their meeting, the nineteen–year old Aubrey Beardsley was a clerk of the Guardian Life and Fire Insurance Company. Without formal training, he devised what he called "a new world of my own creation ...quite mad and a little indecent."[12] The early illustrations such as "The Lady of the Lake Telleth Arthur of the Sword Excalibur" clearly imitate the Kelmscott style. Merlin and the Lady of the Lake in nightgown–like garments and Arthur in bat's–wing armour stand in a crowded landscape, the whole surrounded by a dense inter-laced border of flowers and acanthus leaves. Long before he had finished the five hundred and eighty–five chapter headings, bor-ders, initials, ornaments and full or double–page illustrations (for which he was to be paid £250), Beardsley had developed a simpler style based on a whiplash line and abstract floral images, the "Art Nouveau" look. He had also developed a more dramatic use of starkly contrasted black and white.

In content as well as form, Beardsley was so innovative that he departed entirely from the chivalric ethos of his text. Instead of engaging energetically in tournaments or riding into the forest to seek adventures which involve performing "noble acts of chivalry," his knights recline langorously, use their swords as walking sticks or stand about in dreamy contemplation of phallic floral arrange-ments. The centre of interest in the text, they must share the illustrations with sensuous angels, leering satyrs, heavy–lidded femmes fatales, and androgynous nudes. A reviewer for *Figaro* (April 20, 1893) condemned Beardsley's drawings as "flat blas-phemies against art." They could also be seen as blasphemies against the idealism of Arthurian romance and the respectability of Victorian society. In Malory's ethic, evil is repugnant and ul-timately unsuccessful. The machinations of the fées — Morgan, Hallowes and Anneure — are thwarted, the evil knights are killed or converted, and the contentious Guenevere finds sanctity by becoming a nun. Beardsley takes his attitude to the female charac-ters not from Malory but from the Romantics who "made of the Fatal Woman an archetype which united in itself all forms of seduction, all vices and all delights."[13] As Tristram and Isolde drink the fatal potion, her Medusa locks presage his doom (Fig. 7). When Hallowes lures him to the Perilous Chapel, Lancelot responds with a gesture of self–destruction suggesting castration. The *Morte Darthur* illustrations are witty, technically innovative and aesthetically appealing — but they are not Malory.

The publication of a four–volume fine edition of Edmund Spenser's *Faerie Queen* (1894–7), illustrated with wood engravings by Walter Crane, reaffirmed the Kelmscott ideal. Like Morris, Crane believed that "books which have been considered by their printers and designers as works of art as well as of literature give double pleasure since they satisfy more than one sense."[14] Any area on the book page not devoted to text should be filled with design. Some illustrations obviously draw on late medieval manuscripts like the Douce *Guiron,* where the border contains not only botanical decoration but also figural panels that complement the central picture (Fig. 8). For example, Crane's densely ornamented depiction of the enthroned Duessa gazing into a mirror, (the medieval sign of Pride), is surrounded by border representations of the other Deadly Sins as humans riding iconographically appropriate animals. This design realises Spenser's text and exhibits Pre–Raphaelite delight in symbolism. Crane's Prince Arthur, whether as chivalric monster–slayer, rescuer of the oppressed, or genealogist, embodies such Victorian ideals as duty, muscular Christianity, and imperial power.

Crane regarded handengraving, which he himself had learned during an apprenticeship to W.J. Linton (1857–1860), as a process that enslaved the workers by making them part of a factory–style assembly line. At the same time, he was uneasy about the new photographic process because it encouraged the artist to rely on large masses of black and white. The solution, according to artists like Eric Gill, was to eliminate the middlemen—the photographer, the printer, the etcher, the router, the mounter—because each degraded the original work. The artist should be free to satisfy his own conscience and to show respect for "the thing itself," i.e. the medium. Wood–engraving was the technique which best ensured that a work of art would be "primarily a thing of Beauty in itself and not a representation of something else."[15]

This was also the attitude of the French artists and publishers who pioneered the handsome illustrated books known as *livres d'artiste.* Henry Kahnweiler's publication of Guillaume

Apollinaire's *l'enchanteur pourrisant* (1909), with illustrations by André Derain, revived the art of wood engraving on the continent. The text is based on the Old French *Prose Merlin* story of Merlin's fatal love for Viviane; having learned his magic, she incarcerates the enchanter in the forest of Broceliande. Apollinaire's Merlin has a decayed body but a living spirit that converses with Viviane (the embodiment of evil beauty) and other visitors to his grave.

Apollinaire's aim was to express in his prose–poem "les racines s'etendent très loin, jusqu' aux profondeurs celtiques de nos traditions."[16] Derain, however, felt no obligation to recreate the text literally. The artist's task was to express the text's spirit and underlying significance, using the technique that seemed most appropriate – in this case, the "old–fashioned" woodcut. Rather than recreating an impression of medieval Brittany, he resorts to a naive primitivism that makes the time and place of his woodcuts independent of the text. His forest is a jungle of vines, serpentine roots and exotic, tulip–like flowers with only an occasional hawthorne blossom as a subtle allusion to the original myth. And his human figures are Gauginesque nudes whose grotesque movements convey powerful emotions, although their identity as characters is not always clear.

Another artist who used the wood engraving to free himself from the limits of historical time and geographical space while maintaining the spirit of his text was Robert Gibbings (1899–1954). His acquisition of the Golden Cockerel Press in 1924 enabled him to be artist, book designer and publisher. Having received a commission to illustrate the *Morte Darthur* for the Limited Editions Club of New York, he fulfilled an early desire "to do some decorations for really first class books." Decoration is the key to his approach. In the *Morte* designs, the continuum is provided by rhythmic arrangements of stylized foliage and chivalric images which take account of the wood block's grain. The non–naturalistic style produces the legendary, timeless quality that is inherent in "the matter of Britain." Here, as in Malory, the golden age of chivalry is recreated through isolated images of martial, courtly and Christian ritual—a kneeling knight presenting his sword hilt first, a pair of mounted knights with raised spears loping through a forest, jousting knights charging one another, demure damsels shrinking into stylised foliage, chalices and crucifixes, castles and pavilions, arms and banners.

Illustrations related to specific incidents are few and those few convey a macabre humour. A naked Elaine dances away from Lancelot's sword. Lancelot, wearing only a shirt, his hair standing on end, swings madly at an arrangement of arms interwoven with plants. A toothy Giant of St. Michael's Mount gnaws on a baby's limb while three trussed infants are being barbecued over the bonfire (Fig. 9). Despite the flatness of design, the restricted texture, the simplistic transitions between black and white, and the decorative rather than representational intention, Gibbings is a satisfactory illustrator of Malory because he conveys the energetic and exuberant physical activity of his source.

While black–and–white wood engravings have remained a favourite mode of Arthurian illustration, the introduction of colour into the process has also produced some fine books, notably Gwyn Jones' prose translation of *Sir Gawain and the Green Knight* (1952) illustrated by Dorothea Braby for the Golden Cockerel Press. The colour range is restricted to shades of rose and green, suggesting the antitheses of warmth and coolness, natural and supernatural, sensuous castle life and dangerous forest hunt. What Gwyn Jones describes as "the gracious and aristocratic air, the polished manners and good breeding" of the characters are visually conveyed through elegant fifteenth–century costumes, graceful postures and fine proportions (Fig. 10). Though Braby believes, like Derain and Gibbings, that "the engraver must be master or nothing," her insistence on conferring with the translator about every pictorial detail has resulted in a more literal evocation of the fourteenth–century text than artists like Gibbings and Derain aimed at.

One cannot discuss twentieth–century Arthurian illustration without acknowledging the influence of Arthur Rackham (1867–1939), one of the most technically proficient and original artists employed in illustrating the *Morte Darthur* (1917). This "Paintre–Sorcier" recreates the milieu of medieval romance where the "historical" world of time and space is penetrated by the otherworldly. He produces a "faerie" atmosphere by using line drawings delicately tinted with watercolours and by mingling elements from different genres. The twisted roots, grasping branches and rough bark of his trees incorporate human features while the caricatured physiognomies of his people take on animal characteristics. The possibility of metamorphosis is convincingly conveyed (Fig. 11).

Rackham unblinkingly recognises the existence of evil. The bodies of Ironside's victims dangle like rag dolls from treetops. The fire–breathing dragon clutches Lancelot's foot, as the fair-haired hero in fifteenth–century armour prepares to rid society of this oppressor. "How Mordred was slain by Arthur and how by him Arthur was hurt to death," with its dark ground, bat–like combatants, ominous birds and fragmented bodies, recalls Goya's disasters of war iconography. Contrastingly, the Grail's golden radiance, the richness of costume as Tristan and Isolde prepare to drink, the great bouquet of roses and bowl of fruit on Mark's table and the blossoming woodlands of Guenevere's maying evoke the courtly world's transient joy and beauty. The fact that ominous, bare–branched trees, serpentine roots, turgid waters and thorny thickets keep appearing in the work of recent illustrators like Virgil Burnett[17] and Alan Lee[18] indicates that Rackham's depiction of the Perilous Forest is definitive.

Since its publication in 1485, Caxton's edition of Malory's *Morte Darthur* has largely determined the context of Arthurian illustration.[19] In recent years, however, the field has been enlarged not only by illustrated editions of other medieval texts but also by original Arthurian literature. Errol Le Cain's picture book, *King Arthur's Sword* (1968), combines the forms of historiated initials and decorative borders with foliage and birds, rectangular framed miniatures, and the consecutive narrative of the Bayeux tapestry. The deliberate primitivism, relying on straight lines rather than Gothic curves and on two–dimensional cut out, is in effect comic rather than elegant. The incipient shape–shifting of Rackham's illustrations is here extended to create a world entirely magical, containing rose–coloured knights, a black gowned, dunce–capped Merlin, a blue–haired Morgan and a mauve Arthur, who generously forgives his sister for turning herself into a great black bird and flying away with Excalibur.

The eccentricities of T.H. White's conclusion to *The Once and Future King*, titled *The Book of Merlyn* (1977), find visual equivalents in Trevor Stubley's black and white drawings. Traditional materials, such as Geoffrey of Monmouth's association of Merlin with the building of Stonehenge, are combined with anthropomorphic animals, natural history subjects, and caricatures, notably Merlin himself, to produce the kind of eclectic "world" where realism and fantasy congenially mingle. George Sharp's illustrations for Joy Chant's *The High Kings* (1983), a collection of Celtic stories set in the context of Arthur's life, represent another pictorial trend. As Louis Rhead had urged earlier in the century, Sharp evokes not the High Middle Ages of castles and mailed knights but the milieu of the "historical" Arthur, fifth–century Britain. The colours are the subdued tones of a sepia print and of Rackham's autumnal scenes. Outlines are blurred to produce misty landscapes. Great tumuli, jagged peaks, ochre waters and contorted branches convey nature's hostility to the tormented half–naked humans. A specifically Celtic ambience is suggested by the torque and the metal mirror (cleverly used as roundels that enclose a face), by interlace designs and small drawings of harps, brooches, crosses, by the characters' museum piece jewellery and weapons. Only the young women look too refined and sophisticated for these Dark Age warriors.

In the Middle Ages, creating a work of art was an act of worship, its beauty an intimation of divinity. Though many attitudes changed after the Renaissance, the idea that good art was moral art persisted until challenged by "art for art's sake" in the late nineteenth century. An ethical motive is apparent in Holman Hunt's allegorical treatment of the Lady of Shalott and in the many juvenile versions of Malory, where the illustrations focus on heroes like Lancelot who embody physical beauty, loyal friendship, courage, self–sacrifice, and sportsmanship. However, the opportunity for didactic instruction alone does not explain the continuing allure of Arthurian romance. Perhaps the "cosmic homesickness" of the Pre–Raphaelites is a persistent condition that makes each of us long for a legendary past where, with Edward Burne–Jones, we may find the "magical land that I dream about."

University of Alberta

NOTES

[1]For a more detailed discussion see Muriel Whitaker, *The Legends of King Arthur in Art* (Cambridge, England, 1990). The standard reference for medieval Arthurian art is R.S. Loomis and L.H. Loomis, *Arthurian Legends in Medieval Art* (London, 1938).

[2]M. Alison Stones, "The Earliest Illustrated Prose Lancelot Manuscript," in *Reading Medieval Studies*, 3 (1977), 3–44.

[3]On Arthurian heraldry see Gerard J. Brault, *Early Blazon, Heraldic Terminology in the Twelfth and Thirteenth Centuries with Special Reference to Arthurian Literature* (Oxford, 1972); Michel Pastoureau, *Armorial des chevaliers de la Table Ronde* (Paris, 1983) and *L'hermine et le Sinople: Etudes d' Héraldique Médiévale* (Paris, 1982).

[4]For an explication of the courtly milieu in French Arthurian romance see A.E. Auerbach, *Mimesis, the Representation of Reality in Western Literature,* trans. Willard R. Trask (Princeton, 1953), 123–42.

[5]Bonn, Universitätsbibliotheck HS 526; London, B. L. Additional MSS 10292–4 and Royal MS 14E iii; Manchester, John Rylands University Library MS fr. 1; Oxford, Bodl. Douce MS 215; New York, H.P. Kraus, Catalogue 165, no. 3.

[6]Edmund G. Gardner, *The Arthurian Legend in Italian Literature* (London and New York, 1930). On Italian illumination,

see François Avril, *Dix Siècles d'enluminure italienne (VIe-XVe Siècles)* (Paris, 1984).

[7]For a description of the woodcut series, see Edward Hodnett, *English Woodcuts 1480-1535* (Oxford, 1973 [1935]).

[8]Rossetti describes the visit and his reaction to it in a letter to William Allingham dated January 23, 1855. *Letters of Dante Gabriel Rossetti*, ed. O. Doughty and J. R. Wahl, 4 vols. (Oxford, 1965), I, 238-39.

[9]George Somes Layard, *Tennyson and his Pre-Raphaelite Illustrators* (London, 1894), 3. See also *Ladies of Shalott: A Victorian Masterpiece and its Contexts*, An Exhibition by the Department of Art, Brown University, 23 February-23 March, 1985 (Providence, R.I., 1985).

[10]See Helmut Gernsheim, *Julia Margaret Cameron: Her Life and Photographic Work* (Millerton, N.Y., 1975); Charles W. Millard, "Julia Margaret Cameron and Tennyson's 'Idylls of the King,' " *Harvard Library Bulletin* 21/2 (April, 1973), 187-201; Mike Weaver, *Julia Margaret Cameron 1815-1879*, catalogue of an exhibition arranged by the John Hansard Gallery, The University, Southampton (London, 1984).

[11]A fine example of a *Morte Darthur* in the Kelmscott style is the 504-page folio limited edition printed by C. H. St. John Hornby's Ashendene Press in 1913.

[12]Beardsley's version of the enterprise is given in a letter to G.F. Scotson Clark written ca. Feb. 15, 1894. See *The Letters of Aubrey Beardsley*, ed. Henry Maas, J. L. Duncan, W.G. Good (London, 1971), p. 43.

[13]Mario Praz, *The Romantic Agony*, trans. Angus Davidson (London, 1971), 209-10.

[14]Walter Crane, *William Morris to Whistler. Papers and Addresses on Art and Craft and the Commonweal* (London, 1911), 75.

[15]Eric Gill, Foreword to R. John Beedham, *Wood Engraving,* rpr. as *Foreword to a Treatise Upon the Craft of Wood Engraving* (Vancouver, 1967), 4.

[16]Gerard Bertrand, *L'illustration de la poèsie a l'epoque du cubisme 1904–1914: Derain, Dufy, Picasso* (Paris, 1971), 16.

[17]See Virgil Burnett's line drawings for *Sir Gawain and the Green Knight,* trans. Theodore Silverstein (Chicago and London, 1974) and his lithographs for the Folio Society's *Sir Gawain and the Green Knight,* trans. Keith Harrison (London, 1983).

[18]See Alan Lee's forty-five watercolour illustrations for *The Mabinogion,* trans. Gwyn and Thomas Jones (London, 1982) and the Arthurian section of David Day's *Castles,* ed. David Larkin (New York, 1984).

[19]See Muriel Whitaker, "Illustrating Caxton's Malory" in *Studies in Malory,* ed. James W. Spisak (Kalamazoo, Mich., 1985), 297–319 and 10 plates.

Children's Reading and the Arthurian Tales

Jane L. Curry

Children were undoubtedly from the beginning a part of the audience for the romances and ballads of King Arthur and his court, and with the coming of the printed book they remained a part of that general audience. Many of Caxton's books, from Aesop to the *Morte Darthur,* would have had a strong appeal for the child whose family was prosperous enough to own them, and the very rarity of Caxton's Malory— two known copies and a single sheet— may be in some measure a result of its popularity with the young. Children can in two or three generations read a family favorite to tatters, and the odds against early editions of Malory's Arthurian adventures surviving even a century of such usage would have been high. That Malory continued to be popular with the young is suggested by Roger Ascham's protest in 1570 at its "open mans slaughter and bold bawdrye," despite which,

> Yet I know, when Gods Bible was banished the Court, and Morte Arthure receiued into the Princes chamber. What toyes, the dayly readynge of such a boke, may work in the will of a yong ientleman, or a yong mayde, that liueth welthelie and idlelie, wise men can iudge . . . [1]

And children still knew the tales in other guises. John Milton, himself drawn as a boy to tales of Arthur's knights, was to comment in the following century that Arthur was "more renowned in songs and romances than in true stories,"[2] — and fortunately so, for after William Stansby's 1634 edition of Malory's "true stories" went out of print, there was no other until 1816. Arthur was to make a number of minor literary appearances in the latter seventeenth century, but in the eighteenth he fell out of literary fashion. Kept alive by popular literature, the "drolls" performed at fairs[3] and, it is reasonable to assume, storytelling, Arthur had in that

very rational century gone "underground." The audience for traditional lore consisted not only of the common folk, but of children
from a wide variety of backgrounds, and provided a profitable and
growing market for the printers and sellers of ballad sheets and
chapbooks. Direct evidence of reading preferences is scant, but
what is known of the reading preferences of schoolboys indicates
that their choices were predominantly the chivalric tales.[4]

Chapbooks were easily read to pieces, and among the chivalric
tales Arthurian survivors are rare. Moreover, little record is left to
indicate the strength of the Arthurian popular tradition in print,
but that the history of Arthur was common knowledge is suggested
by the appearance in chapbook form of the adventures of such
unlikely Arthurian knights as the heroes of *Jack the Giant Killer,*
Tom–a–Lincoln, and *Tom Thumb.* As in Thomas Love Peacock's
later *Sir Hornbook; or, Childe Launcelot's Expedition* (1814), the
settings "In the reign of famous King Arthur" are often little more
than a touch of Arthurian gilding intended to add to the tales'
appeal. Jack and Tom Thumb continued to appear in chapbook
versions on into the nineteenth century, by which time the trade
was directed almost exclusively to children, and a late *Jack the
Giant Killer* suggests the appetites of that audience: "Jack was a
boy of bold temper; he took pleasure in hearing or reading stories
of wizards, conjurors, giants and fairies; and used to listen eagerly
while his father talked of the brave knights of King Arthur's round
table."[5]

The revival of a general interest in King Arthur was prompted
by two undistinguished 1816 editions based on Stansby's Malory of
1634, and by Robert Southey's 1817 edition of Caxton's *Morte
Darthur.* Southey in his introduction recalls that "When I was a
schoolboy I possessed a wretchedly imperfect copy, and there was
no book, except the Faery Queen, which I perused so often, or with
such deep contentment." He goes on to suggest that "were it again
modernized ... and published as a book for boys, it could hardly
fail of regaining its popularity."[6] The adult audience would inevitably follow. But the suggestion seemed to pass unnoticed.

Tennyson, born in 1809, also met the tales as a boy. An omnivorous reader, from the age of twelve he had the run of his father's excellent library, which contained one of the 1816 editions.[7] And it was, in turn, in response to the popularity of Tennyson's *The Idylls of the King* that James T. Knowles "compiled and arranged" *The Story of King Arthur and his Knights of the Round Table* in 1864, describing it as "an endeavour to carry out the suggestion of the poet Southey."[8] Knowles's book, arguably still the most attractive of the abridgments of the *Morte*, was followed by others until, by the turn of the century, a virtual industry of abridgers and adaptors was at work to introduce Malory to children. But most versions, not only those intended for use in schools, were less concerned to offer entertainment than to present a Masterpiece of Literature in English, and oral exemplar. Given the modernized spellings and (to varying degrees) simplified language, the entertainment was readily available to young readers, but to judge from the prefaces, the intention of many compilers was frankly didactic. Fortunately a certain respect for the original text, however uneven and unscholarly, restrained adaptors from active moralizing. Children could enjoy the action and color (perhaps especially the gore) without considering that they were being "improved."

Some nineteenth–century abridgers and adaptors, concerned to shape a "clearer and more consecutive story," went, as did Knowles, to Geoffrey of Monmouth "and other sources."[9] Charles Henry Hanson (1898) cites as additional sources the *Merlin, Sir Gawain and the Green Knight,* and the *Mabinogion.* Few went much further afield. Several— Knowles, poet–academic Sidney Lanier in *The Boy's King Arthur* (1880)) and, later, artist–writer Howard Pyle in a four–volume retelling (1903-10), did achieve clear and coherent narratives and, significantly, theirs have proved versions with staying power. All three are still in print. A number of other compilers appear to have chosen tales on the basis of entertainment value or personal preference. Theirs and workmanlike compilations such as those of Margaret Vere Farrington

(1888) and Mary MacLeod (1900) were, if less popular, still widely read.

So long as the compilations of tales were firmly rooted in the *Morte Darthur,* the degree of modernization of Malory's language appropriate for young readers was a matter of concern. Abridgment as well as adaptation led naturally to a simplification of prose style, but the retention of archaic forms and formalities of speech served both to establish a courtly atmosphere and to create the sense that a range of feeling and action higher than that of everyday life exists and can be aspired to. Such formality would have presented no particular problem for young readers until well into the twentieth century, for a majority of the children who made up the reading audience would have had at least a passing acquaintance with the *thous* and *hasts* and *thinkests* of the King James version of the Bible. True archaisms were another matter. Knowles avoids them and strives for a prose style at once formal and comfortable, but Lanier, a professor of English at Johns Hopkins, while freely abridging, shows in *The Boy's King Arthur* a scrupulous regard for Malory's language, bracketing where he substitutes words and using italics within brackets to indicate the meaning of a preceding archaic term: "Then stood the realm in great [danger] for a long while, for every lord made him strong, and many weened [*thought*] to have been king."[10]

In contrast, Howard Pyle's *The Story of King Arthur and his Knights* (1903) and its three companion volumes are stiff and splendid with syntactical inversions and elaborate archaic diction such as *hight, avaunt, cantels, bedight* and *ween,* undefined and often made no clearer by the context. Nevertheless, Pyle's wholehearted delight in his antique idiom gives it an almost incantatory power, and has drawn many young American readers into the enchantment that binds him. English children have consistently resisted the spell, long preferring Henry Gilbert's *King Arthur's Knights: the Tales Retold for Boys and Girls* (1911). Gilbert claimed to write in simple language, and so, in comparison with Pyle, he did.

Later twentieth–century retellings, while employing prose styles increasingly simple and direct, nevertheless almost invariably retain some element of formality, even if, as in Desmond Dunkerly's four small mass–market volumes of *Tales of King Arthur* (1977), it is only the dignity that comes with a careful plainness. Some, like Roger Lancelyn Green's *King Arthur and his Knights of the Round Table* (1953), currently the most widely available ("popular" is perhaps too strong a word), rely on mild syntactical inversions. One of the most distinguished of contemporary versions for young people, Rosemary Sutcliff's trilogy *The Sword and the Circle, The Light Beyond the Forest* and *The Road to Camlann* (1979-81) is notable for its range and flexibility of prose style. The novels are for the most part poetic in their simplicity and easy in their small formalities, but Sutcliff's prose can also rise to repeat Malory's richness in Sir Ector's lament for Lancelot ("thou that were never matched of earthly knight's hand") at the tales' ending.

‡

Beyond the practicalities of choosing stories and a style attractive to children, it was, well into the twentieth century, the didactic intention of compilers and adaptors which influenced the selection of tales and shaped their narratives. Moral underlining, chivalry as the inspiration of a new secular morality, Christian Grail mysticism, censorship and Bowdlerization, and the pedagogy of useful fact – all have been aimed at the heads of unsuspecting children.

"Indeed," Henry Gilbert writes in his preface, "the great and simple lesson of chivalry which the tales of King Arthur teach is, in a few words, to merit 'the fine old name of gentleman'."[11]

Considering the tendency of children to read primarily for narrative sequence, much of the lesson material was aimed past their heads, but nevertheless King Arthur as a superior sort of cultural enforcer had a considerable impact. Mark Twain, alarmed by the chivalric phenomenon, attacked it with *A Connecticut Yankee in King Arthur's Court* (1889), but to no avail. In the half

century to follow, those adapting the tales for children were, as
Southey wrote of Sir Kenelm Digby's influential *The Broad Stone
of Honour* (1822), full of "exaggerated admiration of chivalry" and
"determined not to see the evils connected with it."[12] In America
that uncritical admiration led in 1893 to the founding by Congrega-
tional minister William Byron Forbush of the Order of the Knights
of King Arthur for boys.[13] The purpose of the popular youth
organization was to ". . . bring back to the world, and especially to
its youth, the spirit of chivalry, courtesy, deference to womanhood,
recognition of the *noblesse oblige*, and Christian daring, an ideal of
that kingdom of knightliness which King Arthur promised he
would bring back when he returns from Avalon." The order's
meetings employed "ritual, mystery and parade," and hero–worship was encouraged by, among other practices, "the reading
together of heroic books" and competition for "the sacred
honor of 'the Siege Perilous' for athletic, scholarly or self–sacrific-
ing attainments." The plan was "thoroughly Christian." Similarly,
the Boy Scout was from the first conceived of as a knight errant,
and his familiarity with the Arthurian tales is assumed in the
"Knight's Code" of Lord Baden–Powell's *Scouting for Boys* (1908),
rules ostensibly established by King Arthur and inspiring innumerable latter–day quests and good deeds.

The edition of the tales Baden Powell recommended to Boy
Scouts was U. Waldo Cutler's *Stories of King Arthur and his
Knights* (1914),[14] a prim version in which no hint is given of
Arthur's dubious begetting or Lancelot and Guinevere's guilt.
Moral patterns must not embody moral error. For more than a
century most versions of the tales adapted for children tiptoed
around the adultery and incest so central to the tales. As a consequence of omissions, distortions or outright tampering by adaptors
who saw themselves as the moral guardians of young readers, any
sense of the evil consequences of broken faith was weakened or
lost, leaving the tales little more than a string of adventures.

Concerned to mask Uther's deception of Igraine and Arthur's
conception out of wedlock without actively revising events, a

number of adaptors have relied on neat verbal footwork. Knowles's Uther, "Gerlois being killed in battle," determines to marry the widowed Igerna, obtains some carefully unspecified aid from Merlin and, as the narrative shifts quickly away from Igerna in Tintagil, is "at length happily wedded."[15] Pyle, forty–odd years later, is still more circumspect, saying only, "he took to wife a certain beautiful and gentle lady, hight Igraine. This noble dame was the widow of Gerlois, the Duke of Tintegal."[16] Doris Ashley (1922), with masterly word–waffling, manages to imply that Igraine is unmarried, but Stewart Campbell (1955) eschews the favored technique of simply–not–saying, and converts the Duke of Tintagil into Igraine's guardian. Sidney Lanier and Mary MacLeod avoid such side–stepping by beginning with the birth of Arthur, but Clifton Johnson (1916), unwilling to allow any room for doubt of Arthur's legitimacy, has his Sir Ulfius originate the idea that Uther wed the widowed Igraine, and Arthur is conceived with neither shape–shifting nor sin. The magical deception of Igraine appears to be the element most distasteful to those telling the tale to children. Even G. B. Harrison's *New Tales from Malory* (1939), otherwise unusually frank about the sexual aspects of the tales, omits any reference to it. Constance Martin (1948) shows Uther's illicit desire and his determination to have his way, but backs off with "...killed him in battle, and then married the beautiful Duchess."[17]

Similarly, most versions avoid dealing with Arthur's begetting Mordred on Morgause of Orkney (or, in a number of versions, Morgan), Mordred himself is most often identified as Arthur's nephew, not nephew–son, and Green distances him even further by giving no direct name to the relationship, identifying him only as Morgan's son and Agravaine's cousin. G. B. Harrison provides a rare exception to the tradition of evasion and cover–up, saying of Morgan that "the king loved her greatly, as she loved him. And afterwards she had another son who was called Mordred."[18] Merlin, revealing to Arthur that Morgan is his sister, warns that "you have done a thing that God is displeased with. Your sister

shall have a child that shall destroy you. . . ."[19] Young readers were
free to understand as much as their experience allowed, and Harrison's frankness was not approached until, forty years later, Rosemary Sutcliff's Margawse is "skilled in the sweet dark ways of
temptation" and Arthur realizes "that he had done one of the
forbidden things, and that because of it, in one way or another, he
was doomed."[20] Versions which omit the incest must as a result
omit Arthur's ominous dream of the invasion of the kingdom by
griffins and serpents, Merlin's prophetic interpretation of it, and
the resultant thematic emphasis on the consequences of wrongful
actions and broken faith. (R. L. Green, on the other hand, by
over–reliance on such prophecies, ends in conveying less a sense
of unity than of disunity papered over with assertions to the contrary.)

In dealing with Lancelot and Guinevere's adultery, writers for
children have found vagueness as useful as evasion. While most
versions recognize Lancelot's attachment to the queen, the majority allow the reader to understand it as a devotion at once romantic
and Platonic. The lovers' betrayal of Arthur is in many versions
characterized simply as their "treason," and though children might
puzzle over what treason is meant, the urge to discover what happens next would carry them "safely" past. The Arthur of Dr. Edward Brooks's version (1900) believes Guinevere "at fault," but
again the nature of the fault is nowhere hinted at. Beatrice Clay
(1901) takes care to imply that Lancelot and the queen are innocent of the accusation, but Henry Gilbert is more direct; there
is no affair, and Lancelot goes to Guinevere's chamber strictly in
the role of her champion, to confer about the apple–poisoning
charge brought against her. Medieval scholar Philip Schuyler
Allen, perhaps reluctant to distort the love affair, omits it entirely.
Alice M. Hadfield (1953), without making any explicit distinction,
manages to suggest a high courtly, but not carnal, love. Ultimately,
in the tidied–up versions the Round Table is seen to fail not
because of the flawed actions of good men, but because of hostility
from without.

Not all versions are so timid about sexual matters. Barbara Leonie Picard's treatment of Lancelot and Guinevere's adultery in *Stories of King Arthur and his Knights* (1955), like Harrison's version a generation earlier, is at once direct and circumspect, allowing young readers to understand as much or little as their knowledge affords. And among the retellings of single tales or groups of unrelated tales, a light and even more straightforward approach to sexual matters allows Winifred Rosen's *Three Romances* (1984) of Sir Gawain and Dame Ragnell, Enid and Geraint, and Merlin and Niniane, to explore the theme of sovereignty in good humor. Gawain's comic innocence in the marriage bed— he has only a "foggy kind of impression" of the marital duty Dame Ragnell requires of him— and Merlin and Niniane as they "[make] joy out of mind and time" give the debate a new liveliness. That Rosen's tales are frank without being sexually explicit, as are some teen–age novels, allows any younger readers to keep their own "foggy kind of impression" about what is going on.

‡

If in the latter twentieth century the sexual silence has been broken, it nevertheless continues to be observed by many writers of children's versions of the tales. Violence, on the other hand, is not only an important factor in the appeal the tales have for children, but has always been acceptable. Even the primmest of versions can glory in smiting and skewering, and Malory's vivid account of the fatal combat between Mordred and Arthur survives in painful detail in almost all retellings from Knowles's to the present, including the unexpectedly respectable *The Knights of the Round Table* (1950), by that unlikely Arthurian, Enid Blyton. If some retellers wince away from Mordred's thrusting himself up Arthur's spear, they do not blink at the blow that cleaves the king's helmet and "brayne panne." Indeed, Knowles, Lanier, Hansen, MacLeod and a number of others grimly retain that quaintly graphic "brain pan" of Caxton's edition. Modern writers are no less stern. Anthony Mockler's *King Arthur and his Knights* (1984) is strewn with "swopped"–off heads, and in her trilogy Rosemary Sutcliff effectively slows and deepens the tragedy by a descriptive heightening of the violence of Malory's account of the final conflict: "And when Sir Mordred felt his death wound within him, he gave a great yell, savage and despairing, and thrust himself forward upon the spear–shaft, as a boar carried forward by its own rush up the shaft of the hunter, until he was stayed by the hand–guard...."[21]

For all the gore served up in the one hundred and twenty–odd years in which Arthurian tales have been abridged or retold for children, there seems rarely, if ever, to be a calculated indulgence in visceral effect for its own sake. A morality of violence is implicit: that power or might does not make right, but carries an obligation of service in righting wrongs and defending the defenceless. This cumulative lesson of "right violence" and the right exercise of power impresses itself on young readers with a minimal resort to moral underlining. Neither the value, nor the inherent danger in such lessons—the righteous arrogance of power which Twain condemned—can easily be dismissed.

Since 1900, over one hundred and thirty—probably well over—Arthurian books have been published for children. Few years have passed without one new retelling, whether a compilation or single tale, and in a number of years as many as five or six have been published. The bibliography of juvenile Arthuriana is not complete, but it is interesting to note that the years in which it appears that books about King Arthur were thinnest on the ground were 1914-19 and 1940-45. It is difficult not to assume that for writers, if not for young readers, lessons in right violence must have seemed superfluous.

‡

In the latter half of this century a number of single tales have been published as books for young people, among them E. M. R.

Ditmas's excellent novel–length *Gareth of Orkney* (1956), Ian Ser-
raillier's verse *The Challenge of the Green Knight* (1966), Rosemary
Sutcliff's *Tristan and Iseult* (1974), and Selena Hastings's *Sir
Gawain and the Green Knight* (1981) and *Sir Gawain and the
Loathly Lady* (1985), illustrated by Juan Wijngaard in a style that
echoes the brilliance of medieval illumination.

The single tale or a grouping like Rosen's *Three Romances* can
allow the writer a greater sense of freedom to shape the story to
his or her own vision, but quite early in the century writers had
already begun tentatively to assert their independence of Malory
and the earlier sources. Having become a staple of child culture in
the English–speaking world, the Arthurian tradition was also to
become the subject of embellishments, reworkings, invention, and
plundering. Allen French's *Sir Marrok: A Tale of the Days of King
Arthur* (1902), an elaboration on Malory's passing reference to a
knight whose wife turns him into a werewolf, is an inventive tale in
which the Arthurian setting and appearances by Arthur, King Pellinore and Tristram are integral to the story. Tales featuring invented characters include the essentially domestic adventures of
Catherine Owens Peare's *Melor, King Arthur's Page* (1963) and,
also for younger readers, Clyde Robert Bulla's more robustly adventurous *The Sword in the Tree* (1956). In the '60s, with the surge
in popularity of fantasy novels for the young, Arthur and his
knights took to materializing in twentieth–century Britain. They
are at the center of a dislocation of time in William Mayne's
Earthfasts (1966), and in Jane Curry's *The Sleepers* (1968) are
awakened prematurely from their long sleep. Merlin is a central
character in Peter Dickinson's *The Weathermonger* (1968) and in
Susan Cooper's five–novel sequence *The Dark is Rising* (1965-77).
Cooper's Merriman is a Merlin surviving into the present and
serving as helper–advisor to the young protagonists. Dickinson's
Merlin, stirred from his enchanted sleep, is at the root of the
"Changes" which sweep Britain into a new Dark Age. As Fred
Inglis says of *Earthfasts*, the Arthurian tales are "an extraordinary
power line to the imagination of many writers."[22]

For the most part, stories and novels employing Arthurian
settings and characters in original narratives — even those which,
like *The Weathermonger,* are bizarre in their invention — do not run
counter to the traditional tales in the liberties they take. Rather,
the tales run parallel with them, or provide points of departure. In
The Sleepers Arthur and his knights, sleeping in a cavern under the
Eildon Hills, as in local Scottish legend, come under threat from a
Morgan le Fay who has survived into the modern world. The
liberties taken are at times broadly comical — Morgan and Mordred, as the agents of darkness, operate under the cloak of the
Morgan Sand and Gravel Company's excavations — but Arthur
himself is taken seriously. Found first by the children of archaeologists working on the site, he and his Romano–British knights
are awakened into a time at once past and present and travel to a
Londinium coexistent with the present–day London so that they
may set sail at last in Pridwen for Avalon. Though much of the
novel is a less than reverent comic extrapolation, underlying both
the comedy and adventure is a narrative urge to reconcile the local
and the larger, central Arthurian tradition.

But there are writers whose approach to legend and tradition
is much less restrained. And it is not only in original stories that
the tales are regarded as a reservoir of motifs or compounds of
free–floating elements which may be freely recombined. Perhaps
most notable, because it purports to be a retelling, is Antonia
Fraser's *King Arthur and the Knights of the Round Table* (1954), in
which Igraine, a maiden, rejects Uther and remains obdurate until
Merlin hypnotises her and leads her to Camelot. Mordred and
Morgan plot to gain the throne at the death of Uther. Young
Arthur lends Kay not the sword from the stone, but his own, and
keeps the magical one. And Morgan bewitches Gawain, who with
Mordred seizes Guinevere and accuses Arthur of betraying the
kingdom to the Norsemen. Motifs, characters and events are re-
designed at will.

Anthony Mockler's *King Arthur and his Knights* (1984) can be
equally startling. Observing in his foreword that "there is no

'correct' or 'incorrect' version of the Arthurian legends, but a myriad variations,"[23] Mockler cites as sources not only *La Mort le Roi Artu*, the Welsh legends and Geoffrey of Monmouth, but T. H. White and J. R. R. Tolkien. The influence of White's *The Sword in the Stone* (not, as is often supposed, written for children) lies predominantly in the insistently humorous tone of the first chapters, and *The Lord of the Rings* is the source of decorative Tolkienisms rather than an imaginative integration of traditional and original material. Moreover, many of the allusions to the *Ring* trilogy betray an imperfect recollection of that work, but since Mockler makes a point in the preface of having deliberately avoided re–reading both the White and Tolkien, his transformations and errors of fact are both accidental and intentional. The implication would seem to be that the spontaneous "influence" is more authentic in storytelling terms than a writer's deliberate and informed shaping of those influences, but since Mockler does not make the same claim in regard to his use of the earlier sources, his motive remains obscure.

The use of traditional materials in Susan Cooper's *The Dark is Rising* sequence is deliberate, and effective in the novels' terms, but nevertheless disquieting to some adult readers, not so much because liberties are taken, but because Cooper subverts the convention of fantasy literature that the supernatural has effective power in the real world. The final novel, *Silver on the Tree*, underlines a point Cooper has made earlier: that, ultimately, action on the supernatural/symbolic level, however stirring, has no significance in the real world of men. Arthur returns in *The Grey King*, but Britain is no better off for it. In *Silver on the Tree* Merriman/Merlin tells the children, "We have delivered you from evil, but the evil that is inside men is at the last a matter for men to control," and Arthur is no longer "somewhere sleeping."[24] At the novel's end, Arthur and a throng of figures from British myth and legend sail off to Avalon at the back of the North Wind. There will be no more magic, no other Return.

This twentieth–century skepticism, by emptying the figures of legend and the evils they confront of potency and significance, would seem to underlie the broad freedom some writers exercise in manipulating and reshaping the tales. It is a rejection of tradition that is combined with a deep–rooted attraction. Cooper's novels are powerfully written and popular, and young readers drawn to the fantasy are unlikely to notice how strongly it is undercut. Most contemporary stories for children and young people, though, are still content to let sleeping Arthur lie – or at least to say with Neil Philip's *The Tale of Sir Gawain* (1987) that "Some say he will come again to save us from ourselves, but how or when that is to be I do not know."[25]

Philip's short novel is at once original and traditional. Firmly rooted in Malory while drawing also on sources ranging from Chrétien to John Heath–Stubbs's *Artorius*, it is told in the at times passionate, at times elated, elegiac or querulous voice of the gravely wounded Sir Gawain. Imposing a sense of unity upon the tales through the perspective of Gawain's recollections and reflections – hardly an innovation in narrative terms – the *Tale* is in its way a radical departure from earlier Arthurian retellings for children and young people. If, as Sutcliff observes, her trilogy comes at the end to be "much closer to the modern novel,"[26] *The Tale of Sir Gawain* is the thing itself.

It would seem, with the appearance in the 1980s of the Sutcliff trilogy, the brilliantly illustrated Hastings *Gawain* stories and Philip's novel, and with new titles continuing to appear, that in books for the young the Arthurian tradition continues to recover and renew itself. If that recovery were to lead in time to a shift in the popular awareness of the Camelot of legend as a citadel of impossible fairytale perfection to that of a city in which mortal men strive to protect the powerless and pursue the good, and falter, and fail, and still hold to that good, so much the better for us all.

Stanford, California

NOTES

[1]Roger Ascham, *The Scholemaster* (London, 1570), 27v.

[2]Quoted in Robert Southey, "Introduction," to Sir Thomas Malory, *The Byrth, Lyf, and Actes of Kyng Arthur* (London, 1817), vii.

[3]Sybil Rosenfeld, *The Theatre of the London Fairs in the Eighteenth Century* (Cambridge, 1960), 85, 91, 97, 125, 138, 140.

[4]Margaret Spufford, *Small Books and Pleasant Histories: Popular Fiction and its Readership in Seventeenth–Century England* (Cambridge, 1985), 72, 75.

[5] n.a., *Jack the Giant Killer* (Otley, Yorkshire, c. 1850?), 1.

[6]Southey, "Introduction," xxviii.

[7]*DNB* 56:66; Mark Girouard, *The Return to Camelot: Chivalry and the English Gentleman* (New Haven, 1981), 178.

[8]James T. Knowles, *The Story of King Arthur and his Knights of the Round Table* (London, 1862), ii.

[9]Knowles, ii.

[10]Sidney Lanier, ed. *The Boy's King Arthur, Being Sir Thomas Malory's History of King Arthur and his Knights of the Round Table* (London, 1880), 1.

[11]Henry Gilbert. *King Arthur's Knights: the tales retold for boys and girls* (Edinburgh, 1911), vii.

[12]Southey, quoted in Girouard, 63.

[13]William Byron Forbush, *The Boy Problem* (New York, 1907), 101-02.

[14]Girouard, *Return*, 196. Re: *Scouting for Boys*, see 255.

[15] Knowles, 13.

[16]Howard Pyle, *The Story of King Arthur and his Knights* (New York, 1965), 1.

[17]Constance M. Martin, *King Arthur and his Knights* (London, 1948), 6.

[18]G. B. Harrison, *New Tales from Malory* (London, 1939), 24.

[19]Harrison, 27.

[20]Rosemary Sutcliff, *Road to Camlann*,10.

[21]Sutcliff, *Road*,122. Cf. Vinaver, *Malory,* 3:1237, ll. 15-18.

[22]Fred Inglis, *The Promise of Happiness: Value and Meaning in Children's Fiction* (Cambridge, 1981), 256.

[23]Anthony Mockler, *King Arthur and his Knights* (Oxford, 1984), xii.

[24]Susan Cooper, *Silver on the Tree* (London, 1977), 267.

[25]Neil Philip, *The Tale of Sir Gawain,* illus. Charles Keeping (Cambridge, 1987), 100.

[26] Sutcliff, *Road*, dust jacket, back flap.

Edwin Arlington Robinson: Arthurian Pacifist

Valerie M. Lagorio

If one were to ask an American Literature class about Edwin Arlington Robinson's poetic canon, their answer might include "Miniver Cheevy", "Richard Corey", "Mr. Flood's Party," and possibly, if they have read Yvor Winters, "Eros Turannos." This is a meager harvest of fame for a poet who, over a period of forty years, wrote twenty volumes of high-quality poetry, and won three Pulitzer prizes: *Collected Poems* (1921), *The Man Who Died Twice* (1924), and *Tristram* (1927), the latter bringing him long overdue success. His three long Arthurian narrative poems, *Merlin* (1917), *Lancelot* (1920), both written during World I and the Armistice, and *Tristram* (1927) have undeservedly fallen into obscurity. Hopefully, like Alfred, Lord Tennyson's *Idylls of the King* they will enjoy renewed popularity and scholarly attention in the wake of the Arthurian renascence of the late twentieth century.[1] This essay will concentrate on the *Merlin* and *Lancelot* and explore one major theme: Robinson's pacifistic use of the Arthurian apocalyptic to comment on America's and Western civilization's involvement in World War I, and by that use, to tap into one of the most enduring and powerful mythic elements in the legend.

The Arthurian apocalyptic is embedded in the great medieval histories and romances dealing with King Arthur and his realm, with Arthur as a Last World Emperor, ruling in the Golden Age of the Round Table, Modred as the Antichrist, the Last Days of terror and dissolution, and the hope of a better world to come.[2]

Beginning with Geoffrey of Monmouth's *Historia Regum Britanniae*, and continuing through the Vulgate romances, Wace's *Roman de Brut*, Layamon's *Brut*, the alliterative *Morte Arthure*, the stanzaic *Morte Arthur*, and Malory, the rise, promise, and tragic finale of Arthur's world is held up as a cautionary *speculum* for contemporary societies, with a concomitant warning on the destructiveness and futile wastes of war. The high aspirations of the Round Table, doomed by human venality and unjust wars of world conquest and revenge, end in the pyrrhic victory of the final Battle, when only a dying Arthur and a faithful remnant of his followers remain. Nowhere is this hollow triumph more succinctly and movingly depicted than in Malory:

> So sir Lucan departed, for he was grevously wounded in many places; and so as he yode he saw and harkened by the moonelyght how that pyllours and robbers were come into the fylde to pylle and to robbe many a full noble knyght of brochys and bees and of many a good rynge and many a riche juell. And who were nat dede all oute, they slew them for their harneys and their ryches.[3]

Robinson knew Malory well, and felt a special affinity with him, as both lived in times of political and social upheavals, Malory with the 100 Years War and War of the Roses, and Robinson with World War I and its aftermath. Like Malory, Robinson

> . . . was seeing a tragedy unfolding which, in its pity and vastness, had no parallel in recorded history. An age was crumbling before his eyes; crumbling, because the men who might have had the vision to guide it were irresponsible or trapped by their own passions, betraying what they most cherished. There was a Light . . . and it would survive, but meanwhile the darkness would be terrifying. Robinson reached out for a parable into which he could pour his sense of cosmic disaster, his grief and his hope.[4]

He found that parable in Malory's *Morte Darthur*. Robinson's two apocalypses begin at the end, when Camelot's Golden Age is finished, and concentrate on the pattern of betrayal and wars which led to the Armageddon at Salisbury. Yet, in the Arthurian tradition, both conclude with the promise of a new age and the spiritual regeneration of humankind.

Robinson intended that his *Merlin* and *Lancelot* be read as companion poems, and commented on them in various letters. He stated that both are World War poems, dealing with the passing of an old order and beginning of a new.[5] Asked if the works were wartime allegories, with Lancelot as Germany, Arthur as the British Empire, Gawaine as America, and Camelot as Western civilization, Robinson allowed that there is some symbolic significance, but warned against too allegorical a reading, as both "may be read just as well as narrative poems with no inner significance beyond that which is obvious."[6] In Laurence Perrine's view, with which I agree, they are not topical poems, but "apply as pertinently to the Second World War period as they did to the First. Both portray a world that is trembling in the balance. Camelot tumbled and went down to destruction, as the pre-war world of Europe and America did . . . for similar and eternal reasons—the disregard of moral laws,"[7] which is Robinson's special focus.

The story of *Merlin* is taken from Malory and the Vulgate *Merlin*, as summarized in S. Humphrey Gurteen's *The Arthurian Epic*, which inspired Robinson's novel treatment of the love affair between Merlin and Vivian.[8] Regarding the character of Merlin, Robinson wrote: "I have made him, without any legendary authority, such a lover of the world as to use Arthur and his empire as an object lesson to prove to coming generations that nothing can stand on a rotten foundation."[9] Robinson conveys the impending doom threatening Arthur's kingdom with three dominant leitmotifs: the mirror, which is central to his apocalyptic purpose, using the Arthurian world as a mirror for all ages to see the causes for the decimation of his and their world; specks, standing for moral and spiritual imperfections; and black and crimson clouds, storms, and ominous darkness, a motif which is also prevalent in the *Lancelot*.

They are alarmed over the prospect of Merlin's return to the court
from Brittany, at the request of a demoralized and beleaguered
Arthur. In a flashback, Robinson tells how Merlin, the great sage,
prophet, and kingmaker, has gone into a willing exile in
Broceliande to share a ten-year love idyll with Vivian. In a departure from the Malory and Tennyson accounts of their liaison,
Vivian is a twenty-five-year-old enchantress, who,from childhood
has revered and loved Merlin as a person first, and powerful
magician second. She is no schemer, anxious to learn his secrets
and then imprison him forevermore. And Merlin is no doting
senex amans but a mature, vibrant man at the height of his powers.
It is because he can do nothing further to guide Arthur or avert the
fall of the Round Table that he has fled to Brittany and a life of
love with Vivian. After ten years, Merlin is summoned by Arthur,
returns to Vivian, and, realizing that he, like Arthur, is subject to
Time and Change, leaves her for the last time. He returns to
Britain after Lancelot's rescue of Guinevere from the pyre and the
inception of Gawain's vendetta against Lancelot. Discouraged,
but seeing hope in the two lights of a woman's torch and the Grail,
Merlin sees only Dagonet, and goes off with him into the stormy
night.

On Merlin's first meeting with Vivian in edenic Broceliande,
he is greeted warmly by her and is totally enamored. As he gazes
on her youth and beauty, however, he has a cataclysmic vision of a
castle with the flaming sky behind it, as if all of Camelot, his
forsaken city, were on fire. He also remembers anew the pain that
fought in Arthur's eyes over losing him (IV, 48). As Vivian pours
him a welcoming cup of rare wine, she remarks: "I fear there may
be some specks," or lees, to which Merlin replies, with a sad
anxiety, equating specks with other more serious imperfections:

> There are specks everywhere. I fear them not.
> If I were king in Camelot, I might
> Fear more specks. But now I fear them not. (V, 68)

Here Merlin is expressing his longing for freedom from responsibility and for the refuge of love. However, he cannot overcome his feelings of guilt for having abandoned Arthur, even though he can do nothing to prevent the collapse of Camelot, which he has foreseen from the beginning, and about which he warned Arthur, but to no avail. This thought of Arthur and Camelot again brings the frightening vision of the end:

> There came
> Between him and the world a crumbling sky
> Of black and crimson, with a crimson cloud
> That held a far off town of many towers
> All swayed and shaken, till at last they fell,
> And there was nothing but a crimson cloud
> That crumbled into nothing, like the sky
> That vanished with it. (V, 64-65)

This vision will recur, "as through a cracked and clouded glass," (VII, 112), the shattered mirror of Arthurian glory, at the poem's end, when the seer leaves Camelot for the last time, and the fall is no longer portended but actual.

When Merlin is summoned to Camelot by the king, he justifies his departure to his angry lover, who rightly sees Arthur as her main rival:

> This time I go because I made him King,
> Thereby to be a mirror for the world;
> This time I go, but never after this,
> For I can be no more than what I was,
> And I can do no more than I have done. (V, 73)

This last statement is prophetic, for, in their painful meeting, Arthur cries out:

> ... I am still
> A king—who thought himself a little less
> Than God; a king who built his palaces
> On sand and mud,and hears them crumbling now,
> And sees them tottering, as he knew they must.
> You are the man who made me to be King—
> Therefore, say anything. (III, 25-26)

But Merlin, who had predicted it all, can give him little comfort, except, "say not you have lost, or failed in aught/ Your golden horoscope of imperfection" (III, 26-27), and disconsolately returns to Broceliande. Distressed in spirit, he increasingly roams about his prison of love, apart from Vivian:

> He wondered, when she was away from him
> If his avenging, injured intellect
> Might shine with Arthur's kingdom a twin mirror,
> Fate's plaything, for new ages without eyes
> To see therein themselves and their declension. (VI, 77-78)

Thus Merlin bitterly sees that he has become Arthur's mirror, just as Arthur mirrors Camelot, and the specks in both mirrors are the reflection of a world that is speckled.

   A furious Vivian scornfully dismisses Merlin's concern for Arthur and his mission:

> I know this king; he lives in Camelot,
> And I shall never like him. There are specks
> Almost all over him. Long live the king,
> But not the king who lives in Camelot,
> With Modred, Lancelot, and Guinevere—
> And all four speckled like a merry nest
> Of addled eggs together. You made him King
> Because you loved the world and saw in him
> From infancy a mirror for the millions.

> And all four speckled like a merry nest
> Of addled eggs together. You made him King
> Because you loved the world and saw in him
> From infancy a mirror for the millions.
> The world will see itself in him, and then
> The world will say its prayers and wash its face,
> And build for some new king a new foundation.
> Long live the king!

This cynical rejection of Arthur's importance to his now and future worlds contrasts sharply with Bedivere's forthcoming millennial prediction. Moreover, it crystallizes Merlin's realization that their love idyll is over, and that he must leave Vivian and Broceliande forever. The only place he can go is back to Camelot.

Meanwhile, Lancelot has rescued the queen, inadvertently killed Gareth and Gaheris, and fled to Joyous Gard. Dagonet, the fool-knight, is discussing these calamitous events with Bedivere and a vengeful Gawaine, and, as Robinson's surrogate, accuses Lancelot of making a war of love, the king a war of madness Gawaine a war of hate, and Modred a war of his ambition, "And somewhere in the middle of all this/ There's a squeezed world that elbows for attention." He concludes fatalistically that only when all men are rational or rickety, there may be no more wars (VII, 102-3). This looks ahead to the strong denunciation of war in *Lancelot*, and particularly to Lancelot's assessment of the irrational and selfish reasons for war in Book VII, 7. Dagonet's despair is countered by Bedivere's optimistic observation:

> We pass, but many are to follow us,
> And what they build may stay; though I believe
> Another age will have another Merlin,
> Another Camelot, and another King (VII, 103)

a view of human history consonant with Robinson's guarded idealism and belief in humanity. The phrase, "Another Camelot,

broods on warfare as a bloody harvest, a field of waving men shorn
by Time's indifferent scythe, and the King, Gawaine, Modred, and
Lancelot "all spent, and all dishonored, and all dead" (VII, 105).
His reflections are interrupted by the returning Merlin, who explains his unwillingness to meet with the king at this time: Arthur,
who was "to be a mirror wherein men/ May see themselves, and
pause" (VII, 119), is no longer a paragon to be emulated, in the
mirror for magistrates tradition, but a speckled human being, a
warning exemplar, and Merlin, as a speckled kingmaker, is similarly finished.

The mage and fool-knight go off into the night as final darkness falls over Camelot; but a note of hope, reconciliation, and
renewal is sounded when Merlin speaks of two fires that are to
light the world: the torch of woman and the Light that Galahad
found. According to Robinson, the torch of woman is to be taken
literally, and the Light is "the light of the Grail, interpreted universally as a spiritual realization of Things and their significance. I
don't see how this can be made any more concrete, for it is not the
same thing to any two individuals."[10] For this author, Robinson is
speaking of the creative force of love, human and divine. Not
surprisingly, Robinson did not consider the poem sad, for he found
nothing especially sad about the end of kings and the redemption
of the world,[11] which is the essential message of the *Merlin*.

Just as *Merlin* presages the fall of Camelot, so *Lancelot*
explores the reasons for that fall, relying for the most part on
Malory's *Book of Sir Lancelot and Queen Guinevere* and the *Morte
Arthur*. It covers the fateful tryst of Lancelot and the queen, his
rescue of her and slaying of Gawain's two brothers in the melee,
the flight to Joyous Gard, its subsequent siege by Arthur and
Gawain, the papal interdict, Guinevere's return to Camelot,
Lancelot's exile, the war at Benwick, Modred's revolt, and the last
battle at Salisbury. Robinson's character development of
Gawaine, Guinevere, and especially Lancelot, torn between his
love for the queen and his calling to the higher spiritual life symbolized by the Grail, has been justly acclaimed. And his depiction

of Arthur as a tragic *roi faineant* is pathetically apt, as he now, more than ever, mirrors the Waste Land of his disintegrated empire and world: "Like a sick landlord shuffling to the light/ For one last look–out on his mortgaged hills" (IV, 37) . . . "He stared and shivered like a sleepwalker,/ Brought suddenly awake where a cliff's edge/ Is all he sees between another step/ And his annihilation" (IV, 38).

But the poem's apocalyptic thrust centers around the topic of war, which Robinson consistently associates "with a feeling of waste and tragedy. No longer is it the theater of glory or heroism, nor, as in Tennyson, the weapon of God."[12] Robinson's anti–war sentiments are concentrated in Books VI and VII, which deal with the siege of Joyous Gard, but they pertain as well to the battles of Benwick and Salisbury, and directly address the battle horrors of World War I.

As in Malory, it is Gawaine who goads and drives Arthur to attack Joyous Gard, where his army, "disheartened with unprofitable slaughter/ Fought for their weary King and wearily/ Died fighting" (VI, 56). Because Lancelot's nobility prevents him from fighting his liege and Gawaine, the siege drags on. One night, Lancelot and a disgruntled Bors gaze down "In angry silence upon Arthur's horde,/ Who in the silver distance, without sound,/ Were dimly burying men" (VI, 56). This starts a litany of references to mists shrouding the dim work of Arthur's men, and to the "sacrificial hundreds" who fill "rainy graves" (VII, 72 and 94), a litany which conveys Robinson's special concern for the death of common soldiers, caught up in the quarrels of the mighty few. This democratic intrusion into the chivalric world, where battles of individuals and armies are the sole province of the nobility, evokes the image of the youth of the Western world, the humble unknowns, fighting and dying in Europe in the first Great War.

In another striking allusion to the high cost of war in human lives and the insanity of warfare, Bors, infuriated by Lancelot's noble forbearance and inaction, asks:

> How many of these tomorrows
> Are coming to ask unanswered why this war
> Was fought, and fought for the vain sake of slaughter?
> Why carve a compost of a multitude,
> When only two, discriminately dispatched,
> Would sum the end of what you know is ending
> And leave to you the scorch of no more blood
> Upon your blistered soul? The Light you saw
> Was not for this poor crumbling realm of Arthur,
> Nor more for Rome; but for another state
> That shall be neither Rome nor Camelot,
> Nor any that we may name. Why longer, then,
> Are you and Gawaine to anoint with war
> That even in hell would be superfluous,
> A reign already dying, and ripe to die?
> I leave you to your last interpretation
> Of what may be the pleasure of your madness. (VI, 58-59)

Guinevere also caustically condemns Lancelot's "slow game of empty slaughter":

> Tomorrow it will be
> The King's move, I support, and we shall have
> One more magnificent waste of nameless pawns,
> And of a few more knights. God, how you love
> This game! (VI, 61)
>
> . . . . . .
>
> How many thousand men
> Are going to their death before Gawaine
> And Arthur go to theirs — and I to mine! (VI, 64)

Responding to Guinevere's lament for the hundreds who have died for her, Lancelot underscores the irrational motivations for war, recalling Dagonet's speech in the *Merlin* (VII, 102). Like Dagonet, he lays the blame on the powerful, privileged few:

> They died because Gawaine went mad with hate
> For loss of his two brothers, and set the King
> On fire with fear, the two of them believing
> His fear was vengeance, when it was in fact
> A royal desperation. They died because
> Your world, my world, and Arthur's world is dying,
> As Merlin said it would. No blame is yours.   (VII, 79)

After the papal interdict, which ironically ends "an endless war with *pax vobiscum*" (VI, 70), Guinevere reluctantly rejoins Arthur, Lancelot goes into exile, and another "long sorrow" and "longer war" ensues at Benwick. It ceases only when the treasonous Antichrist Modred, "the Almighty's instrument/ Of a world's overthrow" (VIII, 101), summons a war-weary Arthur back to Britain, "with an army brisk as lead" (VIII, 102).

At this point, Robinson innovates a conciliatory farewell meeting between Lancelot and the dying Gawaine, who asks forgiveness, and penitently says bidding prayers for all caught in Camelot's tragic end—Arthur, Guinevere, his brothers,

> And for ourselves,
> And all who died for us, or now are dying
> Like rats around us of their numerous wounds
> And ills and evils, only this do I know—
> And this you know: The world has paid enough
> For Camelot. (IX, 104)

Robinson felt that this was the most significant line in the two poems,[13] realizing that the high price paid for the temporal might and spiritual sterility of Camelot, as well as of Western civilization, would also continue to be paid by succeeding generations. Having lived with the exploded myth of "the war to end all wars," he wrote in 1919:

> Meanwhile, we shall have the League of Nations to play with while Germany is getting herself and Russia together

for another grand smash. You will see from this that I
have no faith in any social scheme that doesn't see beyond
a moonshine millenium. Sometimes I wonder if it would
take much to set me yelling for an absolute monarchy in
this country—assuming that we haven't got one. The world
is a hell of a place; and if life and the universe mean
anything, there is no reason to suppose that it will be
anything else. This, as I understand it, is the true optimism.[14]

And in 1934, aware of the rise of dictatorships and growing threat
of World War II, he made a prophetic statement worthy of Merlin:

Today I have been thinking about Hitler, and of what one
neurotic fanatic may yet do to us and drag us into. It's all
right to say it can't happen, but unfortunately it can. The
more I try to make a picture of this world for the next
hundred years, the more I don't like it, and the gladder I
am that I shall be out of it. But something better will come
sometime, we'll hope . . .[15]

After Gawaine's death, Lancelot raises an army and races to
Britain to assist Arthur, only to learn

> Arthur was dead,
> And Modred with him, each by the other slain;
> And there was no knight left of all who fought
> On Salisbury field save one, Sir Bedivere,
> Of whom the tale was told that he had gone,
> Darkly away to some far hermitage
> To think and die. There were tales told of a ship. (IX, 108)

This terse account recalls Malory's summation of the king's last
battle and the destruction of the Round Table, but Robinson omits
the Excalibur incident, Arthur's journey to Avalon, and the
promise of his return. For, in Lancelot's words, Arthur's world is
a "played–out world" which had best be dead, as "there are worlds

enough to follow," recalling Bedivere's prophecy of "Another Camelot, and another King" (IX, 109-10).

Lancelot goes to Almesbury for a farewell meeting with Guinevere. As a result, he is no longer torn between his love for the queen and the Light of the Grail. He now must search for peace because he has made "the world a ruin of war" (IX, 128). He hears an inner consoling voice:

> Where the Light falls, death falls; a world has died
> For you, that a world may live. There is no peace.
> Be glad no man or woman bears for ever
> The burden of first days. There is no peace. (IX, 127)
> . . . . . .
> You have come to the world's end, and it is best
> You are not free. Where the Light falls, death falls
> And in the darkness comes the Light. (IX, 128)

And the poem ends with Lancelot riding on alone and, in the darkness, finding the Light.

This closure complements and reaffirms the positive ending of *Merlin*, and reflects Robinson's view that, beyond the end of Arthur's world, and all worlds, there is the possibility of spiritual salvation for the individual and for society. As Christopher Brookhouse points out:

> This answer may have been what first attracted him to the Arthurian material and to Malory, for this solution has long been implicit in the Arthurian story, and especially in Malory, who confronted the chaos and failure of worldly undertakings with the spiritual vision of the Grail.[16]

Robinson is not alone among twentieth–century poets and authors in seeing in the Arthurian legend what Frank Kermode has termed the recurring historical sequence of empire, decadence, hope of renovation, progress, period of transition, and final catastrophe which continues to be invoked in times of crisis.[17]

Others, particularly T. H. White, in his *Once and Future King* and *Merlin*, use King Arthur, the Round Table, and Camelot to mirror our modern age, with its recurring major wars, and strongly voice their anti–war sentiments and hopes for the future.[18] But few can equal Robinson's pacifistic and amelioristic message for his contemporaries and for us today: Remember that the world has paid enough for Camelot, but there will be another Camelot, another king — another world leader — and another world.

University of Iowa

NOTES

[1]Edwin Arlington Robinson. *Collected Poems. Merlin, Lancelot, Tristram* (New York, 1927). All quotations in this study are taken from this edition and identified by book number and page. For an incisive comparison of Robinson and Tennyson, see Laurence Perrine, "Tennyson and Robinson: Legalistic Moralism vs. Situation Ethics," *Colby Library Quarterly* 8 (Dec., 1969), 416-33.

[2]See my "The Apocalyptic Mode in the Vulgate Cycle of Arthurian Romance," *Philological Quarterly* 57 (1978), 1-22.

[3]*The Works of Sir Thomas Malory*, ed. Eugene Vinaver, III (Oxford, 1967), 1237-38.

[4]Hermann Hagedorn, *Edwin Arlington Robinson. A Biography* (New York, 1938), 306.

[5]Winfield Townley Scott, "To See Robinson," *New Mexico Quarterly* XXVI (Summer, 1956), 168.

[6]*Selected Letters of Edwin Arlington Robinson*, edd. Ridgely Torrence, Hermann Hagedorn, Lewis M. Isaacs, and Louis V. Ledoux (New York, 1940), 160.

[7]Laurence Perrine, "Contemporary Reference of Robinson's Arthurian Poems," *Twentieth–Century Literature* 8 (1962-63), 74-75.

[8]Laurence Perrine, "The Sources of Robinson's Arthurian Poems and His Opinions of Other Treatments," *Colby Library Quarterly* 10 (June, 1974), 337.

[9]*Selected Letters*, 112.

[10]*Selected Letters*, 113.

[11]*Selected Letters*, 142.

[12]Perrine, "Contemporary Reference," 77.

[13]*Selected Letters*, 113.

[14]*Selected Letters*, 115.

[15]*Selected Letters*, 175.

[16]Christopher Brookhouse, "Imagery and Theme in *Lancelot*," in Ellsworth Barnard, ed., *Edwin Arlington Robinson: Centenary Essays* (Athens, GA, 1969), 129.

[17]Frank Kermode, *The Sense of an Ending: Studies in the History of Fiction* (London, 1966), 28-29.

[18]See my "King Arthur and Camelot, USA, in the Twentieth Century," in *Medievalism in American Culture*, edd. Bernard Rosenthal and Paul Szarmach (SUNY Binghamton, 1989), 164ff.

Charles Williams' *Taliessin Through Logres* And *The Region of the Summer Stars*

Judith Kollmann

W hen Charles Williams died in 1945, his friends were convinced that his Arthurian cycle of poems remained incomplete. *Taliessin through Logres* (published in 1938)[1] was to have been the first installment, and then, as Anne Ridler notes, "the collection which followed was to be called *Jupiter over Carbonek*. . . . *The Summer Stars* were never meant to be more than Work in Progess."[2] No doubt Williams' own somewhat apologetic introduction to *The Region of the Summer Stars* (1944)[3] has reinforced the impression that this is simply a miscellaneous collection: "These poems are part of a series of poems which began with *Taliessin through Logres,* but these, generally, are incidental to the main theme."[4] C. S. Lewis, observing "I do not know whether he would so have arranged them if he had lived to complete the cycle,"[5] recommended a chronological rearrangement of the thirty–two poems for the convenience of reading and critical discussion, clearly implying that, inasmuch as the cycle was unfinished, no real purpose was to be gained by dealing with the poems in their published order. And as a consequence, subsequent criticism of the poems has continued the tradition of assessing them irrespective of context. In dealing with the Arthuriad as Lewis and others[6] have done, one unquestionably obtains a clearer perception of the legendary materials, the themes and the intellectual substance of the poems — and such explication has been badly needed for these beautiful but difficult lyrics.

However, in the process of analyzing the poems out of context, something of the poet's art has been overlooked and his emphases blurred. For in spite of Williams' disclaimer, *The Region of the Summer Stars* is neither irrelevant to the main theme nor, structurally speaking, is it an incomplete miscellany. Rather, it is a complete, self–contained cycle. Moreover, when the two cycles are read sequentially, they form a complementary and competing diad, becoming one aesthetic whole. While the Arthuriad may remain unfinished, it is, nevertheless, complete.

Taliessin through Logres begins with a "Prelude" that recapitulates the early Christian centuries, the Arthurian myth and the failure of two dreams (of Arthur's Logres and of a universal Christian Empire). The cycle then recounts the Arthurian legend from its inception in "the word of the Emperor" (19), the arrival of Taliessin, the summoning of Arthur to his destiny and the flowering as well as the fall of the kingdom. But the cycle concludes not so much with Arthur's death as with the salvific action and the triumph of Lancelot's Mass. *The Region of the Summer Stars* also begins with a "Prelude." This one recounts the conversion of Greece and Rome to Christianity, the early apostasies and heresies, and the Church's expectation of the Parousia, the Second Coming, in the form of the Grail. In the following poems this cycle also returns to Taliessin, recounting his development as a poet, and then describes events during the height of the kingdom. *Summer Stars* concludes, in "The Prayers of the Pope," with a second triumphal and salvific Eucharist. Although they do not repeat material, the two cycles are developed along parallel lines and tell the same story twice, from beginning to end, in such a form that they may be compared to the image of the stone and shell from Book V of Wordsworth's *Prelude*, an image that Williams borrowed and used in both cycles. As Karl Göller has described it, "the fifth book [of the *Prelude*] . . . begins with a dream of the poet. In the midst of a desert, a mounted Bedouin appears bearing a stone in one hand, in the other a shell of exquisite beauty. The stone stands for the doctrine of Euclid, geometry, and the shell for poetical song, poetry. The stone and shell become the poles of Williams' thought, and symbolize for him order and life."[7] Taliessin informs the reader that there is "everywhere a double dance of a stone and a shell" (88). He is reflecting Williams' own conviction that a major goal of life and art is to perceive the double dance that pervades the created universe, and this vision of the double dance, and ultimate unity, is sustained in the structure of the Arthuriad as a whole. *Taliessin through Logres* may be considered the stone: it describes the ordering (and dis-ordering) of the Arthurian world through the efforts of, mainly, the male characters. Reason, especially as evinced in mathematics and the mathematical aspects of life and art (in, for example, poetry, magic, metaphysics and human physiology) are emphasized; and this cycle may be considered the masculine aspect of the Arthurian legend. *The Region of the Summer Stars* is the shell: describing the hope for a meterial and spiritual Empire (and the loss of that specific hope) it is concerned mainly with women or with those men whose natures partake of the feminine. It is also concerned with the emotional (organic) aspects of poetry, magic and other pursuits of human intellect, the interior freedom of self, societal harmony, and other nurturing processes. It may, therefore, be considered the feminine half of the cycle.

However, before summarizing and discussing each cycle, it is necessary to define six terms that are essential to an understanding of Charles Williams' work. These are: image; The Way (or Path) of the Affirmation of the Images; The Way (or Path) of the Rejection of the Images; exchange; substitution; and co–inherence.[8]

Of "image" Williams wrote in *The Figure of Beatrice*:

> I have preferred the word image to the word symbol, because it seems to me doubtful if the word symbol nowadays sufficiently expresses the vivid individual existence of the lesser thing. Beatrice was, in her degree, an image of nobility, of virtue, of the Redeemed Life, and in some sense Almighty God himself. But she also remained Beatrice right to the end.[9]

But for Williams the word image was more than a fresh synonym for an overused term. Image also reflected a significant element of his theology: namely, that while no thing is God except God, and while all things possess their own identities and their diversity, all are reflections (or images) of God. Moreover, to the degree that they reflect the Triune Unity, they themselves are unified.

The two Paths, of Affirmation and Rejection, indicate the two life–styles that Williams felt were open to humanity. Those who Affirm the Images are simply those who, living in the world, affirm it as good. Those who Reject the Images are those who by–pass the material world (insofar as a creature may) for the more spiritual one of self–denial and prayer. Those who affirm consist of the vast majority of people; they are those who marry, raise families, compose poetry, perform magic, and rule kingdoms. Those who reject the world become ascetics — monks, enclosed nuns, hermits.

Both Paths, correctly followed, lead to salvation, and both engage the individual in two activities that are simultaneously practical and theological. These are the activities of exchange and substitution. Both were given theological license by Christ, Who, exchanging His innocence for man's sin, substituted Himself for mankind. The Crucifixion then becomes the prototype for man's practise of exchange and substitution; and consequently it also becomes the basis for peaceful human society, the foundation of the human community for which Williams' usual symbol was the City (any city, all cities, but ultimately the New Jerusalem). In the Arthuriad, Camelot, Carbonek, Byzantium all represent the height of human interraction.

And finally, the correct pursuit of either Path may lead an individual, if he or she possesses the necessary metaphysical insight, to a perception of co–inherence — of a cosmos ordered by the laws of reason (mathematics and science) on the one hand, and by nurturing love and emotion on the other, so that the infinite variety of the cosmos dances in complex, unified harmony. Moreover, the nature of co–inherence is such that, while it can be damaged, it cannot be finally destroyed except by its Creator.

The "Prelude" to *Taliessin through Logres* introduces the scene upon a universal as well as specific scale, placing Arthur's kingdom within the greater context of world events. The entire

Arthurian story is implicit in this short poem: once there was glory
and light in the world, because for a brief moment (in the seventh
century A.D.) the wills of God and the Byzantine Emperor were
unified in the common goal of converting the entire Empire to the
glory and light of orthodox Christianity. As part of this grand
concept, "the word of the Emperor established a kingdom in
Britain" (19) but success is defeated on two fronts: the kings of
Logres (including Arthur) insist on "a fallacy of rational virture"
(19) which destroys Logres, while "the Moslem destroyed Byzantium" (19), destroying the Empire.

The second poem, "Taliessin's Return to Logres," introduces
the poet Taliessin as he recounts the story of his journey to Arthur.
Disembarking in England, he rides, skirting a desolate wood until
he arrives at Arthur's camp.

The third poem, "The Vision of the Empire," is one of the
longest in the *Taliessin* cycle. As its title suggests, "The Vision"
describes the nature of an idealized Byzantine Empire whose
human Emperor is an image of God and whose political ideals are
at one with the deity's intentions for mankind; this is, as the refrain
of the poem indicates, an Empire whose "organic body sang
together" (24), even if success was short–lived. The Byzantine
Emperor, understanding this concept of unity, is extending
spiritual and administrative order as he converts the world to
Christianity and subjects it to law, creating peace. It is in this
context that the Emperor authorizes the creation of Logres and
fosters intellect in the schools of Gaul. As a result, humanity works
to create society.

However, harmony is threatened by the opposition of wills.
The basis for this lies in Original Sin, and Williams recounts his
interpretation of the Fall in this poem. He begins by interpreting
Genesis 1:27 to mean that, when God created mankind, both male
and female were created simultaneously and were equally images
of Himself.[10] Furthermore, because *adam* is a collective noun
meaning "mankind", Williams chose always to consider "the
Adam" a plural entity, implying that although one member was

male and the other female, they were, as Gen. 2:24 suggests, "one body,"[11] and that this state of androgynous unity was an ideal image of human perfection because, according to Gen. 1:27, God's own self includes the feminine and the masculine. Original Sin, as it is described in "The Vision of the Empire," is the separation of the unified Adam into "a double entity" which "spewed and struggled, good against good" (28). To illustrate such divisive effort ("the wars of identity" [28]), Williams introduces the figure of the headless and handless Emperor, P'o–lu, a supernatural being who walks on a Far–Eastern ocean accompanied by headless octopi. He is not a direct opponent of God (nothing, in Williams' schema, is), but rather he is an enemy of the Byzantine Emperor and of Nimue, a Mother–Nature figure who controls the sea–forest of Broceliande. P'o–lu therefore constitutes a threat to the order of nature and society, but in spite of his existence the organic body of the Empire sings together. The poem ends with a paean requesting that the organic body, which includes the parts of the human body as well as the nations of the Empire, "bless . . . [the Lord], praise him, magnify him forever" (30-31).[12]

The next three poems deal with the creation of Logres, and are among the few in the cycles that approach narrative; the majority are lyrical meditations. In "The Calling of Arthur," not only does the young king, summoned by Merlin, arrive at last on the stage, but also Bors and Elayne are introduced. The old king, senile and decadent King Cradilmas,[13] is ineffective during a winter of war and famine, and it is Bors, the active soldier, who fights for peace, while "his wife Elayne behind him/ mends the farms, gets food from Gaul" (33). Lancelot, bringing men and supplies, arrives as others of Arthur's followers assemble.

"Mount Badon" tells the story of the battle from Taliessin's perspective as the leader of the reserves. He is waiting, in "a passion of patience" (35), for the moment to charge. As he does so he has a vision in which he sees Virgil struggling to create *The Aeneid* and finds that war and poetry fuse into one entity in "the pen of his spear" (35)while:

> The Aeneid's beaked lines swooped on Actium;
> the stooped horse charged; backward blown,
> the flame of song streaked the spread spears
> and the strung faces of words on a strong tongue (35).

The power of poetry has given the poet the ability to wait for the right moment to act, and, therefore, Taliessin wins the battle and the war for Arthur.

"The Crowning of Arthur" deals slightly with the coronation. The real topic is the significance of this ritual, and that is explained by means of the heraldic banners of Arthur and his vassals, which represent not only the subjected nobles but also the now-disciplined bestial elements of man and, to a degree, nature. At the moment of success, however, the tragedy is anticipated as Williams touches on three weaknesses already present: first, Lancelot escorts Guinevere, already falling in love; second, the poet asks whether "the King [is] made for the kingdom, or the kingdom made for the king," (39); and third, he alludes to "the dolorous blow" (39).

The seventh poem, "Taliessin's Song of the Unicorn," acts as a transition to the central part of the cycle. Taliessin first recounts the story of the capture of the unicorn by means of a maiden. The unicorn's horn is a phallic symbol, but one which is, as far as the girl is concerned, "to her no good," for the unicorn is "a snorting alien love," an untamed "shouldering shape" (40). Therefore it is appropriate that she betray the unicorn to the hunter. Then the girl will lie "with the gay hunter and his spear flesh–hued" (40). However, in western civilization the unicorn can also have a religious significance; in this case the animal symbolizes Christ.[14] In the latter half of the poem the image shifts to a religious one; here, though, the unicorn represents not Christ, but God–as–Father. Now Taliessin views the girl's potential differently; if she is willing to give herself to intercourse with God–as–unicorn, she can become "the Mother of the Unicorn's Voice" (41) — that is, Christ.

In "Bors to Elayne: The Fish of Broceliande," the king is building Camelot, and Bors, home on a visit, describes the effect a song of Taliessin's (presumably that of the unicorn) had on himself. Bors has plucked a metaphorical fish out of the song and he drops the imaginary creature in Elayne's hand, envisioning it swimming through her body, which becomes simultaneously a running mountain stream as well as woman's body.

The ninth poem, "Taliessin in the School of the Poets," deals with the creation of poets as Taliessin visits their school. Since Taliessin is thinking about poetry, it is natural for him to think about the master of poets, Virgil; and from Virgil the poet to Virgil the man is an easy step. By the end of the poem, "the young poets studied precision"; but "Taliessin remembered the soul" (48). As the following poem, "Taliessin on the Death of Virgil," makes clear, the soul Taliessin is thinking about is Virgil's. Virgil was the righteous pagan who died before the coming of Christ, and who, as Dante's guide, was forced to turn away from Paradise and return to Limbo.[15] Dante had agonized over the question of Virgil's salvation, but had found no solution to this theological dilemma. In "The Death of Virgil" Williams resolves Dante's problem: all concerned Christian poets, living, dead, or yet–to–live, join together in an infinity that transcends past, future and present; and, by means of exchange and substitution, Virgil is saved:

> Virgil was fathered of his friends.
> He lived in their ends.
> He was set on the marble of exchange (50).

In "The Coming of Palomides," the Islamic knight arrives to fall in love with Iseult, seeing in her the perfection of geometry, the perfect harmony of intellect and beauty. However, his love is flawed; he discovers that "division stretched between/ the queen's identity and the queen" (54). Due to her illicit love for Tristram, the queen's self has become sundered from her function as queen. The questing beast, the symbol of the sexually bestial in man, has inserted itself "in the blank between" (55) Iseult's self and her position.

In the twelfth poem, "Lamorack and the Queen Morgause of Orkney" Morgause is equated, by her lover Lamorack, with stones. She is "primeval rock" (54), her eyes "a dark cavern" (55), while "her hand discharged catastrophe" (56). Worse, she is Arthur's sister, and, as such, Arthur's other self. Things have gone very wrong in Logres: out of the King's egotism (Williams views egotism as a form of spiritual incest) and lust, the king commits physical incest, and Mordred is engendered.

In the thirteenth poem, "Bors to Elayne: On the King's Coins," Elayne (whom Bors now perceives as a corn–mother, representative of "organic salvation" [61]) is implicitly contrasted with the stone–Morgause on the one side and with the king's new concept of minting coins as the medium of exchange on the other. He calls the minting a "convenient heresy" (62), since exchange ought to be purely a theological function, not an economical one.

In "The Star of Percivale," Taliessin sings, and a slave–girl wants to worship him because of the song. He refuses to allow this, directing her impulse into the correct religious channel, and she experiences a genuine epiphany. As the sun rises, the court assembles for Mass: Balin the Savage strides about impatiently; Arthur, caught in self–love, contemplates the elevated host, but "in the elevation beheld and loved himself crowned" (65); and Lancelot, looking at the consecrated host, can only see in it "a ghost of the Queen" (65). All the nobles demonstrate the irony of this formal Mass, which is juxtaposed to the quiet moment before dawn when another image of Christ, the day–star, was elevated in the sky, and a nonentity within the social structure had been offered, and received, grace.

"The Ascent of the Spear" is also concerned with a slave. This one has been placed in the stocks because of too much pride.

With Taliessin's help, she learns humility, gentleness, and courtesy.

In "The Sister of Percivale," Taliessin is watching a slave draw water from a well when Blanchefleur (called Dindrane in *The Region of the Summer Stars*), sister to Percivale and Lamorack, arrives at court. The slave and the princess at first appear to be polar opposites: one is at the nadir of society, the other at the height; only the slave's naked back is seen, juxtaposed to Blanchefleur's magnificently clothed front; one labors at drawing water, the other arrives escorted by her brothers to the sound of trumpets. But the women are a "double grace" (70), the reversed images of one another, opposites, yet the same, one the back and base, the other the front, of the same image — of Christ: "the face of Blanchefleur was the grace of the Back in the Mount." [16] Taliessin finds himself in love with Blanchefleur.

In "The Son of Lancelot," Galahad is born. Brisen's magic has tricked Lancelot into making love with King Pelles' daughter, Helayne, in order to beget Galahad. And Lancelot, attempting to contend with his equivocal moral situation, goes mad. His insanity becomes expressed in bestial terms as it metamorphoses him into a were-wolf, which lies in wait to kill his new-born son.[17] Merlin saves the child by shape-changing into another wolf and carrying the boy to Blanchefleur, now in a convent, for nurturing, while Lancelot is taken to Carbonek, where he is healed. In the Empire, which had been threatened (with famine, wolves and Moslems), order is restored by the Emperor.

The eighteenth poem, "Palomides Before His Christening," deals with Palomides' conversion, a process which is described in terms of a surrealistic climb to the top of a mountain, where Palomides finds both a cave and the questing beast. There he remains, trying to subdue himself by means of himself alone. At last the beast leaves, but Palomides has become an emaciated skeleton; his spirit resembles a bat, and he terrifies even himself. Then, in a manner reminiscent of Ezekiel's vision of the valley of bones (Eze. 37:1-14), he is revitalized, and Palomides comes, humbled, to Camelot, ready to be made a fool, and ready to be baptized.

With the nineteenth poem, "The Coming of Galahad," the cycle turns to its conclusions, to resolutions neither tragic nor, finally, destructive, but primarily triumphal. This poem, the sixth from the end, is balanced with the sixth from the beginning ("The Crowning of Arthur"). Both poems celebrate the advent of a charismatic savior: Arthur of a physical kingdom, Galahad of a spiritual one. Both poems treat their ostensible subjects in exactly the same way: they begin after the glorious and famous events. In "The Crowning of Arthur" the glorious events are summarized in one line; in "The Coming of Galahad," in three. In both poems Taliessin interests himself with the meaning of the action. In this case he does not stare out over the city looking at banners; instead, he goes down to the bottom of the castle. From this deliberately assumed position, in a conversation with Gareth (who is serving his year as kitchen–boy) and with a slave–girl, Taliessin points out that all of them (Galahad, Gareth, slave, king's poet) are equally essential to Camelot and the universe.

The main topic of their discussion, and the main topic of the poem, is, as Karl Göller has indicated,[18] a reflection of Wordsworth's dream–vision from Book 5 of the *Prelude*, the dream of the Arab who holds a stone and a shell. They are the two poles of the human mind, and the dreamer is offered a choice between them, a choice he never explicitly makes. However, in Book 14 Wordsworth uses the term, "the *mens sensitiva*" ("the feeling intellect"), a phrase of which Williams was very fond because it expresses the right choice — namely, both: the combination of emotion and analytic intellect makes poetry, magic, governance and all human endeavor possible. Palomides is an example of a character (appropriately enough, an Arab) searching for this balance; but Galahad (because he is the closest human image of Christ in the cycle) melds the stone and the shell when he completes a symbolic action:

'To-day
the stone was fitted to the shell,' the king's poet said;
'when my lord Sir Lancelot's son sat in the perilous sell (89).

Still, Taliessin emphasizes that he has seen "the double dance of a
stone and a shell" (88) elsewhere. In fact, it is to be found
everywhere: in nature ("the Druid oak"), in sexuality ("The gay
strokes of Caucasia"), in study ("the parchments of Gaul"),
institutional religious observance ("the altar stone of Lateran or
Canterbury") and in governance ("the tall Byzantine hall") (89).

The twentieth poem, "The Departure of Merlin," begins the
dissolution of Arthur's kingdom as characters begin to leave it.
Merlin's purpose is completed when Galahad arrives in court, and
he returns to Broceliande, melting into the trees. In the following
poem, "The Death of Palomides," another departure is in
progress. At peace with himself, the universe and God, Palomides
is dying in a small hut where he has shared the mystical experience
of the Way of Rejection with two old Jewish men, followers of the
Kaballah.

In the twenty–second poem, "Percivale at Carbonek," the
entry of Carbonek by the Grail knights (Galahad, Percival, Bors)
is effected immediately after Galahad prays "for Lancelot's pardon" (99), a deliberately ambiguous phrase. Galahad seeks not
only his father's forgiveness of himself (i.e., Galahad) for having
been born, but also forgiveness for Lancelot's own sins. Bors is
given the task of carrying the pardon back to Lancelot.

In "The Last Voyage" Williams first describes two wall paintings hanging "in the hall of Empire" (102). One depicts Solomon,
the father of sorcery, "the grand master of all creaturely being/ in
sublime necromancy" (102). The other shows Virgil, the grand
master of poetry, awarding Taliessin a poet laureateship as Homer
looks on in the background. Then Williams describes the Grail
knights' voyage in the magic ship of Solomon to Sarras. The
knights themselves are described in alchemical terms, while the
dead are present in the form of Blanchefleur's body and Dinadan's

heart, which "burned on the sun" (105). In the final stanza Williams repeats a line from "The Calling of Arthur": "The King's friend landed, Lancelot of Gaul" (33 and 106). Once again, Lancelot brings men and supplies to Logres, but this time he is too late. Arthur is dead, Mordred overthrown. However, the moment is not tragic; instead, it is a moment of healing, for

> At the hour of the healing of Pelles
> the two kings [Arthur and Pelles] were one, by exchange of
> death and healing (106).

In the last poem of the cycle, "Taliessin at Lancelot's Mass," Lancelot, who has not been consecrated to the priesthood, is nevertheless licensed to celebrate this Mass:[19] "I came," states Taliessin,

> to his altar when dew was bright on the grass;
> he—he was not sworn of the priesthood—began the Mass
> (107).

And, as Lancelot performs the ritual, he becomes a necromancer, for all the dead lords of the Round Table come to the Mass, joining the living in concelebration. Guinevere achieves repentance in her convent cell, and from the "queen's substitution the wounded and dead king/ entered into salvation to serve the holy Thing" (107). As the Mass continues, it becomes a re–enactment of Pentecost, the Passion and the Resurrection for the participants. Taliessin experiences himself "rising in the rood" (109), achieving a joyous crucifixion, a union with deity that transcends all poetry. The Arthurian world is assumed into the Godhead: "the Table ascended; the glories intertwined" (109).

When the plot and structure of *Taliessin through Logres* is laid bare, the Arthuriad appears geometrically precise and even simple: the cycle consists of twenty–four fairly short poems that follow the traditional chronological sequence of the Arthurian legend. The first six poems are concerned with the establishment of Arthur's rule; the central twelve deal with the apogee of Arthur's kingdom and its subsequent decay; the concluding six describe the dissolution of the physical kingdom and triumph of the spiritual one. However, this foundation sustains a complete reinterpretation of the Arthurian legend and a vast, complex synthesis of Williams' poetics and theology, as well as his literary and historical scholarship.

Williams was a poet of ideas rather than emotions. Even in his novels, his characters tend to be embodiments of thought rather than realistic personalities. In these compact, intellectual lyrics the characters are complex enough to be believable, rarely being flat or simply allegorical; yet they remain important primarily for their symbolic functions.

Of all the characters, Taliessin is the most constantly present, evident to some degree in thirteen of the twenty–four poems. He is seen as a man as well as a poet and visionary, and although he is usually an observer rather than a participant, at times he becomes involved with events, or, more often, with characters. Because of all these factors he is not only an individual but a representative of the characteristic male role in the Arthuriad: like Bors, Percivale, Galahad and Palomides, he represents the human male's rightful search, by means of the passion that directs his life, for the "Grail" (that is, Christ). But while the Grail knights are more concerned with forms of love directed towards others, and Palomides for solitude and self–denial, Taliessin finds his passion and salvation in art. It is man's task to pursue his Path, whether of Affirmation or Rejection, actively; and all the males are typified by action, by search. Thus the typical masculine role in the cycle is dynamic: it creates – it makes a poem, summons a king, feeds the starving, seeks a Grail, founds and rules a state or an Empire, rescues a child. And since action, and the meaning of action, is a dominant theme in *Taliessin through Logres,* masculinity dominates the cycle. It is no accident that God–as–progenitor overshadows the cycle, or that the imagery is dominated by beasts, hard objects, or geometric shapes such as porphyry stairs, cut or uncut hazel-wood, the moon, spears, skeletons, stones, and the pentagram; or that colors tend toward the pure, brilliant tones of heraldry: red, white, silver, black.

Women are not unimportant in *Taliessin,* but they are secondary to the males. The role of the female in both cycles is passive and, often, static; but never stagnant or insignificant. Women perform few actions and rarely make journeys. If they do travel, it is so they can reside at their destinations for what are (obviously) years. Whether she follows the Path of Affirmation or Rejection, the woman's task is to provide or to nurture—whether she provides bread or children, whether she nurtures an infant or a rose garden—and to make action (on the part of the males) possible. When Merlin and Brisen, the twin children of Nimue, appear, they are obedient to these roles: Merlin, who is also Time, goes to intercept and summon Arthur to his kingdom. Later, as wolf, he streaks across Logres, carrying Galahad to safety. When he departs, he goes to Broceliande. Brisen, who is Space, travels to Carbonek, where she remains, preparing the place for the begetting and birth of Galahad, and, this done, she is not mentioned again. Blanchefleur goes to a convent, to prepare for Galahad's nurturing; when she travels again it is only to die, and be transported, passively, to Sarras. Elayne, Bors' wife, is "mother of children" (63), lives at home, and is the main example of the ideal domestic woman. Not all the female characters have to be engrossed with *kinder* or *küche,* but all the women who achieve salvation are providers and nurturers of something. Even Guinevere's repentance is seen in terms of fertility and motherhood:

> In Blanchefleur's cell at Almesbury the queen Guinevere
> felt the past exposed; and the detail, sharp and clear,
> draw at the pang in the breast till, rich and reconciled,
> the mystical milk rose in the mother of Logres' child (107).

The main image associated with women is that of some aspect of planet earth—geography, geometry, water, grain, fish. The first edition of *Taliessin through Logres* contained an illustration of the Empire superimposed by a recumbent female figure whose head lay in England, breasts in Gaul, genitals in Jerusalem and buttocks in Caucasia.[20] Williams viewed the earth as feminine ("Mother Earth" is nothing new) and women as an expression of the same femininity. Consequently Nimue is a sort of Mother Goddess who is in charge of the sea–forest, Broceliande;[21] and Elayne is equated with fish, water and grain, while Morgause becomes stone and cliff.

In the Arthuriad the major theme is, as I have suggested above,[22] the vision of a co–inherent universe. This vision is expressed by everything in *Taliessin*, including a number of sub–themes, of which a few of the more significant are the existence and nature of sin; the ethic of work; the place of eros; and the individual's search for self–perfection.

Williams explains the nature of sin in "The Vision of Empire" when he describes Original Sin as the decision, on the part of the unified, diadic male/female Adam, to revolt against the unity of the cosmos. The result of this decision is that the Adam becomes divided against itself, splitting into two persons. The essence of all subsequent sin is merely a repetition of the same decision, although, of course, the forms of sin are multiple and the results vary: division can occur within oneself, within human relationships, and against nature.

As men act, they either use things rightly and bring them to fruition, or they distort the gifts of creation and themselves. This concept is to be seen most clearly in Williams' exploration of the subjects of work and eros. The ethic of work is questioned in "The Crowning of Arthur" when Taliessin asks whether "the king [is] made for the kingdom, or the kingdom for the king?" (39). In other words, is man made for the work, or is the work made for the man? For Williams, only one answer was possible: man exists to serve his work. Those in the Arthuriad who refuse to do so define their goals as egotistic self–fulfillment, twisting the rightful into the wrongful. The prime example is Arthur, whose incorrect assumption leads to the egotistic conclusion that he can take any woman he happens to desire, and, in addition, to "rational fallacies" such as the minting of coins. Those who serve their work include (besides Taliessin) Galahad, Bors, Merlin, Blanchefleur, and, in the end, Palomides.

"The Song of the Unicorn" makes clear that sexuality is an integral element of God–as–Father and of His love for the world; therefore, as with all things, used rightly it can be glorious. Abused, it becomes one of the most destructive of forces. Not only Arthur, but Lancelot and Palomides experience the repercussions of abusing their erotic impulses — Lancelot because of unethical use, Palomides because of excessive denial of his animal nature. In Williams' theology one cannot deny any aspect of one's innate, hence God–created, self.

Erotic impulses are not limited to the males. Morgause and Elayne represent two poles of feminine sexual behavior — Elayne the domestication of eros by means of Christian marriage and fruitful procreation, Morgause the sterility of passion undisciplined, aptly symbolized by stones.

If an individual follows his (or her) chosen Path correctly, he (or she) will ultimately be taken into unity — into God. This begins to happen to Taliessin when, in "Lancelot's Mass," he feels himself rising in the rood, and to Palomides, when, dying, he recognizes the co–inherence of all things. This union is what constitutes perfection, nor is the search for such perfection a selfish activity because the Paths of Affirmation and Rejection (one of which must be followed) lead automatically to the practice of exchange and substitution, through which human community develops. But since the existence of divisive individuals prevent the advent of a perfected society, what is left is the goal of individual perfection and, above all, the salvific effect of the Trinity, through Whom, during "Lancelot's Mass" the dead are assumed into heaven and the living healed.

The Region of the Summer Stars forms a complement to *Taliessin through Logres*, completing images, making manifest themes that are latent in *Taliessin*, and, in essence, "rounding out" the Arthuriad. Like *Taliessin*, *Summer Stars* is narrated largely by Taliessin, but his perspective shifts. He becomes more of a participant — not in great exterior events, but in personal experiences in matters of faith, friendship, poetic development, and love. And while *Summer Stars* begins with Taliessin's experience and ends with Mordred's internal monologue and the Pope's prayer, the central section of the cycle is devoted to three women: Guinevere, Dindrane (Blanchefleur in *Taliessin*), and one or more Circassian slave girls, so the cycle becomes overtly feminine. Moreover, the males who become most fully human (Taliessin, Merlin and the Pope, Deodatus) are androgynous. Taliessin is over–shadowed by the will of the Emperor and by God–as–Procreator. *Summer Stars* is dominated from its beginning by Christ, Who is the nurturer of mankind, the self–sacrificer, the gentler, and, in short, more feminine aspect of deity. The dominant imagery of the cycle is that of softer, generally organic shapes such as lamb's wool, the Circassian rose, and snow flakes, while colors tend to be those of living things: cream, gold, crimson, emerald.

The "Prelude" to *Summer Stars* takes the broadest possible perspective on the topics of this cycle. This time the emphasis is upon theological issues rather than socio–political ones, upon Greek and Roman paganism, the coming of Paul the Apostle to the Classical world, and the establishment of Christianity in Rome. Paul preaches of the simultaneous double nature of Christ as God and man — the "twyfold Nature of the golden Ambiguity" (119) — and Williams describes the inability of the Greeks to accept this concept. Rome, however, finding no difficulty with the idea, influences Byzantium into accepting the interpretation, and the Empire settles to await the Second Coming in the form of the Grail: "in a rich container, the Blood of the Deivirilis" (121).

The second poem, "The Calling of Taliessin," is concerned first with the development of Taliessin into a poet, and then with

his calling (by Merlin) to a greater destiny as the king's poet of
Logres as well as the lord of a household that will become the
spiritual counterpart to the worldly Round Table. Taliessin's
development is characterized throughout by metamorphosis, by a
shape–shifting that has his foster–father, Elphin, wondering who,
or what, Taliessin actually is. When Taliessin does describe himself, he describes the essence of all poets:

> 'My heritage is all men's; only my age is my own.
> I am a wonder whose origin is not known' (124),

and adds that his imagination leaps all space and all time, that his
"true region is the summer stars" (125). The "Prelude" had
already suggested that "the summer stars" signify hope (121);
therefore Taliessin implies that not only his vocation, but that of
all poets', is one of giving hope. He concludes by describing
himself in a riddling verse:

> It is a doubt if my body is fish or flesh,
> therefore no woman will ever wish to bed me
> and no man make true love without me (125).

When Taliessin leaves Elphin's pagan court in order to ascer-
tain the truth of rumors he has heard about Christianity, he approaches the forest of Broceliande, and on its outskirts sees "a
faint light" that "grew double" until it "divided to a man and a
woman" (129), becoming Merlin and Brisen. They are twins, so
close to being one entity that Taliessin "heard speech flow/ out of
the masculine mouth of the twinned form" (129). The three make
camp together, and during the night, in a dream–vision, Taliessin
sees Merlin conjure by means of the pentagram. The spell does not
become complete without Brisen, whose shadow forms a bridge
between Broceliande and Logres. Williams describes Broceliande
as "Mystically...the making of things"[23] and therefore a foundation of the world, while Logres, headed by Guinevere as queen, is

also the head of the Empire. The metaphor of woman as base and
as head has been expressed before in the cycles (notable in "The
Sister of Percivale"), but now Williams extends the image until the
feminine principle of creation frames and overshadows the earth.

In the third poem, "Taliessin in the Rose Garden," the emphasis upon the feminine becomes even more explicit. To Taliessin, who is walking in the queen's rose garden, appears a tableau
of three women: Guinevere speaking to Dindrane, and a slave
behind them. Guinevere, "the consummate earth of Logres" (140),
is dressed in green, the color of spring and growth, theologically
the color of hope. In addition she is composed of gold and rose:
her hair is blonde, "her arm was tinged/ with faint rose–veins"
(140). Taliessin experiences a vision in which he perceives, by
means of the queen, the affinity of all things. Guinevere is not only
the earth of Logres but, simultaneously, an "anatomical man," the
figure used in medieval and renaissance works of astrology to
illustrate the correspondence between the microcosm (the human
body) and the macrocosm (the signs of the zodiac, and, therefore,
the heavens).[24] Heaven and earth become unified in the form of
the queen. It is a vision of co–inherence that is broken by a recollection of Cain's murder; however, the vision is healed by the
recollection of Christ's redemptive action.

In "The Departure of Dindrane" attention shifts from the
queen to the other two persons of the tableau, to Dindrane, and,
in particular, to the slave. Dindrane's decision to enter a convent
and her escorted trip to it serves as the occasion for a consideration of the relationship between servitude and freedom. Arthur's
kingdom observes the Mosaic law, and the slave will shortly have
completed her seven years of servitude. She will have to decide
among three choices: a dowry and marriage in Logres; a return to
her home; or perpetual slavery in Taliessin's household. First the
girl recognizes that, although Dindrane is a princess and she a
slave, they are alike in the fact of bondage:

The cell of her own servitude was now the shell
of the body of the princess; therefore, closer, of hers (149).

And she realizes that "in her heart,/ servitude and freedom were
one and interchangeable" (149), in part because she sees that
although Dindrane has chosen the Way of Rejection and Taliessin
the Way of Affirmation, both are paths of service, and servitude is
a universal human necessity for all those who choose unity.
Bondage is a just and necessary state for man, who is half rational
and half beast — a state aptly symbolized in the poem by the image
of the centaurs (one of the few animal images in *Summer Stars*).
The centaur, half human, half horse, has traditionally been
representative of man's mixed nature, of his aptitude for wisdom
and also his potential for irrational violence.[25] The slave freely
chooses slavery and is, paradoxically, made free by her choice.

In "The Founding of the Company," Taliessin is asked by
Dinadan to lead a group that has developed informally around
Taliessin's household. The poem discusses man's dispensability
(Taliessin's taking the leadership is an excellent joke since it is a
superfluous job) and describes the ideal functioning of this group
as it exercises exchange and substitution among its members.

In "The Queen's Servant" Guinevere asks Taliessin for a servant to work in her rose garden, and he sends her a slave who
accepts the charge, observing, "So./ Freedom, I see, is the final
task of servitude" (160), a comment Göller finds sarcastic;[26] however, in the light of the conclusions drawn in "The Departure of
Dindrane," it is simply a logical, if paradoxical, deduction. Taliessin becomes a magician, in a lavishly sensuous passage, creating
clothing for the slave from conjured Circassian roses and golden
lamb's wool that shower her from the air.

"The Meditation of Mordred" is in abrupt contrast to all the
poems in *Summer Stars*, for the Arthurian version of Cain has
arrived upon the scene. The poem, unlike any other, is an interior
monologue, totally self–directed, and as ruthless a self–portrait as
any by Robert Browning. Arthur has taken his knights to besiege

Lancelot in France, leaving Mordred, like Absalom,[27] "rest[ing] on his palace roof" (165), plotting to betray his father and expounding his cynicism regarding Arthur's ideals. The height of his ambition is solitude and the hope of imitating "a small Emperor," who lives "beyond P'o–lu," (167) and who tortures his wives.

In the final poem, "The Prayers of the Pope," the Pope Deodatus is waiting in St. Peter's Church to sing the Christmas Eucharist. As he waits he prays for the world, which is in chaos. The Round Table has fallen and anarchy reigns everywhere as barbarian tribes push into Europe. The Goetian necromancers have summoned the dead to rise as armies, Mordred is bent on destruction, and the Grail, received "within the land of the Trinity" (176-178), has been removed permanently from earth. P'o–lu attempts to destroy the Empire by stretching forth the tentacles of his giant octopods. But the Pope prays, his prayer becoming a summation of the paradoxical nature of the Trinity and mankind's relationship to It; and, as he prays, peace is restored. The forces of cosmos extend, and the roots of Broceliande, reaching down and through the sea, grasp the tentacles, immobilizing them forever. With that, the zombie armies disintegrate, P'o–lu drowns, Mordred dies, and the barbarians lose impetus. Advent has ushered in a new cycle of history[28] as the Pope celebrates Mass. Arthur and Logres are gone, as is the dream of a Byzantine Empire and a unified Christianity; the High Prince (either Galahad or Christ–as–Grail) is hidden. But "consuls and lords within the Empire ... felt the Empire/ revive in a live hope of the Sacred City" (179). The Sacred City is Rome; and the new hope rests in Roman Christendom.

Thematically, *Summer Stars* is, of course, concerned primarily with finding fresh ways to describe co–inherence, and does so by turning its attention from the masculine to the feminine, by expanding the scale, and by examining philosophical and theological issues more overtly. *Taliessin* concentrates mainly on Arthur's kingdom and its fall. *Summer Stars* deals with the larger context: although set in Logres, Williams' interest lies in moving from the

particular to the general, and from the microcosmic to the macro-
cosmic. Thus, "The Calling of Taliessin" begins by describing the
growth of one boy into a poet, but this develops quickly into a
discussion of the nature and mission of all poets. "The Departure
of Dindrane" begins with a slave's personal need to choose between freedom and slavery and ends with a philosophical–
theological discourse on the interrelationship of bondage and
liberty and the necessity of both for mankind.

Most notably, the significance of the feminine element expands geographically and theologically. In *Taliessin* the feminine
principle is part of the geography of the Empire, and Nimue rules
Broceliande, but her powers are not explicit. In the *Summer Stars*
Nimue is shown to control the planet's roots in the oceans, and the
feminine principle extends, by means of the zodiac and the cone of
the Earth's shadow, to the stars. Theologically, the feminine influence is made so universal because Williams views femininity as
an integral part of the Godhead. In part, this is no doubt due to
Genesis 1:27, but Williams also chose to associate femininity with
Christ. For one thing, Venus, the planet of love, is also the day-
star, which was equated with Christ in the Book of Revelation: "I,
Jesus . . . am of David's line, the root of David and the bright star
of morning" (22:16), and Williams had already alluded to this
relationship in *Taliessin's* "The Star of Percivale." Moreover, Williams repeatedly emphasizes that Christ is "the twy–natured single
Person" (121), by which he means not only that Christ is God and
man, but that also, as the perfect human being, His nature par-
takes of both male and female. The further implication is that all
Christians must emulate His androgynous nature. Women physically and involuntarily do so, through menstruation:

> Only the women of earth,
> by primal dispensation, little by themselves understood,
> shared with that Sacrifice the victimization of blood (122).

Men must find other ways. That is why Taliessin maintains it is doubtful whether his body is "flesh or fish" (125); why Merlin is so strongly twinned with Brisen (128-129); and why Deodatus seems "in his trance of prayer a third twin/ of Merlin and Brisen, masculine touched with feminine" (168).

If *The Region of the Summer Stars* did not exist, *Taliessin through Logres* would stand on its own as an intact, if somewhat Spartan, Arthurian cycle. If the *Summer Stars* existed alone, it, too, would probably succeed in standing alone, although not as effectively as *Taliessin*. The two cycles need each other: Taliessin offers the foundation, a solid skeletal sub–structure, while *Summer Stars* fleshes out the story, the theology, and the philosophy more opulently. It is interesting that few critics have attempted to explain *Taliessin* without at some point resorting to *Summer Stars*. The two cycles form a poetic Adam, a double dance, in their structure as well as in their content, as together they attempt to fuse the total experience of western civilization — its history, myth, legend, theology, mathematics, science, pseudo–science, magic and literature — into one comprehensive vision of mankind's ever–recurring dream of making a new society, a heaven on earth. When this fails — and, because of the divisiveness of sin, it inevitably must — the world is repeatedly redeemed by the miracle of the Eucharist: "the Body salvaged the bodies" (179).

It is a glorious vision. But whether Williams succeeded in his ultimate hope that he had written great poetry is yet to be determined. However, it is certain that his Arthuriad is one of the most creative versions of the Arthurian legends written in the twentieth century, and one of the very few that has approached the topic from a symbolic and theological perspective rather than a historical one.

The University of Michigan–Flint

NOTES

[1](London). All citations from either *Taliessin through Logres* or *The Region of the Summer Stars* will be from the following: Charles Williams and C. S. Lewis, *Taliessin through Logres, The Region of the Summer Stars, Arthurian Torso* (1974; rpr. Grand Rapids: 1976). As no edition of the Arthuriad contains line numbers, all numbers following quotations refer to page numbers.

[2]Charles Williams, *The Image of the City and Other Essays,* sel. and intro. Anne Ridler (1958; rpr. London, 1970), 174.

[3]Rpt. in Grand Rapids, 1976, ed., 117-18.

[4]Williams and Lewis, *Taliessin,* 117.

[5]Williams and Lewis, *Taliessin,* 279.

[6]Among these scholars are Charles Moorman, *Arthurian Triptych: Mythic Materials in Charles Williams, C. S. Lewis, and T. S. Eliot* (1960; rpr. New York, 1973); Karl Heinz Göller, "From Logres to Carbonek: the Arthuriad of Charles Williams," in *Arthurian Literature* I, ed. Richard Barber (Woodbridge, 1981), 121-73; and Beverly Taylor and Elisabeth Brewer, "Charles Williams, *Taliessin through Logres* and *The Region of the Summer Stars*; C. S. Lewis, *That Hideous Strength,*" in *The Return of King Arthur: British and American Arthurian Literature since 1800* (Cambridge, Eng., 1983), 245-61 (Williams material only). Glen Cavaliero, *Charles Williams: Poet of Theology* (Grand Rapids, 1983) discusses the poems sequentially.

[7]Göller, 152.

[8]For further information, see Charles Williams, "The Way of Affirmation," in *Image of the City,* 154-58; also Mary McDermott Shideler, *The Theology of Romantic Love: A Study in the Writings of Charles Williams* (1962; rpt. Grand Rapids, 1966); and Robert J. Reilly, "Charles Williams and Romantic Theology," in *Romantic Religion: A Study of Barfield, Lewis, Williams and Tolkien* (Athens, Georgia, 1971), 148-89.

[9] *The Figure of Beatrice: A Study in Dante* (1943; rpt. New York, 1961), 7-8.

[10] Gen. 1:27: "God created man in the image of himself, in the image of God he created him, male and female he created them."

[11] Gen 2:24: "This is why a man leaves his father and mother and joins himself to his wife, and they become one body."

[12] The line is a doxology from the Benedicite Omnia Opera, *The Book of Common Prayer.*

[13] In *The Works of Sir Thomas Malory,* ed. Eugene Vinaver (1954; rpt. London, 1964),19, a King Cradilmans is one of the eleven rebellious kings of the North. Williams has combined this figure with the motif of the impotent ruler of the waste lands as well as the decadent Roman Emperor, Nero.

[14] Malcolm South, "The Unicorn," in *Mythical and Fabulous Creatures: A Source Book and Research Guide,* ed. Malcolm South (Westport, 1987),14.

[15] *Purgatory,* XXX. 43-54.

[16] Göller, 147-48, discusses the imagery of the human body and the back in particular. He suggests that "The origin of the image is possibly to be seen in Exodus XXXIII. 23 which states that Moses may only see the back of God." This is entirely possible; Williams may also have had in mind Jesus' back during the Sermon on the Mount.

[17] Modern lycanthropy cases have been diagnosed as schizophrenia. See Charlotte F. Otten, ed., *A Lycanthropy Reader: Werewolves in Western Culture* (Syracuse, 1986).

[18,] See above, 3.

[19] It is not known why Williams departed from his source (presumably Malory) here, but perhaps he had 1 Peter 2:9-10 in mind: "...you are a chosen race, a royal priesthood, a consecreated nation, a people set apart to sing the praises of God who called

you out of the darkness into his wonderful light. Once you were not a people at all and now you are the People of God; once you were outside the mercy and now you have been given mercy."

[20]This illustration is reproduced in Alice Mary Hadfield, *Charles Williams: An Exploration of His Life and Work* (New York, 1983),150.

[21]Williams writes ["Notes on the Arthurian Myth," in *Image of the City*, p. 179]: "Broceliande...is regarded as both a forest and as a sea—a sea-wood...Mystically it is the 'making' of things. Nimue is the Nature of Creation as the mother of Merlin (Time) and Brisen (Space)...She [Nimue] is almost the same state represented by the Emperor's Court, but more vast, dim, and aboriginal."

[22]See p. 3.

[23]"Notes," 179.

[24]See especially *The Tres Riches Heures of Jean, Duke of Berry,* Intro. and Legends, Jean Longnon and Raymond Cazelles (New York, 1969), F. 14v. for the earliest illustration of anatomical man in European art. It is interesting to note that two male figures are depicted, back and front; the one facing front is androgynous.

[25]Judith J. Kollmann, "The Centaur," In *Mythical and Fabulous Creatures*, ed. Malcolm South (Westport, 1987), 231-32.

[26]"From Logres to Carbonek," 146.

[27] 2 Sam. 16:22.

[28]Williams and Lewis, *Taliessin,* 111. Lewis points out that Williams had read Yeats' *A Vision*.

Trends in the Modern Arthurian Novel

Maureen Fries

While the medieval Matter of Britain may be conveniently divided into chronicle and romance traditions, modern versions of Arthurian story have emerged in a wider variety of genres. Drama and various sorts of poetry, even film and — more recently — television, have served as vehicles for the traditional stories and newer variants upon them. But the most surprising development in the last hundred years has been the emergence of Arthurian prose fiction, which both in number and variety has provided a seemingly inexhaustible source of inspiration. Over two hundred novels alone, and a somewhat lesser number of short stories, have appeared since 1884.

Such numbers and a concomitant variety of modes make any consideration of modern Arthurian fiction in a short span a difficult task. There is the matter of comprehensiveness, which even book–length studies have been unable to achieve.[1] There is taxonomy, which is always arbitrary. And there is the perennial problem as to whether one should speak of only the best and most enduring works, or include lesser and even inferior ones as well, especially if they represent interesting or even unique experiment. Some of my decisions on these dilemmas have been made easier by the format of this volume — science fiction and fantasy, and children's literature, for instance, are covered in separate chapters. Others I have not hesitated to make on the bases of uniqueness or enduringness or abiding interest. What follows, then, is one scholar's perception of twentieth–century trends in the Arthurian novel.

To begin with, an American tradition of Arthurian comedy has wound its uneven way through most of the decades of this century. Perhaps, even probably, inspired initially by Mark Twain's *A Connecticut Yankee in King Arthur's Court*, it includes novels by James

Branch Cabell, John Erskine, John Steinbeck, and Thomas Berger.
Cabell's *Jurgen: A Comedy of Justice*, published in 1919 as part of
his series, *The Biography of the Life of Manuel* — of which it is the
most popular and probably the best volume — concerns itself with
the adventures of Jurgen, a sometime poet turned pawnbroker. On
quest after his missing wife, Lisa, he pursues a picaresque series
of amatory adventures. Restored to youth and apparently inexhaustible sexual virility, he revisits his own past and sadly altered
first love, and then has affairs and/or "marriages" with a variety of
women, including Guinevere and the Lady of the Lake (here
known as Anitas, an anagram to Insatia).

Jurgen's Arthurian episodes are imaginative but bizarre, and
decidedly atraditional. Freeing Guinevere from a troll king, Thrag-
nar (from whom he also steals Caliburn), Jurgen undertakes a
passionate affair with her (approved by her father) which is interrupted by her departure to be married. His own departure with
Anitas for Cocaigne follows, as does his enjoyment of her un-
limited sexuality. Offered both the widowed Guinevere's hand and
renewed access to Anitas's body at the end of the book, he prefers
instead to return to the creature comforts offered by his now
rescued wife.

In *Jurgen*, both Arthurian and non–Arthurian episodes alike
emphasize sexual euphemism and double entendre. The ancient
Arthurian symbol Caliburn becomes a smirking phallic emblem,
and the powerful Lady of the Lake a panting sexual athlete — all of
the ludicrously grateful women Jurgen beds, for that matter, could
be called Insatia. Cabell obviously wanted to take advantage of the
new freedom of sexual expression his post–Freudian era seemed
to offer, and of which the book's famous trial offered one of the
first tests.[2] Paradoxically, the real social tensions between sex and
character in previous Arthurian stories disappear in the novel's
atmosphere of (what Jurgen himself calls) "glorified brothel."

Sex and society interact in quite different fashion in two
mostly forgotten novels by John Erskine, *Galahad: Enough of His
Life to Explain His Reputation* (1926) and *Tristan and Isolde:*

Restoring Palamede (1932). Following Malory's and Tennyson's accounts, Erskine chooses in *Galahad* to concentrate on Lancelot and the three women in his life—Guinevere, Elaine daughter of Pelles, and Elaine of Astolat—as well as on the title character. Lancelot conceives Galahad upon an Elaine wholly uninterested in any Grail mission, with whom he also lives after the traditional madness brought on by Guinevere's jealousy. When he does return to the Queen, it is to defend her from a treason Erskine creates by combining the usually separate stories of Meliagrance and Mador de la Porte. The author also invents Guinevere's adoption of Galahad as her protegé, a fosterage which fails when the young man discovers his patroness's sexual connection with his father. After the death of the Astolat Elaine (and Guinevere's belated discovery that there were two Elaines, after all), Lancelot, as traditionally, turns religious.

As had E. A. Robinson in his contemporaneous Arthurian poems, Erskine ruthlessly suppresses all traces of the supernatural in Arthurian story. To fulfill her Grail role, Elaine uses no magic but only cunning and sexual attraction to lure a finally willing Lancelot to bed. When Galahad goes on a quest, it is not after the Grail but to the rescue of a besieged castle and maiden—a futile errand, as it happens. Nothing in Erskine's Galahad would have fitted him for the Grail achievement anyway—he is a narrow-minded moralizer in whom it is difficult to be interested, and of whose Grail quest (reported at the end of the book by Lancelot's confessor) it is hard to predict success.

Another search is the theme of Erskine's *Tristan and Isolde: Restoring Palamede*. The Saracen hero is, like Galahad, an unworldly outsider when he arrives at the Cornish court. Enchanted by the inflated chivalric stories told him in his Eastern home by his Christian slave, Palamede sojourns first to a disillusioning France where he discovers that knightly life is not the wise and beautiful alternative he had expected. As in earlier versions of his story, he falls into a hopeless and unrequited love for the Irish Isolde—and, in an Erskinian twist, her cousin Brangaine conceives a similar passion for him. Into Palamede's disillusionment with the uncouth Mark, the philandering Tristan, and the decidedly unpedestaled Isolde, Erskine weaves such traditional narremes as Tristan's involvements with King Farnom's daughter and Segwarides' wife (Segwarides is not here, as in Malory, either Saracen or sib to Palamede), as well as his marriage to the other Isolde. At the end of the story, after Palamede (and not Mark) strikes Tristan his death blow, the Saracen departs for his homeland with Brangaine in lively pursuit.

As in *Galahad*, spiritual and supernatural elements are deleted. Palamede's timeworn trademark, the Questing Beast he must pursue, disappears; Tristan and Isolde need no love potion— Erskine ascribes their loving each other to "what they were, and they were young"; [3] an ubiquitous hermit is merely a reformed knight who unavailingly proselytizes Palamedes. On the other hand, the author's use of the medieval motif of the tying of Brangaine to a tree takes on new (perhaps Eliot–inspired) resonance as Mark's gardeners' attempt to reenact a fertility rite, as well as providing Palamede with an occasion to rescue and endear himself to Brangaine.

Besides inventing previously unexplored segments of Palamede and Galahad's careers, Erskine's chief innovation is the characters' endless dialogue. Beyond the mere wordiness which results in both novels, this technique often strikes the wrong, or at least a falsely Arthurian, tone—as in Lancelot's incongruous inability to imagine being in love and not wanting children (so much for his famous declaration rejecting family life in Malory), or Segwarides' wife's rebuke to her husband. Nathan Starr has well noted the shallowness of this attempt "to make the land of Logres and Lyonesse as smart and as up–to–date as a Park Avenue drawing room." [4] Such technique, moreover, makes the books seem a curious relic of the 1920s and 1930s rather than a valid translation of the Arthurian past into modern idiom.

Another curious 1930s novel is John Steinbeck's *Tortilla Flat* (1935), the Arthurian aspect of which has been neglected by comprehensive books on the Tradition proper but not by Stein-beck scholars.[5] Like several other American authors— Twain and Robinson, for example—Steinbeck was affected by an early ad-miration for Malory which led to a lifelong employment of Ar-thurian themes in his work.[6] His unconventional attempt to recast such themes in terms of post–World War I American life resulted in *Tortilla Flat*, a 1935 narrative centered on a cast of typically Steinbeckian loners and drifters.

Arthurian intentions appear in the "Preface" of the book:

> No, when you speak of Danny's house you are understood to mean a unit of which the parts are men, from which came sweetness and joy, philanthropy and, in the end, a mystic sorrow. For Danny's House was not unlike the Round Table, and Danny's friends were not unlike the knights of it.... In the end, this story tells how the talisman was lost and how the group disintegrated.[7]

Danny and his friends, California *paisanos* and mostly war veterans, fall rather than are called together when their leader inherits his grandfather's two houses. Their communal life erupts into picaresque adventures revolving (mainly) around their stealing of food and drink and (very secondarily) their seduction of and by various women. Once they accidentally burn down one of Danny's houses, the band crowds into the remaining one, which they deliberately burn down after the death of their leader.

Into this story Steinbeck attempts to weave various Arthurian motifs: the fellowship for mutual aid and (here only intermittent) social service; the quest, by which they discover a forbidden geological marker rather than a grail; the otherworldly vision, a sight of St. Francis granted to a pack of dogs rather than men; the hero's madness in the forest; and the holocaust which signals the fellowship's dissolution. But the actuality of the *paisanos'* deeds accords ill with the Steinbeckian rhetoric of encomium or the chapter headings meant to be imitative of Caxton's for his edition of Malory's *Morte*. The gap between the narrator's (however mock) idealism and the characters' basically selfish universe never closes, and we are left with yet another comic modern analogue which fits but poorly into the tradition to which it aspires.

The best American example of modern Arthurian comedy is Thomas Berger's *Arthur Rex: A Legendary Novel* (1978). Grounded mainly in Malory's *Morte* but utilizing other medieval Arthurian romances, particularly those centered on Gawain, Berger's story ironically retells (often reinvents) incidents ranging from Arthur's conception to his transportation to Avalon. Besides its eponymous hero's, the novel deals with the stories of Merlin's infatuation with the Lady of the Lake; Tristan and both Isoldes; Lancelot and all his females (both Elaines as well as Guinevere); Guinevere and her rescues, tantrums and (here not holy) end; Gawain and his triumphs and faults; Gareth, Pellinore, Percival and Galahad; and, memorably, Morgan le Fay and Mordred, here confederated in anti–Arthurian schemes.

As Malory did, Berger unifies his diverse materials with a consistent auctorial tone. His ironic view is steady and spares no one or nothing, neither Arthur himself nor the Grail (which Berger thoroughly secularizes). The young Arthur is pompous, and the young Guinevere a freckled hoyden (in spite of also being the most beautiful of women); Lancelot is initially pious, and Gawain moves from lechery to holiness; Kay is a frustrated gourmet chef, and Lamorak loves Morgause first for revenge; Morgan le Fay turns from evil to malignant and then to real good, thus restoring some of her original archetypal significance. Voiced through these and other characters, as well as its bemused narrator, *Arthur Rex* achieves a richness of texture reminiscent of Malory's.

Varied voicing as well as comedy enriches the work of T. H. White, the most enduringly popular of modern British Arthurian novelists. White's novels, *The Sword in the Stone* (1938), *The Witch in the Wood* (1939) – retitled *The Queen of Air and Darkness* – and *The Ill-Framed Knight* (1940), were published together with *The Candle in the Wind* as *The Once and Future King* (1958); and *The Book of Merlyn* (1977), with some overlapping material, was issued posthumously. While White's major source is Malory, his first book, *Sword*, is an inventive *enfances* of Arthur unknown to previous literature, in which the boy prince is tutored by an eccentric Merlin who guides him, through shapeshifting him into various beastly forms, to the wisdom he will need on his coronation as king at the end of the book. *Queen* alternates the *enfances* of Gawain and his brothers under their brutally indifferent mother, Morgause — who seduces Arthur into Mordred's conception at the book's end — with Arthur's victorious campaign against the rebellious kings. *Knight* counterpoints Lancelot's adventurous and amorous career (with Guinevere and Elaine) with the developing Orkney feud with Pellinore's kin and the Grail Quest, climaxing with Lancelot's healing of Sir Urre. *Candle* retells the tragedy of the Round Table's fall in its traditional outline: the machinations of Mordred and Aggravain, the guilty loves of Lancelot and Guinevere, the feud of Lancelot and Gawain precipitated by the latter's brothers' deaths, to which is added Arthur's failed, final attempt to harness Right to Might; it ends on the eve of Arthur's last battle as he bequeaths his story to the page Thomas (Malory) to tell. *Merlyn* brings the sage back to Arthur on that same evening, to try to take the King back to the animals to learn how to abolish war.

The *Merlyn*, didactic and unsuccessful, need not concern us here. But the tetralogy which precedes it — revealed in a recent MLA survey to be the most taught of all modern Arthurian works — is a considerable and original achievement. From the comedy of the first book through the tragicomic second, the novels move to ever more tragic recognition of the fatality inherent in Arthurian story. White's concerns, both ecological (he was a naturalist) and political (he was an uneasy pacifist), make this one of the most individualistic and autobiographical of retellings. While the shift in tone from the jolly and avuncular first (and some of the second) book to the pessimistic and tragic in the third and fourth books of the tetralogy, and the misanthropic in the Merlyn, disconcerts some readers, White's version of the story nevertheless stands as the finest homage to Malory our century has yet produced.

Different both from White's mixed tragicomedy and the more pronouncedly comic American novels of Cabell, Erskine, and Steinbeck are a trio of British novels roughly contemporaneous with them, in which the concept of the Holy Grail emerges as mystically important for modern times. The first of these, Charles Williams's *War in Heaven* (1930), centers upon a power struggle between the forces of good and evil. The latter are represented by a retired publisher, Persimmons, and his confederates, Dmitri and Manasseh; the former by Archdeacon Davenant (who has discovered his church's old chalice's identity as the Grail from an archeological treatise published by Persimmons), Kenneth Mornington and the Catholic Duke of the North Ridings — identified with Galahad, Bors and Percival respectively. Persimmons, who dabbles in the occult, seeks to use the Grail to sacrifice an innocent child as well as to unite Davenant's soul with the body of a murdered man. Both are saved by Prester John (whose name is drawn from a non–Arthurian medieval legend), bearer and guardian of the Grail, whose celebration of a Grail mass climaxes with his own (and the Grail's) disappearance and the death of the saintly Archdeacon.

Less orthodoxly religious, in that it depends not upon the more usual Christian but rather upon the (perhaps earlier) Celtic significance of the Grail, is John Cowper Powys's *A Glastonbury Romance* (1932). This immense novel (1174 pp.) turns upon an inheritance which Canon Crow leaves, not to his relatives, but to his nurturing friend John Geard, a lay preacher who plans to use the money to finance a non–denominational Glastonbury religious fair and to enshrine the holy spring as a place for healing. As mayor, Geard is opposed by one of the dead man's grandsons, Philip Crow, a successful businessman who wants to develop the nearby caves for tourism and as tin mines; and Crow is opposed in turn by the Communist Dave Spear. Such oppositions Powys sees as part of the First Cause's dual nature; they are embodied in the character of the antiquary Owen Evans, who has a sinister fantasy life but – fastened to a cross as Christ in the religious festival's passion play – so suffers the Atonement that he is permanently injured. But even Geard's "miracles" – which may or may not occur – at the Grail fountain cannot prevent the sea from inundating Glastonbury, and the Mayor is drowned trying to rescue his enemy Philip Crow.

A third British novel, C. S. Lewis's *That Hideous Strength* (1945) – the final volume of his Space Trilogy (including also *Out of the Silent Planet* and *Perelandra*) – has Grail–centered characters and settings. Mark and Jane Stoddard, an estranged young couple, are involved, respectively, with the good– and evil–centered communities of the novel. Mark is initially ambitious to join the research activities of N.I.C.E. (National Institute of Coordinated Experiments), a sinister organization of fascistic scientists and technocrats seeking to create a superior race, which all but enslaves the surrounding area. This Wasteland society is opposed by a Christian community assembled at St. Anne's and presided over by Ransom (who has a wounded foot and is also known as Mr. Fisher–King), the hereditary Pendragon, which Jane – whose visionary dreams reveal N.I.C.E.'s evil – reluctantly joins. Both sides seek the aid of Merlin, in suspended animation nearby and the repository of the primitive power both need. Emerging not as the black magician N.I.C.E. had hoped for but as a force for good, Merlin destroys the evil characters, and then both he and Ransom depart to other spheres, while Jane returns obediently to her husband.[8]

While critics have concentrated on the likenesses of Lewis's and Williams's narratives as Christian parables, and the differences from both in Powys's Celticized version, these three novels have more in common than any of the works previously considered. All three posit a crucial opposition between forces for good and evil which is somehow related to the Grail. All three seek to show the emergence of these ancient archetypal forces in modern society, among characters many of whom are ordinary, but some of whom are Arthurian avatars. All three involve a saviour–figure who disappears at the end. Finally, both the Oxford Christians Williams and Lewis and the Celticist Powys are concerned with the primacy of spiritual values as opposed to worldly ones.

A different trend in both British and American works dating from early in this century and produced in a surprising quantity which still shows no signs of abating, is the novel based in the social sciences — an awkwardly named category which springs variously from concerns historical, anthropological and archeological. Here only a few of the scores of such novels can be considered. One of the best is *Sword at Sunset* by Rosemary Sutcliff (1963), author also of Arthurian children's books. Told retrospectively in the first person — a mode which was to be popular with the authors of similar novels — by an Artos who is half Roman and half Welsh hillfolk, the story is framed by its hero's lying gravely wounded at Glastonbury. Nephew and favorite of Ambrosius, the young Artos is magically seduced by his half–sister Ygerna (a hill woman) out of hate, to produce Medraut, his fated foe. His followers include Gwalchmai, a former brother at the monastery, who becomes a healer, and Bedwyr, half Breton and half–Welsh — a talented harper and horseman who takes Lancelot's role in the story. Here Artos marries his queen for her dowry of one hundred knights — his discovery of his incest with Ygerna has made him all but impotent. As he and his queen almost starve through a terrible winter, however, he conceives a child upon her. But their small daughter dies just before Medraut comes to court, and the Queen blames Artos. It is in her grief and her nursing of him that Guenhumara finally takes Bedwyr as her lover. Their discovery, as traditionally, by Medraut leads to Artos's banishing them, but Bedwyr returns to join the final battle against the king's rebellious son. As also traditionally, Medraut and Artos wound each other fatally; then the king, stricken in the groin, turns Britain over to Constantine and retires to wait for death.

Similar in several respects but quite different in others, especially tone, is Parke Godwin's *Firelord* (1980). A Romanized

Artorius, natural son of Uther – chief magistrate of the Dobunni – and older half–brother to Kay, also tells his own story, again from Glastonbury. He early discovers both a "genius" or prophetic facet of himself (personified as Merlin) and, as a soldier under Ambrosius, a separate, faëry identity he realizes while young during a six–months' sojourn with the Prydn. (Late in the book, this double nature is explained as the result of his mother's being a changeling.) As one of the husbands of this euhemerized and matriarchal people's queen, Morgana, he fathers a son, Modred, before Merlin recalls him to his "tallfolk" self to fight the Saxons. First named Count of Britain by Ambrosius (who teaches him the necessity of cruelty to enemies for survival), he eventually succeeds him as emperor. But Guenevere, whom he marries for love and who loses the only child she can ever conceive in an attempt to save her life, turns to Lancelot (who has married Eleyne) out of sadness and the emptiness of the impersonal life she comes to share with an Artorius whose co–regent she effectually is. When Morgana, her son and her followers come at the King's invitation to court, an insanely jealous Queen has them all killed except Modred, who escapes. Banished by Artorius, Guenevere and Lancelot first revolt against him, but then the Queen makes peace. Wounded by one of the army of Prydn and changelings Modred has collected, Artorius, after Modred is killed, is carried gravely ill to Avalon.

Both Sutcliff and Godwin create convincing earlier worlds in which to set their Arthurs – not those imitations of the High Middle Ages which stretch in a long line from Malory to White, but richly detailed and authentic–seeming post–Roman British societies, with a variety of tribes, including faërie. Both frame their stories to provide an Arthur–narrator looking back upon his life from his last wounding; each of these narrators speaks in an individuated voice which seems honest, devoid of self–pity and – in Godwin's hero – often genuinely humorous. Both heroes early conceive a child in an Otherworld peopled by the Little People of Celtic myth. Both marry strong queens, and in each case the loss of a child triggers the queen's love for a trusted lieutenant. (Godwin's Guenevere is especially notable for her administrative ability, and she becomes the hero of a sequel, *Beloved Exile*). Keeping the original themes of a royal bastard's revenge, a forbidden love which ruptures a male–bonded fellowship, and the king who must die for his people, these two authors have created authentic modern versions of the legend which – far beyond the often pejorative label of "historical novel" – present Arthur as he might have been had he lived.

Another, similar re–creation, although with somewhat less depth, is the world of Mary Stewart's four Arthurian novels – the Merlin trilogy, *The Crystal Cave* (1970), *The Hollow Hills* (1973) and *The Last Enchantment* (1979), and the sequel centering on Mordred, *The Wicked Day* (1984). Through these two personages, always in a sense outsiders, the story according to Geoffrey of Monmouth and, latterly, Malory, emerges in a rationalized form. *Cave* introduces Merlin, the bastard of Ambrosius Aurelianus by a Welsh princess, to tell his first–person story. After schooling by the sage Galapas (whose home, the Crystal Cave of the title, he will eventually inherit and from which he tells all three novels in retrospect), Merlin seeks and finds his father. Serving first the latter and, after his death, his brother Uther Pendragon, he transports (here in an engineering feat) the Stonehenge monoliths from Ireland and presides at the conception of Arthur (not this time by magic but by disguise and trickery). In *Hills*, Merlin supervises Arthur's education at a distance while he seeks the sword of Macsen Wledig (a Celtic motif conflated with the traditional stone–bound one), which he uses to ensure Arthur's accession to the throne. At the book's climax, the young King is seduced by his revengeful sister Morgause, who conceives Mordred. *Enchantment* continues to pit Merlin against Morgause, who here is the causer of his traditional madness. Loving and loved by Nimue, he teaches her to succeed him as physician and seer to Arthur after he willingly and impermanently retires to his cave, where he tells a visiting (and already cognizant) Arthur of Guinevere's love for

Bedwyr. In *Day*, a sympathetic Mordred becomes as much the unwilling instrument of Morgause's continuing revenge against Arthur as himself an agent. Through an omniscient third–person narrator, but mainly in Mordred's voice, Lady Stewart retells the betrayals — by Bedwyr and Guinevere, by knight against knight in family feud, and finally by Mordred — which lead Arthur to the traditional Wicked Day of his fatal wounding, by a Mordred who is also dying at the end.

It is easy to see why, next to White, Stewart is currently the most–taught Arthurian novelist. Her Arthurian plots are absorbing examples of their kind — the popular romance — and her characters' psychology is mostly convincing. Her rationalization of Merlin's magic (for instance, much of what he knows of others' secrets is gleaned from his youthful forays into the abandoned Roman hypocaust of his home) is also effective. In her creation of *enfances* for both Merlin and Mordred, she enriches our understanding of their subsequent actions. But her self–conscious narrators, especially Merlin, with their occasional bouts of self–pity, come off as less successful than those of Sutcliff and Godwin, and her women — chiefly Guinevere, Morgause, Morgan and Nimue — are less convincingly (and often less sympathetically) rendered.

Interest in Arthurian women has increased in the past few decades, perhaps as much from the twentieth–century rebirth of feminism as from the concomitant search for new narrators from whose viewpoints to tell the old story. Of a number of variously successful examples of this trend, I have space to consider here only the most remarkable, Marion Zimmer Bradley's *The Mists of Avalon* (1982). This immense work — at 876 pages second only to *A Glastonbury Romance* in length — has served, in the few years since its publication, to draw many students into Arthurian courses, if I am to credit my own and others' experience. Like the novels just discussed, the book is set in a post–Roman Britain distinguished by a variety of cultures — here Druidic, Great Motherist, and primitive and Augustinian Christian as well as faërie. All of these elements find a spiritual center at Avalon/

Glastonbury. Bradley employs both first- and third-person voices
to tell her story through its women: Morgaine, as traditionally
offspring of Gorlois and Igraine but also priestess of the Mother
and eventually Lady of the Lake; Igraine, sister to Morgause and,
like her, half-sister to Viviane, Morgaine's mentor and predecessor as Lady; Morgause, Queen of Orkney; Niniane and Nimue, the
latter daughter to Lancelot, Viviane's son, by Elaine; and
Gwenhwyfar, the only woman unrelated to these others and the
bigoted, arch-Christian opponent to their matriarchal Avalon. The
latter is allied with the Druids Taliesin (who has fathered in fertility rites most of the women) and Kevin, whom Morgaine—over-
whelmingly the central character of the novel—eventually sees as
a traitor to the old religions in his surrender of the Grail hollows
to Arthur. Arthur's conception is planned by Viviane, as is
Mordred's upon a horrified and unmaternal Morgaine by Arthur.

Morgaine, sometime seer and healer to Arthur's court, unre-
quitedly loves Lancelot and requitedly Accolon (here son to
Urien, whom as traditionally she marries), and is loved by Kevin,
but finds neither happiness nor real power over events. Indeed,
real empowerment escapes all of the women in the book except
perhaps (and indirectly) Gwenhwyfar, whose narrow Christianity
Arthur adopts. Viviane dies at the hands of Balin as she attempts
to assert the rights of Avalon over Christianity; Nimue's spell on
Taliesin's successor Kevin so redounds on her that she commits
suicide; and Niniane is first used and then killed by Mordred. Even
Morgaine, the most assertive of all these strong women, is at the
mercy of traditional, male-centered events. Her abandonment of
Mordred to Morgause leads to his rejection of her, as well as to
the discovery of the Queen's adultery and the mutual slaying by
father and son. Indeed, for a long period at the center of the book,
Morgaine is a virtual prisoner in the faërie country parallel to the
novel's several other worlds. In the end, Morgaine sees both the
Grail (here originally a sacred object of Avalon) as a universal
symbol and the Virgin Mary as identical to the Great Mother, so

that the claims of her religion are at last reconciled with the triumphant Christianity.

Bradley's is a highly original and compelling vision, and gives voice to those females who have so long remained mute in Arthurian legend. Her plotting is dense and rich, and her characters strikingly differentiated. But one wishes she had had (or accepted) better editorial advice: the novel is so prolix and so often repetitive as to make reading it a decided chore. Its language, moreover, is often trite and sometimes mawkish, and there is a trendiness in some of its details which may not wear well—Gwenhwyfar is afflicted with agoraphobia and hot flashes, for instance, and participates in a sexual threesome with Arthur and Lancelot, and Morgaine agonizes over an abortion. Yet perhaps this last is somewhat unfair in an Arthurian context which has, from its beginnings, always adapted itself to contemporary concerns.

That adaptation continues apace, as do some of the trends in modern Arthurian fiction surveyed in this essay. Two examples culled from *The New York Times Book Review* as I was revising this article will suffice as illustrations. In late 1988, *The Road to Avalon*, by Joan Wolf, was advertised as "imaginative and moving...historical fiction at its finest (*Publishers Weekly*)"; and, in very early 1989, under the headline "King Arthur in Toronto," *The Lyre of Orpheus*, by Robertson Davies, is described (in a full–page review) as about the production of an opera, "Arthur of Britain, or the Magnanimous Cuckold," by a man named Arthur Cornish, "a modern incarnation of a powerful man of the past who also tried to raise the moral tone of his kingdom."[9] Thus the trends represented by Sutcliff, Godwin, Stewart and numerous others, on the one hand, and by Steinbeck, Williams, Powys and Lewis, on the other, continue. While Erskine's or Cabell's dated comedy may not find successors, nor Berger's greater achievement, Bradley's book may be a harbinger of continuing feminist interest. Or a new and unexpected version or versions may provide narrative(s) as yet undreamed of. Such is the chance, and the delight, of the once and future fiction which attends the Once and Future King.

State University of New York College at Fredonia

NOTES

[1]For the most comprehensive attempt, see Raymond H. Thompson, *The Return from Avalon: A Study of the Arthurian Legend in Modern Fiction* (Westport, Conn., 1985). See also Thompson's essay in this anthology.

[2]Cabell's publisher, McBride, and its book department manager were charged with violating the New York Penal Code by The New York Society for the Suppression of Vice in 1920, but the trial ended in acquittal.

[3]*Tristan and Isolde: Restoring Palamede* (Indianapolis, 1932), 63.

[4]Nathan Comfort Starr, *King Arthur Today: The Arthurian Legend in English and American Literature, 1901-1953* (Gainesville, 1954), 45.

[5]See *Steinbeck and the Arthurian Theme*, ed. Tessumaro Hayashi (Steinbeck Monograph Series, No. 5, 1975).

[6] His first book, *Cup of Gold* (New York, 1929), features Merlin in a minor role; his last, the posthumous *The Acts of King Arthur and His Noble Knights* (New York, 1976), is a retelling of part of Malory.

[7] *Tortilla Flat* (New York, 1935), 9-10.

[8]One can only agree with the judgment of Elisabeth Brewer that "an unattractive male chauvinism...comes out when Lewis is concerned with the unfortunate Jane," Beverly Taylor & Elisabeth Brewer, *The Return of King Arthur: British and American Literature Since 1900* [sic: should be 1800] (Cambridge, England, 1983), 264.

[9]*The New York Times Book Review*, 8 January 1989, 7.

Arthurian Legend in Science Fiction and Fantasy

Raymond H. Thompson

One of the most fascinating aspects of Arthurian tradition is the range of literary forms that it encompasses, from beginnings in heroic poems and tales to such relatively recent developments as science fiction and screenplays. As the Middle Ages waned, so did the popularity of such genres as romance and chronicle, in which Arthurian legend achieved its most widespread success. The legend passed out of fashion for more than three centuries, in fulfilment of Sir Thomas Malory's complaint, "For he that was the moste kynge and nobelyst knyght of the worlde, and moste loved the felyshyp of noble knyghtes, and by hym they all were upholdyn, and yet myght nat thes Englyshemen holde them contente with hym."[1] Yet the tides of changing taste that swept Arthur away have turned again, bringing him back to a renewed prominence. Over the past century and a half, his story has spread into literary genres that have evolved since the Middle Ages.[2]

Among these none has been more fascinating than science fiction and fantasy. The proliferation of conventions devoted to these two kinds of writing offer ample evidence of the enthusiasm of their reading public. Academic attention has followed more cautiously, as one might expect; yet it has led to a growing appreciation of the potential and achievements of both genres.

Since science fiction is concerned with the impact of change upon humanity, one would imagine that it would find the cyclic pattern of Arthurian legend a fertile field to explore. The kinds of change that science fiction is most interested in, moreover, are caused by social, political, and technological advances. That these advances are inherent in Arthurian legend is demonstrated by historical fiction which has, for example, pondered the impact upon Arthur's wars of such developments as the *comitatus* and the stirrup.[3] Science fiction, however, is more interested in developments that have not yet taken place, rather than those that have. It starts with the premise, "what if such and such were possible?" As a result the setting for science fiction is usually the future. Since Arthurian legend is rooted in the past, it is approached by science fiction authors in one of two ways: either they return to the past to offer a technological explanation for certain features of the legend, or else they create characters to re-enact Arthurian roles in a society set in the future. To date, few authors have responded to the challenge imposed by these limitations.

Returning to the past has proven particularly discouraging, and few works have tried it. The most famous is Mark Twain's *A Connecticut Yankee in King Arthur's Court* (1889), but since this can also be considered an ironic fantasy, it will be discussed later. Twain's device of sending a modern man back in time to Arthur's day is employed by Robert F. Young in "A Knyght Ther Was" (1963), in which a time-thief's plot to steal the Holy Grail from the castle of Carbonek is thwarted. The short story generates light-hearted humor at the expense of the thief, whose over-confidence in advanced technology leads him from one misjudgement to another. The crowning irony comes when he finds himself marooned in the fifteenth century, and realizes that he is the Thomas Malory destined to write *Le Morte Darthur*. The process is reversed in A. W. Bernal's humorous short story, "King Arthur's Knight in a Yankee Court" (1941), in which Galahad travels forward in time for a brief visit to the New York World Fair.

The other works identify specific features of Arthurian legend as the products of a highly superior extra-terrestrial technology. This is how Andre Norton explains the powers of Merlin and Nimue, the Lady of the Lake, in *Merlin's Mirror* (1975). Nimue convincingly argues against external intervention to accelerate human development, as Merlin and Arthur intend, but the cruelty of her actions and those of her allies indicates lack of concern for the well-being of others. In Rita and Tim Hildebrandt's *Merlin and the Dragons of Atlantis* (1983) Merlin's skills are the product of technology developed in Atlantis and Lemuria, but lost when they are engulfed. Peter Hanratty's *The Last Knight of Albion: The Quest for Mordred* (1986) anachronistically sets Arthur's chivalric world in pre–Roman Britain, then destroys it at the Battle of Camlann with an atomic bomb supplied to Mordred by aliens. Thereafter Percevale, the sole survivor of the Round Table, seeks Mordred in order to avenge his king. Over the years Percevale loses his youthful illusions about life, but when called upon to defend a town against a marauding army, he rediscovers the importance of self– sacrifice, the quality that motivated the best of Arthur's followers. This thoughtful novel comments ironically upon war, showing how pride drives people to acts of folly whose cost they do not realize until too late. It is a cost that everybody, guilty and innocent alike, must pay. Like Norton's, Hanratty's novel raises interesting questions about the price of progress, and it uses the Arthurian setting to demonstrate the timelessness of the issue.

Works in which characters re–enact Arthurian roles in a society set in the future are more numerous. Several make use of the concept of reincarnation for this purpose. Thus in Theodore Sturgeon's "Excalibur and the Atom" (1951), a private detective encounters various reincarnated Arthurian characters before discovering that he himself is Galahad; in K. W. Jeter's *Morlock Night* (1979), a sequel to H. G. Wells' *The Time Machine*, a reborn Arthur, initially unaware of his identity, must restore the power of Excalibur so that he and Merlin can thwart the plans of the Morlocks to use the Time Machine to invade nineteenth–century England; in Peter David's *Knight Life* (1987) a reborn Arthur encounters some traditional friends and foes in the course of his successful campaign to become mayor of New York. A variation on this idea is used in David Bischoff's *Star Spring* (1982), where Merlin and Galahad give assistance during a Grail quest in a computer–generated fantasy world. Although all four afford opportunity for irony, none probe deeper issues.

Elsewhere Arthurian roles are adopted, either consciously or unconsciously, by characters of the future. The hero of Vladimir Nabokov's "Lance" (1952) is named after Lancelot, and his voyage in space is compared to that knight's crossing of the swordbridge into a world from which none return. The Arthurian analogy helps to explain the problem that an earthbound generation encounters in trying to comprehend something so remote from ordinary experience as space travel. The bumbling hero of John Phillifent's "The Stainless Steel Knight" (1961, later incorporated in *Life with Lancelot*, 1963) is also named after Lancelot, and humor is generated by his attempts to live up to the prestige of his name when he finds himself on a world with a culture based upon Arthurian romance. J. F. McIntosh also gives his characters names out of Arthurian tradition in his short story "Merlin" (1960), but their actions do little to recall those of their predecessors.

These last two stories are typical of the casual writing that has given science fiction a bad name among scholars. Fortunately for the reputation of the genre, however, C. J. Cherryh's *Port Eternity* (1982) penetratingly explores the gap between illusion and reality inherent in adapting Arthurian roles. In this novel a private space craft is marooned in another dimension where its occupants find themselves threatened by aliens. Their anxiety is heightened because the staff and crew are "made people," cloned from special genetic combinations, conditioned to follow certain patterns of behavior by "deepteach" tapes, then sold as slaves to "born people." Since their conditioning has not prepared them for this crisis, they have great difficulty in handling it; but in this they turn out to be little different from the born people, who are equally disconcerted by so unexpected an experience.

This examination of human conditioning is thrown into focus by the Arthurian element, for the wealthy owner staffs her space craft with made people modeled upon characters in Tennyson's *Idylls of the King*. When the latter discover their Arthurian personae, they begin to react to each other as to their traditional namesakes, so that the fantasy threatens to overwhelm reality.

Moreover, the plot structure, too, follows an Arthurian pattern: although divided by internal dissension and mistrust, this microcosm of Arthur's court must deal with external invasion; eventually it is overwhelmed and its members borne off to live in a timeless, science-fictional Avalon. Despite flaws, Cherryh's novel thoughtfully and skilfully explores issues that are central to Arthurian legend.

In her Keltiad series, *The Copper Crown* (1984) and *The Throne of Scone* (1986), Patricia Kennealy recreates the ancient Celtic world and its traditions in a space–faring future. Among those traditions is an Arthur whose career is similar in outline, if not setting, to our own. In order to repel alien invaders, the Queen of the Kelts must recover the Thirteen Treasures that disappeared with Arthur after the space battle of Camlann, using as her guide Taliesin's obscure poem, "The Spoils of Annwn." Arthur's exploits themselves will be the subject of a forthcoming book. The series is interesting not only for the ingenuity with which it adapts traditional material and for the active role it gives women, but also for its development of the Arthurian themes of loyalty and the responsible use of power.

Related to science fiction is science fantasy. This creates a secondary world where magic operates, but it offers a scientific explanation, however cursory, for the existence of this secondary world, though not the magic. In John Brunner's *Father of Lies* (1968) this magical secondary world is explained as the creation of a mad child with mutant powers. These transform his immediate environment into an Arthurian fantasy world.

A more common device is to create an alternate universe. In Andre Norton's *Witch World* (1963), the hero sits upon the Siege Perilous in order to gain entry into the Witch World of the title; in Poul Anderson's *Three Hearts and Three Lions* (1953) the hero finds himself in an alternate universe after receiving a head wound, and there encounters Morgan le Fay. In Roger Zelazny's series about the magical world of Amber, Lancelot appears briefly *(The Guns of Avalon,* 1972), and a character named Merlin emerges as the protagonist in the most recent books, though whether he will be identified with the figure from Arthurian tradition remains to be seen.

None of these science fantasy novels use their Arthurian borrowings as more than convenient devices with which to advance the plot. Their focus is upon other matters. Thus while Morgan's conflicting impulses to love and to destroy the hero evoke her intriguingly ambivalent role in Arthurian tradition, it is not a direction that Anderson chooses to explore.

The Arthurian element is more significant, however, in the most recent science fantasy, Michael Greatrex Coney's imaginative *Fang, the Gnome* (1988). Here the legend of Arthur becomes reality when Avalona, the mother of Merlin and mentor of Nyneve, uses her supernatural powers to alter the "happentracks," the many frames of existence created by the different choices that are possible to people.

Most of these works, including those categorized as science fiction, incorporate elements of fantasy; and that authors have found fantasy a more comfortable genre for treating Arthurian legend is proven by a rapid increase in numbers over the past thirty years. Even more than science fiction, however, fantasy has struggled for recognition as a serious literary genre. Too often it is dismissed as mere escapism, suitable only to entertain children until they are ready for more adult writings. Yet in the hands of a skilful author the apparently simplistic world of fantasy is as capable of probing truths about the human condition as the most introspective psychological novel.

Fantasy is distinguished from other literary genres in that the element of the marvelous is crucial. The way in which the marvelous is used separates the two major classifications: low and high. The former confines itself to the primary world with which we are familiar, and it offers no explanation for the non–rational phenomena that occur. Since their impact tends to be mysterious and frightening, such phenomena occur frequently in horror novels. High fantasy, on the other hand, creates a secondary world where non–rational events are accounted for by a supernatural power that is acceptable within that world.

Few low fantasies make use of Arthurian legend, although elements of low fantasy do appear in novels from other categories. The best are two juvenile novels, William Mayne's *Earthfasts* (1966) and Nancy Bond's *A String in the Harp* (1976).[4] By contrast, Irving Cox's "Lancelot Returned" (1957), in which the fantasy of an ugly and neglected idiot girl becomes reality when Lancelot carries her off to Camelot, is typical of the carelessly written short stories in pulp magazines.

In the remaining novels, the response of the characters to the non–rational phenomena that they encounter ranges from confused incredulity to panic–stricken horror. In Mary Mitchell's *Birth of a Legend* (1956) the inexplicable arrival of Lohengrin, the son of Perceval, in a swan-like vessel just in time to defend a maiden in trial by combat reveals that most people are too suspicious to accept a miracle with simple faith. In Charles de Lint's *Moonheart* (1984) an assorted group of people in modern Toronto discover the evil that is within all of us when they get caught up in a terrifying struggle between wielders of magic powers from the past, amongst whom is the bard Taliesin. In Fred Saberhagen's *Dominion* (1982), set in modern Chicago, Merlin shakes off the enchantment that bereft him of power in time to frustrate Nimue's diabolical plan to bring forward from the past an evil sorcerer who seeks to rule the world. In Mary Leader's *Triad* (1973) by contrast, Merlin is deceived again by Niniane in this novel of supernatural possession set in the American midwest. In Philip Michaels' *Grail* (1982), demons seek to possess the sacred vessel so that they may multiply and take over the world.

Apart from a couple of didactic fantasies, like John Cowper Powys' *Morwyn or the Vengeance of God* (1937), which castigates religious and scientific fanaticism, the many Arthurian high fantasies can readily be divided into three main groups: mythopoeic, heroic, and ironic.[5] In mythopoeic fantasy the struggle between good and evil is waged directly between

supernatural powers. The setting is usually contemporary, with
Arthurian figures revived to participate in the struggle. Thus it is
in post–war England that Merlin aids in the assault upon the
representatives of dehumanizing scientific progress in C. S. Lewis'
That Hideous Strength (1945); and it is in modern Mobile,
Alabama, that Morgause and Morgan le Fay serve the forces of
evil in a race to find the Grail and Excalibur in Anne Saunders
Laubenthal's *Excalibur* (1973). Charles Williams' *War in Heaven*
(1930) reveals the limitations of human reason during another
quest for the Holy Grail, here set in contemporary England. Tim
Powers, on the other hand, sets *The Drawing of the Dark* (1979)
during the Turkish siege of Vienna in the sixteenth century. The
forces of good are led by the Fisher King and Merlin, who brings
back from Avalon the spirit of Arthur, temporarily resurrected as
an Irish soldier of fortune.

Less common are mythopoeic fantasies set in Arthur's day.
Gillian Bradshaw, however, returns to the Dark Ages for her
trilogy, *Hawk of May* (1980), *Kingdom of Summer* (1981), and *In
Winter's Shadow* (1982). Gwalchmai (Gawain), in the service of
"Light," helps Arthur lead the struggle against the forces of
"Dark" served by his mother, Morgawse. At considerable cost they
win early successes, only to see them squandered through human
selfishness and misjudgement.

Most recently, a group of modern Canadians revive a sleeping
Arthur so that he can assist the struggle of Light against Dark in
an alternate world, as created by Guy Gavriel Kay in his Fionavar
Tapestry, *The Summer Tree* (1984), *The Wandering Fire* (1986),
and *The Darkest Road* (1986). There he encounters his hound
Cavall, the bard Taliesin, and a reborn Guinevere; he himself
revives a sleeping Lancelot on a raid to Caer Sedat (Caer Sidi). In
her series, Byzantium's Heirs, Susan Shwartz creates another
alternate world in which not only are stories told of Arktos the
Bear, but Olwen, Luned, and Gereint play major roles in *The
Woman of Flowers* (1987).

The protagonists in these mythopoeic fantasies develop a deeper understanding of life, but only at great personal cost. Nor is it clear that the wisdom gained always outweighs the sacrifice required, and this leaves us with a sense of regret, of innocence that has been irretrievably lost. In books for younger readers, like Susan Cooper's series The Dark Is Rising and Alan Garner's Alderley books, this pattern represents growth into maturity with its added burden of responsibility.

The largest group of fantasies is the heroic, in which supernatural beings fade from the picture. Although they may be glimpsed occasionally as fays and demons, they have largely ceded their power to human magic workers, like Merlin, Morgan le Fay, and the Lady of the Lake. Linda Haldeman's *The Lastborn of Elvinwood* (1978) and Roger Zelazny's ironic short story, *The Last Defender of Camelot* (1979), involve a long–lived Merlin in contemporary events, while in Victor Milan's "Soldatenmangel" (1981) he travels forward in time to the religious wars of sixteenth–century Germany. The protagonist of Will Bradley's *Launcelot and the Ladies* (1927), on the other hand, pays brief visits to the past by means of visions. The effect in each case is to teach valuable lessons about the human condition.

It is more common, however, for the action to be set entirely in Arthur's day. The two earliest works are relatively short: Arthur Machen's "Guinevere and Lancelot" (1909) follows Malory's account of the love story, except that the Queen uses a sorcerer's magic spell to entrap the knight; and George Moore's *Perronik the Fool* (1926) offers a radically changed version of Perceval's quest for the Grail.

T. H. White returns to Malory for what is undoubtedly the best–loved modern version of the Arthurian legend. *The Sword in the Stone* (1938) deals with Arthur's childhood, *The Witch in the Wood* (1939) with his early years on the throne, *The Ill–Made Knight* (1940) with the love of Lancelot and Guenever and its tragic outcome. In 1958 these were collected together, revised, and then re–issued as *The Once and Future King*. In the first book

White creates a wonderful world that satisfies childhood's most
heartfelt needs: for knowledge by Arthur's transformation into
various creatures; for adventure by the rescue of Friar Tuck from
a fairy castle; for laughter by comical figures like the bumbling
King Pellinore and the absent–minded Merlin; for love by the
warm response to Arthur's coronation. Yet the bright hopes
darken in the later books. Kindness and friendship are replaced by
conflict and betrayal, and by an aching sense that something
precious has been lost.

Since World War II heroic fantasy has divided into two
streams. Perhaps disillusioned by the cruelties of war that White
found so hard to bear, most male authors have turned to a category
popularly known as sword and sorcery, which introduces fierce
new heroes into a particularly savage Dark Age setting. Walter H.
Munn's *King of the World's Edge* first appeared in magazine form
in 1939 before it was published as a novel in 1966, to be followed
in 1967 by a sequel, *The Ship from Atlantis*. They were bound
together as *Merlin's Godson* in 1976, two years after publication of
a third novel in the series, *Merlin's Ring*. The series begins when
Merlin and a Romano–British centurion lead a shipload of
refugees from the Battle of Camlann to North America, where
they get involved in wars among the native peoples. The
centurion's son later returns and visits Arthur who lies asleep in a
cavern. In both Chris Carlsen's *Berserker: The Bull Chief* (1977)
and David Drake's *The Dragon Lord* (1979) a formidable Irish
warrior helps Arthur in his war against the Saxons. Another
Irishman, this time a warrior bard, has a number of encounters
with Arthur and his warriors, as well as Vivyan, in the course of
the adventures recorded in *Bard* (1981), *Bard III: The Wild Sea*
(1986), and *Bard IV: Ravens' Gathering* (1987). In *Runes* (1984)
and its sequel *Broken Stone* (1985) Richard Monaco breaks with
tradition when he makes a British slave woman and the son of
Spartacus the gladiator the parents of Arthur, and follows their
adventures and those of their young son in the strife–torn years
before Augustus establishes imperial rule in Rome.

Like the composers of many late medieval romances, these authors use Arthurian legend as a vague general background to what are essentially independent and episodic adventures. Theme and character are ignored in favor of action that emphasizes gratuitous and even sadistic violence. In *Merlin Dreams* (1988) Peter Dickinson uses the seer's long, entranced sleep as the frame for a series of perceptive ironic tales.

Recently, however, male authors of heroic fantasy have started to turn from this preoccupation with violence. In *The Wizard of 4th Street* (1987) and *The Wizard of Whitechapel* (1988), the first two books of a lively ongoing series, Simon Hawke creates a future in which magic has largely replaced technology, thanks to the revival of Merlin from his long enchantment. With the aid of Morgan le Fay, her son Modred, and two descendants of her sisters, Elaine and Morgause, he opposes the Dark Ones in their bid to regain power over humanity. Peter Hanratty, on the other hand, returns to the past in *The Book of Mordred* (1988). This deals with Mordred's early years, culminating in his successful quest for the Grail in the company of Lancelot and Galahad. He emerges as an intelligent and idealistic young man whose efforts to help others are constantly frustrated by the ignorance and narrow–mindedness of those around him.

In general, however, it was left to female authors to present a more positive view of the Arthurian world in heroic fantasy, but in doing so they have adapted intriguing new perspectives on the legend. In place of such traditional protagonists as Arthur and Lancelot, they focus more often upon figures long relegated to minor roles. The effect upon Arthurian tradition has been stimulating.

As one might expect, some have placed women at the centre of events. Long victims or prizes of chivalric prowess when submissive, or disrupting influences when they take the initiative, the women of Arthurian legend are emerging from the shadow of the men. Vera Chapman's trilogy of The Three Damosels is imbued with sentimentality, but the young heroines struggle to control their own fate as valiantly as any knight: in *The Green Knight* (1975) Bercilak's lady tries to save Gawain's life; in *The King's Damosel* (1976) Lynett, who guided Gareth to rescue her sister in Malory's *Le Morte Darthur*, gives invaluable service to Arthur and eventually achieves the Grail quest; in *King Arthur's Daughter* (1976) the child of Arthur and Guenevere heroically fights for the throne after her father departs for Avalon. Marion Zimmer Bradley's *The Mists of Avalon* (1982) adopts the point of view of a number of women, but most commonly Morgaine, whose progress towards wisdom and understanding as a servant of the Mother Goddess unifies the novel. The focus thus shifts from warfare to the political and domestic conflicts that raise Arthur to power, and then destroy him. Sharan Newman's Guinevere Trilogy, comprising *Guinevere* (1981), *The Chessboard Queen* (1983), and *Guinevere Evermore* (1985), follows the life of the Queen with sympathy for her predicament in a changing world where she is little more than a pawn in a predominantly male power struggle. "Nimue's Tale" (1988) by Madeline Robins and "Meditation in a Whitethorn Tree" (1988) by Jane Yolen, however, reveal the perils of treating women like pawns.

The women of Arthurian legend are not the only concern of female authors. Yolen's *Merlin's Book* (1986) offers a collection of short stories and poems on the mysteries associated with the figure of Merlin; Phyllis Ann Karr's *Idylls of the Queen* (1982) and "Two Bits of Embroidery" (1988) shed a sympathetic light upon Kay, Arthur's sharp–tongued seneschal; Gail van Asten's *The Blind Knight* (1988) tells how a blind albino youth is trained to knighthood by Uther Pendragon, a prince of Faërie; Chelsea Quinn Yarbro's "Night Mare" (1988) and Morgan Llewelyn's "Their Son" (1988) are both ironic tales about the childhood of Modred and of Merlin's son respectively; Susan Shwartz's "Seven from Caer Sidi" (1988) and Sharan Newman's "Palace by Moonlight" (1988) proclaim the importance of song and legend to us all; *Tristram of Lyonesse* (1949) by Ruth Collier Sharpe recreates the traditional story as gothic melodrama in a disconcertingly anachronistic setting. What many of these works by women share is sympathy for the victims of the power struggles that take place in Arthur's world. They deepen our understanding of the legend by allowing us to view it from an unfamiliar perspective.

Whereas heroic fantasy measures human achievements against high odds to reveal the potential of the human spirit, ironic fantasy measures these same achievements against still higher expectations of the characters or audience to reveal a comic gap. The most famous is Mark Twain's *A Connecticut Yankee in King Arthur's Court* (1889), in which the protagonist, Hank Morgan, travels back in time to Arthur's Britain. Hank takes advantage of his technological expertise to gain power, and he uses his relentless practicality to expose not only the comedy inherent in such features of medieval romance as knight errantry, but also the ignorance and callousness of feudal society. Yet when Hank turns his modern weapons against those who oppose his rule, it becomes clear that Twain's satire is aimed at society in his own day as much as in the past. Indeed the final slaughter of an entire army, electrocuted by wire, mowed down by machine guns, and drowned in a flooded ditch, reveals the futility of our progress. What is the worth of improved efficiency when it is put to such destructive uses?

The popularity of this satiric approach has risen sharply since the publication of John Steinbeck's *The Acts of King Arthur* in 1976. Although it starts as a retelling of the early part of Malory's *Le Morte Darthur*, the novel introduces changes that develop a spirit of disillusionment alien to its source. This process culminates when Lancelot sets out to perform deeds of selfless service as a knight errant, only to find his best efforts frustrated by the selfishness of others. Moreover, this failure mirrors the outcome of his own internal struggle to escape or sublimate his love for the Queen.

The following year saw the publication of *The Book of Merlyn* (1977), the conclusion to T. H. White's *The Once and Future King*.

On the eve of the Battle of Camlann, the aged King Arthur tries valiantly, but with as little success as when he tries to prevent the battle itself, to defend humanity's record to Merlyn and the animals whom he met in the first book. The result is a bitter and didactic denunciation of human folly and barbarism.

Both books had a long wait to be published, Steinbeck's since 1959, White's since 1942, but the remaining satiric novels are more recent in composition. Robert Nye's sardonic *Merlin* (1978) focuses upon the Devil's role in the Merlin tradition to reveal how our baser instincts betray our higher aspirations. Behind the illusion of chivalric ideals at Arthur's court it discovers the reality of licentious perversity. Richard Monaco's continuing account of Parsival's quest for the Holy Grail presently occupies four books, *Parsival or a Knight's Tale* (1977), *The Grail War* (1979), *The Final Quest* (1980), and *Blood and Dreams* (1985). The brutality and destructiveness of the world drive people to seek the Grail; yet their quest not only leads to abandonment of domestic and social responsibilities but at times to fanaticism, both of which serve to make the situation worse.

Although the satiric novels see the Arthurian dream as a foolish, if beautiful, illusion in a bleak and cruel world, other ironic fantasies take a more positive view of their subject matter. For them the failure to live up to lofty expectations is the source of affectionate comedy, rather than bitter regret. In James Branch Cabell's *Jurgen* (1919), the aging protagonist encounters many exciting and beautiful women, including Guenevere and the Lady of the Lake, only to conclude that he is most comfortable with his unattractive, scolding wife. In Gwyn Jones' "Gwydion Mathrafal" (1945), a Welshman is rewarded for defending the honour of Wales against English insults by a vision of Arthur riding forth to the hunt from a ruined fortress. In John Myers's *Silverlock* (1949), the hero learns a fuller appreciation of the wonders of life in the course of picaresque wanderings through a realm filled with memorable characters from literature, including Nimue and Gawain. In Evan Hunter's "Dream Damsel" (1954), a shrewd damsel teaches the hero that dreams are not always as wonderful as one might imagine. Matt Cohen's *Too Bad Galahad* (1972) is a series of very short burlesque accounts of Galahad's discovery of the Grail.

Like Twain, some authors create humor at the expense of both the present and the past by bringing the modern age in contact with the world of King Arthur. Naomi Mitchison's *To the Chapel Perilous* (1955) introduces the press into the world of Arthurian romance, then sends reporters with modern professional standards to investigate conflicting claims about the Holy Grail. Cauldron of plenty, stone, spear, dish, cup — each, it turns out, is authentic to those who believe. Our own special Grail awaits each one of us. In Leonard Wibberley's *The Quest of Excalibur* (1959), King Arthur is confused when he returns from Avalon to the modern British welfare state; in J. B. Priestley's *The Thirty-First of June* (1962), the world of modern advertising is just as confused when it encounters an alternate universe of Arthurian fantasy; and in Elizabeth Scarborough's "The Camelot Connection" (1988), modern psychoanalysis creates more problems than it solves when a romantic young woman and a pop psychiatrist travel back in time to occupy jointly the body of a revived Merlin in an Arthurian world based upon T. H. White's *The Once and Future King.*

The finest ironic novel on the Arthurian legend, certainly of this century, is Thomas Berger's *Arthur Rex* (1978). Berger has a keen eye for the ridiculousness inherent in romance conventions. Thus at the Battle of Camlann he parodies the exaggeration found in medieval romance when 148 knights of the Round Table kill 20,000 foes, Lancelot skewering them on his lance, ten at a time, Percival riding along the front rank, lopping off heads as though scything a wheat field. He also demonstrates his delight in ironic reversal, in his treatment of Meleagant. As a villain Meleagant achieves impressive success, capturing Guinevere, Kay, and even the mighty Lancelot, but when he reforms in an attempt to win the love of the Queen, he lurches from one mishap to another.

Similarly, the effort of Arthur and his knights to create a better world ultimately founders upon the rocks of human imperfection, prompting the King to question its worth as he lies wounded to the death by the treacherous Mordred. He is comforted, however, by the ghost of Gawaine: "For can we not say, without the excessive pride which is sinful, that we lived with a certain gallantry?"[6] This willingness to behave gallantly, even at the cost of looking ridiculous, wins success beyond all expectations for Arthur and his knights.

This ironic reversal, whereby naive and foolish behavior turns out to be the noblest wisdom, is at the heart of all ironic fantasy. The characters have the courage to risk making mistakes and looking foolish, because that is the only way to learn. And the lesson they learn is to keep striving despite disappointment, for that alone can create a better world where love and decency can prevail. Even in the satiric works, the authors prefer the noble–minded folly of their heroes to the destructive cynicism that finally overpowers them.

Arthurian science fiction and fantasy share an admiration for the heroic self–assertion of their characters. In pursuit of the Arthurian dream of a better world, they brave overwhelming odds, self–doubt, fear, and even ridicule. Though doomed to final failure, as the cyclic pattern of rise and fall in Arthurian legend recognizes, they remain committed to that dream. What matter, after all, that our own imperfections will ultimately destroy what we have built, provided we hold back the darkness for even a little while longer?

Acadia University

NOTES

[1] Eugene Vinaver, ed., *The Works of Sir Thomas Malory*, 2nd ed., (Oxford, 1967), 3, 1229.

[2] See James Douglas Merriman, *The Flower of Kings: A Study of the Arthurian Legend in England Between 1485 and 1835*

(Lawrence, Kansas, 1973); Beverly Taylor and Elisabeth Brewer, *The Return of King Arthur: British and American Arthurian Literature Since 1800* (Woodbridge, Suffolk, 1983); Raymond H. Thompson, *The Return from Avalon: A Study of the Arthurian Legend in Modern Fiction* (Westport, Conn., 1985); Norris J. Lacy et al., eds., *The Arthurian Encyclopedia* (New York, 1986).

[3]See, for example, Parke Godwin's *Firelord* (1980).

[4]For a discussion of the fiction for younger readers, see Jane Curry's article above.

[5]For a fuller rationale of these groupings, see Thompson, *The Return from Avalon,* 88-89.

[6]Thomas Berger, *Arthur Rex* (New York, 1978), 483. See also Brooks Landon's article below.

Thomas Berger's *Arthur Rex*

Brooks Landon

Over the thirty years of his distinguished publishing career, Thomas Berger has seen more than his share of reviews as misinformed and misleading as they were meant to be genial: even raves for some of his novels contained astounding errors of fact, not to mention those of interpretation. Through teeth saved from gritting only by a philosophical smile, Berger said nothing. But, in 1978 a reviewer finally went too far and no longer could even the stoic Berger remain silent. You see, James Atlas had insinuated in his generally blundering *Time* review of *Arthur Rex* that Berger *had been careless in a matter of language*. Specifically, Atlas sniffed that Berger's "heroes talk obsessively of 'paps' and 'mammets' (not, as Berger supposes, a variant of mammaries, but a medieval reference to Muhammad)."[1]

Berger's response, in a 9 October 1978 letter to Atlas, was characteristically precise:

Dear Mr. Atlas:

In my use of "mammets" I chose to turn my back on both OED and Webster, who of course trace the word, in its variant spellings, to one or another version of the Prophet's name; on Dr. Johnson, whose note to Hotspur's speech is, simply, "Puppet"; and on Farmer & Henley, who in their celebrated *Slang and Its Analogues* define the term as "A puling girl" and cite passages in *Romeo and Juliet* and Johnson's *Alchemist*.

Instead I went along with E. Partridge in his *Shakespeare's Bawdy*, from which I here quote the appropriate entry in its entirety:

"*mammets*. Female breasts. '*Hotspur*. I care not for thee, Kate: this is no world to play with mammets and to tilt with lips', 1 *Henry IV*, II iii 92-93.

"*L. mamma*, a breast (especially of a woman): an echoic word, symbolizing the baby's gurgle of satisfaction when given its mother's breast. — Cf. *pap*."

That the Oxonians include "pigeon" among the possible meanings of "mammet" and the Websterians not only join them but add "scarecrow" are perhaps other matters — or mammets.

Yours faithfully,
Thomas Berger[2]

And, in what must be a rarity of astounding unlikelihood, James Atlas graciously accepted Berger's argument. Acknowledging in a letter to the author that the OED had indeed been the sole authority for his objection, Atlas duly apologized.

I cite this exchange as evidence of the attention to detail in matters of language as well as of legend in *Arthur Rex*, a novel hailed in the *New York Times Book Review* by a more perceptive reviewer, John Romano, as "the Arthur book for our time."[3] My concern in this essay will be to show ways in which Berger's distinctive allegiances to literary, linguistic, and legendary traditions coalesce in a telling of the Arthur legend that is as faithful to tradition as it is undeniably modern. While I will not attempt here to offer a thorough reading of *Arthur Rex*, I will attempt to limn its salient features, as well as to offer a number of Thomas Berger's own comments about its composition.[4] These remarks, drawn from my correspondence with Berger, offer a unique glimpse into some of the thinking that produced this delightfully complex celebration of the Arthur legend.

In language which could only be the author's, the book jacket informs us that *Arthur Rex* is "Thomas Berger's salute to the age

of Chivalry from his own enmired situation in the Time of the
Cad," but the insistent message of Berger's ninth novel is that in
the continuous mystery of time, the age of Chivalry and the Time
of the Cad are in many ways of a piece. Running through all
distinctions between legendary past and banal present is the unity
of time, *sub specie aeternitatis*. As Berger's Merlin explains to
Arthur, "the curse which shall ruin you eventually is the selfsame
which ruins all men, irrespective of their actions good or evil, and
that is Time, which is the issue of an incestuous act performed by
God on reality" (76).[5]

Aptly described by one reviewer of *Arthur Rex* as "the Green
Knight of American fiction: a mysterious, protean outsider whose
pose of destructiveness masks a fierce reverence for form and
meaning,"[6] Berger has jokingly remarked that "the most difficult
thing in life is to maintain one's belief in one's own hoax" (6
September 1977). This most difficult of tasks constantly falls to
almost all of Berger's protagonists, but, of his fifteen novels, *Arthur
Rex* most systematically explores the difficulties, dangers, and
rewards of sustaining belief in the hoaxes both of the self and of
culture. Substitute *myth* or *legend* for *hoax* and it becomes clear
that in the world of Berger's writing Arthur faces a timeless problem: for all the events and epistemologies that roil his life, Arthur
is finally defined by the complex intersections of the concept of
freedom with the concept of power.

Arthur Rex is obviously Berger's homage to Sir Thomas
Malory and to the line of tellers who have made the Arthur legend
"the Matter of Britain." In it, Berger inevitably brings modern
scrutiny and his sense of humor to the legend of King Arthur, but
he does so in keeping with his self–professed "genuine hunger for
gallantry and a passion for panache." And just as surely as his
characters struggle to meet their own self–perceived responsibilities, this — like all of Berger's novels — reveals his own sense of
responsibility to literary tradition. Indeed, Michael Malone has
recorded Berger's resentment at coming across an Arthurian
screenplay, written by someone who had apparently read "none of

Malory, Chrétien de Troyes, Wolfram von Eschenbach, Alf Tennyson, Dick Wagner's *Tristan* and *Parsifal* and the many other forerunners whose works I ransacked (including two books for children which were my principal sources)." "This unbelievable trashy practioner," Berger exclaimed, "had *invented* his own Arthurian narrative!"[7]

In this matter, his own experience may have stiffened Berger's distaste for invented Arthur stories. Mentioning that some years before he began writing *Arthur Rex* he had attempted an Arthurian narrative starring a dwarf–magician, Berger added:

> But I discovered that any invention which would revise the basic structure and characters of the classic legend was rubbish: unspeakably boring to write and worse to read. That is to say, it is absolutely necessary that all dwarfs be malignant — these legends are not the work of humanitarian legislation, and if one seeks compassion for the stunted, which in life one should certainly have, one should not seek it here. (13 October 1980)

Clearly, Berger is mindful of his obligation to observe fundamental distinctions between the medieval mind which gave rise to these tales and the modern mind which they still engage. In his 1982 foreword to *German Medieval Tales*, Berger discussed some of these distinctions, with a particular eye toward the radical practicality evident to him in both medieval life and literature. Asking his readers how except in surface matters we can distinguish medieval tales from the modern, Berger offers several criteria:

> An immediate and not altogether droll answer might be: in *our* stories the heroes can often be easily identified as the kind of characters the reader of the Middle Ages would have thought not worth creating: the weakling, the hypochondriac, the sniveler, *et al.* Our tolerance for human frailty would probably seem to the medieval man rather the approbation for that which should be deplored.

His hero is exemplary, even when damnable, like Dr.
Faustus.

Medieval narratives are not devious in their means or
uncertain in their moral focus. The principal personages
are clearly named at the outset, their predicaments are
forthrightly indicated, their responses specified.... In the
Arthurian tales the reader is seldom in doubt as to the
virtues, or lack thereof, of the principal figures: Sir
Galahad is not secretly a rascal, nor is Mordred, underneath it all, a decent chap whose only problem consists in
being misunderstood by his father the king.[8]

Berger's retelling of the Arthur legend has a double focus, at
once true to the heroic essence of the myth while searching for the
deeper truths beneath that heroism and its tragic end. He has
indicated the complicated nature of this double focus with the
observation:

We now know that greatness, wisdom, and courage are
necessarily conjoined with selfishness, childishness, and
petulance—had not Winston Churchill been an
egomaniac, Britain would have fallen to Hitler, to give a
political example. What is "old" in the Arthurian myth is
that God loves the knights of the Round Table and hates
their enemies. (11 February 1977)

Or, as Berger has put this dichotomy another way, "The Arthurian legend is essentially infantile: and you must understand
that I believe children are naturally vicious" (2 April 1977).[9] One
of Berger's most compelling characters, Gawaine, most human and
ultimately the wisest of Arthur's knights, suggests some of the
effects of Berger's belief when, late in his life, he is asked by a
brother if he does not long for the old days of action:

'Nay,' said Sir Gawaine. 'I am happy to have had them in
my proper time, but of a life of adventure it can be said
that there is no abiding satisfaction, for when one

adventure is done, a knight liveth in expectation of another, and if the next come not soon enough he falleth in love, in the sort of love that is an adventure, for what he seeketh be the adventure and not the lovingness. And methinks this sequence is finally infantile, and beyond a certain age one can no longer be interested in games.' (361)[10]

By pursuing some of the adult and ironic implications of the Arthur legend, Berger's retelling in no way diminishes the glory of Arthur's attempt or the measure of his achievement, but it does devote greater attention to the cause of the legend's final tragedy. In one sense, that tragedy centers not on the dissolution of the Round Table nor on the estranging of Arthur, Guinevere, and Launcelot, but on the erosion of the innocently idealistic belief that life can be governed by the simple principle of opposing good to evil. Likewise, Arthur painfully discovers that his code of chivalry has as its primary side effect the limiting of the king's freedom to do his own will. That a king may not be free and that doing good may have evil consequences are but two of the many ironies of the Arthur story, and it is those ironic notes that Berger's novel sounds again and again. Complexity finally overwhelms Arthur and even the wicked who oppose him, uniting both "good" and "evil" in the crucible of irony. Berger's narrator specifies that the tragedy of the Round Table lay not in its dissolution but in the cause of its fall, "for this was the only time that a king had set out to rule on principles of absolute virtue, and to fight evil and to champion the good, and though it was not the first time that a king fell out with his followers, it was unique in happening not by wicked design but rather by the helpless accidents of fine men who meant well and who loved one another dearly" (447). Only when engaged in mortal combat with his fellow knight and respected friend, Gawaine, does Launcelot reflect "on the differences amongst men, and how though a company of them might hold the same principles, each member might honestly interpret these in another way" (462).

Nor does complexity spare the evil, even when they try to reform. Berger's Sir Meliagrant captures and imprisons Guinevere, only to be so confounded by that "metaphysical lady" that he reluctantly renounces his evil métier in hope of winning her love. However, "whereas he had been fearsome when vile, he was but a booby when he did other than ill," and his decision to reform leads in quick succession to his being robbed and wounded by a beggar, then killed in a fight he knew he could not win with Launcelot. "This honor," muses Sir Meliagrant before his death, "can be a taxing thing" (175). In somewhat similar fashion, having had little success in her schemes against Arthur, the crafty Morgan la Fey finally enters a nunnery, "for after a long career in the service of evil she had come to believe that corruption were sooner brought amongst humankind by the forces of virtue, and from this moment on she was notable for her piety" (453).

Morgan represents one of Berger's most distinctive contributions to the legend of Arthur: giving the nature of evil intention its day in the court of myth.[11] By giving Morgan a degree of insight that transcends her seemingly simple malevolence (she instructs Mordred, "The great purpose in doing evil is to defy the good, dear boy!"), Berger makes her an appropriately complicated inverse of Guinevere. Both women seek power, but only Morgan understands the significance of her search.

Arthur knows when he formulates his code of chivalry that his efforts, being human, will ultimately fail, but he insists that they can fail gloriously, since glory "doth come only from a quest for that which is impossible of attainment." What he does not know is that strict adherence to a rigid code of conduct may create more problems than it solves, threaten order more than ensure it. What dawns too slowly on Arthur and some of his knights is the realization that the Code of Chivalry, like any system of abstract definitions and principles, comes into conflict with itself if pursued too blindly. After Gawaine's honor demands that he avenge his father's death at the hand of another knight, even though that death was itself justified by the requirements of honor, Arthur sadly notes that the code's guidance begins to blur because "distinctions are sometimes hard to draw, for our obligations do oft war each on each." To Launcelot, Arthur admits that "evil doing hath got more subtle, perhaps even to the point at which it can not properly be encountered with the sword" (392).

In Berger's hands, the warring of obligations to equally compelling rationales for action finally leads the two greatest of Arthur's knights, Launcelot and Gawaine, to fight each other. During that sad fight, Launcelot suddenly understands that "if Gawaine's morality were complex, it was because chivalry in general was more complicated than it seemed, for it is not easy always to know what is the noble thing, or what is brave and generous or even simply decent" (461). One of the many ironies in Berger's narrative is that as these two greatest knights fight to the death, Launcelot prevails in arms even as he begins to understand that Gawaine has bettered him in understanding. Similarly, Arthur's most anguishing discovery is not that he has been betrayed by his queen and his most trusted knight, but that his philosophy has been shallow. Too late comes his tragic epiphany that "to the profound vision there is no virtue and no vice, and what is justice to one, is injustice to another," a sentiment strikingly similar to Nietzsche's conceptual formula for Aeschylus' Prometheus: "All that exists is just and unjust and equally justified in both."

Despite this central flaw in Arthur's great dream, Berger makes it clear that Arthur's legend is not to be judged or reevaluated by the dream's success or failure. Nor in this or any other Berger novel should irony be mistaken for absurdity. The Lady of the Lake assures the dying Arthur that he could not have done better in his life than he did, and the ghost of Sir Gawaine offers to his king the Round Table's poignant epitaph: "we sought no easy victories, nor won any. And perhaps for that we will be remembered" (484).

As with all tellers of the story of King Arthur, Berger's central concern is with reminding us that while the matter of myth and history may not be the same, both may be equally true or equally false. When he describes one of his literary ancestors, Geoffrey of Monmouth as "a shameless mythomaniac," who "was as successful as any modern statesman in fobbing off fiction as fact," Berger is not criticizing either chronicler or politician, but reminding us that language has long been the most important reality (11 February 1977). The final words of Berger's narrator specify that King Arthur "was never historical, but everything he did was true," a distinction maintained in Berger's subtitling *Arthur Rex* "A Legendary Novel." In Berger's view of things the legendary should not be confused with the spurious, particularly since, as his narrator wryly observes, "it is only in the historical world that a reputation can be gained by talk alone, and in the realm of legend only deeds are counted" (427).

Berger illustrates in several ways the literal application of his narrator's claim that all men of Arthur's time "lived and died by legend" and surely agrees with the conclusion that without legend "the world hath become a mean place" (433). Nevertheless, Berger steadfastly refuses to let *Arthur Rex* slip into nostalgia for a lost world of simple heroism and gallantry. Instead, he urges us to contemplate the enduring complexities of the transitory joy and tragedy of the Round Table.

While many critics have noted the importance of the conflict between illusion and reality as a major theme in the Arthur stories, Berger seems much more interested in this conflict at the level of telling or writing itself: his novel questions or exposes many illusions in the "events" of Arthur's world, but does so ever in pursuit of a more rigorous sense of the "reality" of that imagined world; moreover, Berger seems to believe that the application of greater rigor to the presentation of Arthur's world in no way conflicts with an ultimate allegiance to its myths. Here, as elsewhere in his novels, Berger is never contumacious toward the legendary.

Berger's *agent provocateur* in subtly redirecting our attention toward newly understandable aspects of the Arthur legend is, of course, his unnamed narrator — certainly Berger's most original character. It is through this narrator that Berger pays homage to Malory while refusing to make his own the limits of Malory's vision, and it is through this narrator that Berger creates not just another "version" of the Arthur story, but a comment on the traditions of its telling.

The narrator of *Arthur Rex* uniquely mirrors the dilemma of the characters in his story in that his obligations to various narrative traditions "do oft war each on each," while the panache of his prose style rivals the panache of their lives. His telling celebrates Malory and strives to be true to Malory's spirit as well as to the larger tradition of Arthurian legend, but Berger's narrator differs from his masters in at least four major respects. Perhaps most obviously, Berger's narrator follows the conventions of Christian piety, as Malory took great pains to do, but undercuts that phatic piety with much pragmatic assessment and critique of Christianity as a system of belief. Two important corollaries to this subtle shift are that the narrator ever redirects our attention from the norms of knightly conduct to the realities of power and, while respecting the conventions of the age's conception of women to the point of consistently "revealing" his chauvinistic subscription to that conception, even more consistently portrays the women in the Arthur legend as the only characters deep enough and realistic enough to understand its meanings. Finally, Berger so draws his narrator as to use him, both implicitly and explicitly, as a commentator on the language and the literature of the Arthur story.

The narrator's very vocabulary constitutes another kind of commentary generated by Berger's ever present fascination with the stuff of language. A relatively small number of antique words pepper his narration, making it sound appropriate with crisp efficiency. Surprisingly few of those antique usages have to do with technical terms describing arms or dress; lances are "fewtered," castles have "machicolations," and cloth is invariably "samite" or "sendal," but the balance of the narrator's antique lexicon seems chosen for linguistic interest rather than for realistic utility. In this process "harlot" appears as a male modifier, "wench" appears as curse more than simple description, and the near brutal pun on "queen" and "quean" is directed toward Guinevere, each use historically precise. An even more interesting phenomenon, however, lies in the narrator's use of words whose modern sense has acquired enough connotative baggage to overload root meanings — words such as "boor," "villein," "churl," "clown," even "furniture," or words which have somehow been lost in modern commonplaces — as "fell" has disappeared into "fell swoop," "ruth" into "ruthless" and "jade" into "jaded." Thus, in matters philological as well as moral, Berger's narrator proves a remarkably engaging story teller. Inherently a human construct with obvious biases and generally predictable opinions, he may not always compel our agreement, but his pronouncements consistently merit our consideration.

From the outset of Berger's novel, the narrator reveals both his essential allegiance to events as set down by Malory and his intent to establish a distinctive voice for his telling. For example, Malory takes several pages to explain the somewhat tortured sequence of events which preceded King Uther's war on the Duke of Cornwall, while Berger's narrator cuts through all such preliminary explanations and rhetorical façades to the substance of the matter, specifying that substance in a single sentence: "Now Uther Pendragon, King of all Britain, conceived an inordinate passion for the fair Ygraine, duchess of Cornwall, and having otherwise no access to her, he proceeded to wage war upon her husband, Gorlois the duke" (1). Likewise, while the mere presence of the dying Uther on the battlefield is enough for Malory to explain a British victory over the Saxons, Berger's narrator, ever concerned with the powers of language, suggests that Uther's rhetoric proved more instrumental than his presence, as he "urged his host on in such words as these":

> "Cut down the shit–eaters and carve their rotten bellies
> out and wind their stinking guts around their necks and
> drive staves up their dirty arseholes. Rip off their ballocks

and shove them down their muzzles," and so on in language of the greatest eloquence for its effect on the British warrior. (24)

Malory repeatedly invokes the authority of his source, noting that events proceed "as the French book sayeth," but Berger builds his narrative with only an occasional nod to "the old scribes" and with one striking acknowledgement to Malory himself, when Berger's narrator quotes what that "great knight hath written" of the possibility of Arthur's return: "Yet I woll nat say that hit shall be so, but rather I wolde sey: here in thys worlde he chaunges hys lyff" (497). Berger has obviously studied the Arthur legend in its many variants, but has no intention of "following" any of the older scribes. As his jacket cover note cheerfully claims:

> Mr. Berger has ransacked the work of his great predecessors, from Wace to Wagner, for elements he could exploit in this volume (and his debt to his principal master, Sir Thomas, is obvious), but the further he proceeds with his own hallucinations, the more peculiarly personal becomes his narrative.

What he does follow is the *example* of Malory who drew from, mixed together, deleted, expanded on, and sometimes simply copied his own sources. And in celebrating the master's technique, Berger proves himself, if not the better, at least a modern maker, as his telling of the Arthur story displays an unmistakable unity, woven by the point of view of a narrator identified by Berger as "God, I suppose, though not the Judaeo–Xtian one, whom I've never found at all eloquent" (30 October 1981).

The rigidity of hierarchical thinking emerges as the primary— though unacknowledged—target of Berger's narrator, as he relies most heavily on the drawing of hierarchical distinctions to characterize the spirit of Arthur's age. Central to the problem of hierarchical thinking as well as central to the originality of Berger's telling is the blindness of Arthurian men to the wisdom of Arthurian women. "For not even Merlin, with all his arts, could divine the ways of women," but Berger relates this seeming mystery to the also misunderstood nature of power in general. Berger has claimed of *Arthur Rex* that in it "perhaps for the first time since Marie de France, the queens and princesses are permitted their due in the tales, of which they are the traditional survivors; and as Launcelot, invincible on the field, must defer to Guinevere in the boudoir, so must Tristram be shown as the helpless sex–object of two Isolds."

Even more significant in this respect is the emphasis Berger gives to Gawaine's tutoring by the Lady of the Lake which culminates in his finest and most philosophical act—his marriage to and subsequent acknowledgment of the free will of Lady Ragnell. "Thou art not an object which I possess like unto a suit of armor," reasons Gawaine. "Thou art one of God's creatures, and in all fundamental matters thou must answer only to Him" (325). Her enchantment broken precisely by his refusing to exercise a power over her clearly granted him by the hierarchical schema of their time, Lady Ragnell calls attention to one of the many ironies implicit in Berger's presentation, explaining to Gawaine: "And in allowing me mine own choice, thou hast liberated me in more ways than one" (326). In embedding "The Wedding of Sir Gawaine and Dame Ragnell" in his Arthur story, Berger most clearly rejects Malory's depiction of Gawaine and the simple chauvinism of most medieval narratives, for despite the perfunctory condescension of his narrator ("And so with females, of whom the wise man saith, *Turn them upside down, they do look much the same...*"), Berger's women are by far the most interesting characters in *Arthur Rex,* and his most wise. In their reaction to the world around them lies a sure sign that the sensibility behind what has been persuasively called "the Arthur book for our time," is that of Thomas Berger.

University of Iowa

NOTES

[1] James Atlas, "Chivalry Is Dead," *Time*, 25 September 1978, 110.

[2] I am grateful to Thomas Berger for providing me with this correspondence. Subsequent dates in parentheses refer to Berger's letters to me.

[3] John Romano, "Camelot and All That," *New York Times Book Review*, 12 November 1978, 62.

[4] I offer a much extended reading of *Arthur Rex* in the fourth chapter of my *Thomas Berger* (Boston: Twayne, 1989).

[5] All subsequent page references are to the 1978 Delacorte edition of *Arthur Rex*.

[6] Garrett Epps, Review of *Arthur Rex, New Republic*, 7 October 1978, 34.

[7] Michael Malone, "Berger, Burlesque, and the Yearning for Comedy," *Studies in American Humor*, 2 (Spring 1983): 24. Of his own efforts, Berger has detailed:

> ...I dealt with only the half–dozen very greatest knights, and I ignored several of the classic tales. One had here an even greater wealth of material than with *Little Big Man*, but whereas with *LBM* I was concerned with getting into the text at least some reference to every Western theme, with Arthur I felt no such obligation. After all, these legends are nine or ten centuries old, and first appear in written form in the work of such masters as Chrétien de Troyes, Wolfram von Eschenbach, and Gottfried von Strassburg, and then are assembled by Sir Tom Malory in Olympian prose. Like my predecessors I have honored the existing traditions while adding some special emphases of my own.
>
> Insofar as I relied on the sources, they were the oldest. Tennyson has a quaintness that disqualifies him al-

together, and Mark Twain's *Connecticut Yankee* is un-
speakably vulgar rubbish. T. H. White's *Once and Future
King*, which I quickly scanned, was quite properly turned
into the Broadway musical *Camelot*.... (6 November 1977)

[8]Thomas Berger, Foreword to *German Medieval Tales*, ed.
Francis G. Gentry (New York: Continuum, 1983), viii.

[9]Some ten years after making this remark, Berger clarified
that in calling children "naturally vicious," he was calling them
"not evil but human." He concluded: "I am not a Rousseauist: I do
not believe that man is born either free or innocent" (7 August
1987).

[10]One of the most significant of Berger's subtle shifts of
emphasis is that for all the *pro forma* declarations of the primacy
of Launcelot, Gawaine clearly emerges as Berger's "best" knight.
In the Arthurian pantheon of superlative qualities, Gawaine
appears to offer a kind of golden mean. As the Green Knight
explains to Gawaine, "To be greater than you is to be tragic; to be
less, farcical" (214).

[11]Berger's comment on his spelling:

"Morgan la Fey" is my version. Elsewhere...she is usually
called "le Fee" or "le Fey," but that has always annoyed
me. The French for "fairy" is "la fee," and if Malory et al.
used "le" it was probably through ignorance. However,
there are various versions of many of the names; spelling
has never been standardized, to my knowledge, for the
Arthurian legends. I used "Launcelot" so that it would be
pronounced "LAW..." and not the fat "LAA..." used by
Yanks. (21 April 1985)

Walker Percy's Grail

J. Donald Crowley and Sue Mitchell Crowley

> In the concept of the Second Coming the motif of
> Withdrawal–and–Return attains its deepest spiritual
> meaning. . . . In the myth of the Second Coming of Arthur,
> . . . the vanquished Britons consoled themselves for the
> failure of the historic Arthur to avert the ultimate victory
> of the English barbarian invaders. — **Arnold Toynbee**

>   I think
>   that we
> Shall never more, at any future time,
> Delight our souls with talk of knightly deeds,
> Walking about the gardens and the halls
> Of Camelot, as in the days that were.
> I perish by this people which I made, —
> Tho' Merlin swore that I should come again...
>   — **Tennyson, "Morte D'Arthur"**

Since Walker Percy has characterized himself as a Catholic existentialist,[1] it is not surprising that his fictional heroes are questers, that each is *homo viator*,[2] a sovereign wayfarer. Nor is it surprising that both the way and the goal of these spiritual travelers inheres in sacrament. Insofar as Percy's "knights" inhabit a postmodern world, they suffer and confront both the internal monsters of Kierkegaardian dread and despair and the Heideggerrian malaise of everydayness, endemic with its external monsters of a desacralized culture. This double trajectory — a fiction that projects philosophical and theological understandings and values and, at the same time, criticizes the civilization that has lost those values — has marked Percy's work since his first novel, *The Moviegoer*.[3] How, he seems always to have asked, does one speak to a secular culture? How does one begin, particularly in America (and, to be sure, as a Catholic), to begin again, to make a "new earth" or, more properly, renew the old, old one. Possessed of a prophetic–apocalyptic quality in plot and tone, conceived in the complexly linear time structure of the Judaeo–Christian tradition, Percy's works as fictional critique ponder the past and present and thrust forward into an increasingly uncertain future. Binx Bolling of *The Moviegoer* (1961) and Will Barrett of *The Last Gentleman* (1966) are on horizontal searches for faith; Dr. Tom More, a fallen version of his namesake (Percy's own knight of faith — that eminently practical saint who stood against the adultery of his king and tried to save the old church in England, Sir Thomas More), is in *Love in the Ruins: The Adventures of a Bad Catholic at a Time Near the End of the World* (1971) and *The Thanatos Syndrome* (1987) struggling against a wasteland of secularism in which science and sex, both exclusively genital now, reign supreme.

As Percy's theologically based critical commentary has evolved, his readers have become growingly aware that it is born out of a broad sweeping mythical–historical vision. Percy is in his historical understanding greatly indebted to Arnold Toynbee's *Study of History*,[4] particularly to Toynbee's views on the endurance of the Jews in history, and the Incarnation, the god–man, as the ultimate and only lasting conception of withdrawal and return. Though their own religious convictions are quite disparate, Percy is, no less than Toynbee, fascinated with the manner in which the thought of the Mediterranean world was a crucible of Christianity. He is concerned, too, with the negative as well as positive influence of Greek and Roman philosophy on later Christian thought. This long view is personalized in all Percy's fiction because of his overriding need, in the light of his own conversion to Roman Catholicism, to work through what he calls the southern Stoicism of his own ancestors, especially of William Alexander Percy, the man of letters who raised him.

In a 1956 *Commonweal* essay, "Stoicism in the South," Percy makes the connections that will frequently inform his later fiction: preeminent among those ideas are Roman Stoicism, the southern tradition, and the Arthurian legends:

The greatness of the South, like the greatness of the English squirearchy, had always a stronger Greek flavor than it ever had a Christian. Its nobility and graciousness was the nobility and graciousness of the old Stoa. . . . If the Stoic way was remarkably suited to the Empire of the first century, it was quite as remarkably suited to the agrarian South of the last century. . . . It was a far nobler relationship than what usually passes under the name of paternalism. The nobility of Sartoris . . . was the nobility of the natural perfection of the Stoics, the stern inner summons to man's full estate, to duty, to honor, to generosity toward his fellowmen and above all to his inferiors—not because they were made in the image of God and were therefore lovable in themselves, but because to do them an injustice would be to defile the inner fortress which was oneself. . . . For the Southern Stoic the day has been lost and lost for good. . . . Southern society was above all a society of manners, an incredible triumph of manners, and a twilight of manners seems a twilight of the world. For the Stoic there is no real hope. His finest hour is to sit tight-lipped and ironic while the world comes crashing down around him.

It must be otherwise with the Christian. The urban plebs is not the mass which is to be abandoned to its own barbaric devices, but the lump to be leavened. The Christian is optimistic precisely where the Stoic is pessimistic. . . . We in the South can no longer afford the luxury of maintaining the Stoa beside the Christian edifice. In the past we managed the remarkable feat of keeping both, one for living in, the other for dying in. But the Church is no longer content to perform rites of passage; she has entered the arena of the living and must be reckoned with.[5]

Arthurian motifs occur often in the densely allusive texture of Percy's fiction: they serve regularly as paradigms for the southern code of Stoicism in the face of defeat. Where Percy employs the Arthurian legends he does so with two very complexly interrelated intentions. On the one hand, he parodies the chivalric code which he associates with the

Stoicism of the ante- and post-bellum South; on the other hand, he discovers an antidote for that Stoa, that Roman inheritance of aristocratic paternalism, absolute reliance on reason, and heroic resignation before the dictates of fate, in a conception of the human being as incarnate creature, participating both in the fall and its many consequences—most pointedly in a quest, both individual and communal, for the Grail, not as provocative literary and legendary symbol but in its ultimate incarnational meaning as sacrament.

Percy's earliest fictional embodiment of southern Stoicism is Binx Bolling's Aunt Emily Cutrer (a portrait, in fact, of his "Uncle" Will Percy) in *The Moviegoer*. If Binx is the Kierkegaardian aesthete, Emily is the ethical dowager who values manners and doing "the right thing." Certain of Binx's ancestors, like Percy's own, have been well-known military men. Emily's brother Alex, the one with "the Rupert Brooke–Galahad sort of face," (24) died in the Argonne a hero's death held "as fitting since the original Alex Bolling was killed with Roberdaux Wheat in the Hood breakthrough at Gaines Mills in 1862" (24-25). And so, when Binx's little brother dies his aunt explains that he must "act like a soldier" (4). Emily, the darling of her brothers, sees herself as "the female sport of a fierce old warrior gens" (26). After a career in volunteer public service which culminated in Red Cross service in the Spanish Civil War, she has married a well-to-do Creole and settled in the Garden District to become "as handsome and formidable as her brothers, soldierly in both look and outlook, . . . at sixty-five still the young prince" (27). Her husband Jules, participating, if more passively, in her chivalric code, can describe a Tulane goal-line stand against LSU as "King Arthur standing fast in the bloodred sunset against Sir Modred and the traitors" (30). So goes one of Percy's anticly postmodern transmogrifications of Arthurian materials.

Emily regards herself as "an Episcopalian by emotion, a Greek by nature and a Buddhist by choice" (23). A patron of good causes and the arts and possessed of a Socratic manner, she is strongly individualistic, philosophical, serene, and self-righteous. Like the Roman Stoics and Arthur in his defeat, she fears that "the fabric is dissolving" (54) but, adds Percy, "for her even the dissolving makes sense. She understands the chaos to come." She sees the "barbarians at the inner gate" (133) with no one to defend the West, and the future as her own "Dover Beach" of "the going under of the evening land" (54). The world itself is "an insignificant cinder spinning away in a dark corner of the universe," and the reason for human existence "a secret which the high gods have not confided" to her (54). She is the embodiment of William Alexander Percy's devotion to the resignation of Marcus Aurelius. She is less than resigned, however, when she suspects that Binx has betrayed her code by sexually compromising her stepdaughter Kate; Emily, "as erect and handsome as the Black Prince," (221) accuses him of breaking his trust. In fact, Binx and Kate's failed sexual encounter on the train to Chicago is the outward sign of that inner grace which permits their mutual discovery of a deeper intimacy as creatures in despair on a common journey, as co-questers in the religious mode.

Percy symbolizes Emily's moral rectitude and lack of a supernatural religious understanding with a distinctly Arthurian metaphor. As she confronts Binx on his return from Chicago, they both gaze at a letter opener, a small Excalibur, the "soft iron sword she has withdrawn from the grasp of the helmeted figure on the inkstand" (221). Emily realizes that the tip of the blade is bent, and Binx, ever the existential questioner, is acutely conscious now that, years before, he himself had bent it in trying to open a drawer. Emily, relentless Stoic, now accuses him of breaking "sacred trust" that involves the common assumptions of "gentlefolk" who share "a native instinct for behavior, a natural piety or grace," a certain kind of "class," over against the "common" people, who have "enshrined mediocrity" as a national ideal. Emily "raises the sword to Prytania Street" (222-24) and explains that she has tried to "save" him: "More than anything I wanted to pass on to you the one heritage of the men of our family, a certain quality of spirit, a gaiety, a sense of duty, a nobility worn lightly, a sweetness, a gentleness with women—the only good things the South ever had and the only things that really matter in this life" (224). However, Binx will find his Grail, not in an idealized past but rather in the present of the communal feast of fish with his mother and her family, in the Mass they attend together, in his handicapped and holy brother Lonnie's devotion to sacramental Penance and his request for the last rites, and, finally, in his love for and marriage to Kate.

If Percy has given us Binx as his Kierkegaardian "knight of faith," in the "knight" of his fourth novel, *Lancelot*,[6] the reader is confronted with a complete antihero in search of an Unholy Grail. This "grail" Lancelot Andrewes Lamar will define as sin and, then more precisely, as sexual sin. He relives his quest as he makes a deeply perverse anticonfession to an old friend and failed priest-psychiatrist, whom long years ago in his youth he had begun to call "Percival." His unconscious self-revelation continues for 257 pages and forms the basis of the very complex structure of the novel. Lance tells the priest:

> I don't know why I want to talk to you or what I need to tell you
> or need to hear from you. . . . I have to tell you in order to know
> what I already know. . . . Perhaps I talk to you because of your
> silence (85).

The confessor with his "hooded look" speaks only in the last two pages of the novel and then, like the knight of the Wasteland, to infer a question and to imply, cryptically, that there is an answer. At the same time, however, Percy controls Lancelot's narrative in such a way that Percival—who, as much as his Arthurian prototype, has had a life of relentless difficulty and uncertainty in defining his true vocation—becomes extraordinarily present as a character, and the reader begins to understand that, for him as well, "there is something wrong." For Percival will come to know the nature of his own quest only when he hears the story of Lance's antithetical one. As the medieval friends Lancelot and Percival sought each other during their Grail quests, so these two twentieth-century souls are deeply interdependent and, in Percy's word, potentially "intersubjective." They share a story fraught with Arthurian names, symbols and situations, and give that story two possible endings, not totally unlike the divergent destinies of their paradigms. Percy's parodic art leaves little doubt that there are also in *Lancelot* echoes and correspondences to the homecoming of Odysseus, but these are by no means as dominant as the parallels to Arthurian materials in his scheme here of employing myth to illustrate history.

The legendary Launcelot understood his singleminded passion for Guinevere as a guilty love. For a time he wandered in the forest, driven mad by public scorn and personal shame. Though he struggled to tear his two loves asunder in his heart, his one poisonous sin was inextricably bound to his quest, and he was doomed to follow wandering fires to the end of his days. On the other hand, Percival was characterized as "The Pure," that is, possessed, not only of chastity but of purity of intention, purity of heart. All his other endeavors turned to dust because he was destined for a single quest. Readers of Malory will recall that after Launcelot has been sent from "the holy place" where the knight was healed, he curses the day of his birth and comprehends that it is his adultery with the queen and his betrayal of his king that have prevented him from an actual vision of the Sangreal. Then, coming upon a hermitage and a hermit, Launcelot "prayed him for charity for to hear his life" (XI, 190).[7] The hermit, a man of great good will, marvels that the knight looks so "abashed," and he senses somehow that God must love him. The hermit warns Launcelot that, though he is the greatest knight in the world, he has been deeply presumptuous in seeking to be "where His flesh and His blood was" while still unshriven of his "lechery." Though Launcelot makes his confession and is enjoined to do penance, he is nonetheless never free of his love of Guinevere and forgets "the promise and the perfection that he made in the quest."[8]

Percy's Lance has as his hermitage a New Orleans "Center for Aberrant Behavior" following the explosion of his ancestral home, Belle Isle, in which the bodies of his wife and three others are found, and it is only late in the course of the novel that the reader knows that Lance has been incarcerated for having wreaked his vengeance by multiple murder violent and obscene. From the cell Lance and, later, Percival as well look down on both "Lafayette Cemetery," suggestive of both revolutionary chivalry and death, and "Annunciation Street," evocative of new, redemptive life in the Incarnation. This dual view points directly to the opposing choices open to Lance and his old friend at the end of the novel.

Lance sees Percival, in his J. C. (a singular but typical Percy word-play) Penney pantsuit, standing in the graveyard with a woman who is scrubbing the white New Orleans tombs and who apparently asks the priest to pray for the dead. It is All Souls' Day, a feast that (like Christmas) would permit Father John to say three masses, but he apparently refuses the request. Percy seems to be indicating that the priest considers himself unworthy because he himself knows that he suffers from the "sickness unto death." Lance, too, suffers from despair and has a shock of recognition; at the sight of Percival he feels he is "overtaken by the past" and is seeing himself. Lance, however, suffers from what Kierkegaard calls the despair of defiance, truly demonic despair, so what he encounters in Percival is a former self or the self he might have been. Lance invites Percival to "Come into my cell" (3). These two deconstructed – or reconstructed – Arthurian knights then reenact in a radically postmodern and desacralized setting essential elements of the relationship between their literary/legendary ancestors.

In earlier days when he lived at Northumberland near Belle Isle, Percival, though he was not pugnacious but brilliant, obscure and withdrawn, bore the misnomer Harry Hotspur. He was built "like Pius XII" but called Prince Hal because he seemed happy only in whorehouses. "Also," Percy writes in an emphatic fragment – "as Percival and Parsifal, who found the Grail and brought life to a dead land" (10). Now he is Father John, either because he is a loner like the Baptist, or because he loved much like the Evangelist. Like Percival, Lance was part of the gone-to-pot Anglo-Saxon aristocracy which inhabited the River Road, called "the English Coast" since it was an enclave of British gentry united by a crazy-quilt dislike both of Catholics and the Longs. Unlike the Creoles who have mastered the secret of living ordinary lives well, making money and "making" Mardi Gras, their "honorable" families "lived from one great event to another, tragic events, triumphant events, with years of melancholy in between. They lost at Vicksburg and Shiloh, "fought duels, defied Huey Long, and were bored to death between times" (23-24). In contrast to the River Road, Percy characterizes New Orleans proper as a Catholic city, not really part of the

South, a city which has had no heroes in three hundred years and has its cathedral set in the Vieux Carré in a concentration of sin.

The Anglo–Saxon backgrounds shared by Lancelot and Percival have, however, resulted in strikingly different careers. Percival, perhaps because the men in his family are prone to depression and early suicide, has found Louisiana "not good enough for him" and chosen to work in Biafra. Lance, whose life peaked in college when he became a Rhodes scholar, had become a nonpracticing lawyer and a liberal gone sour, devoted on the one hand to rather paternalistic civil rights endeavors and, on the other, to publishing nostalgic essays on Civil War skirmishes in the *Louisiana Historical Journal*. In all this he had rather forlornly repeated the same dilettante efforts of his own father without knowing it. And he had done so because, being one of Percy's seemingly incurable romantics who puts his most cherished ideals just out of his reach, he is drawn, like his father (and, to be sure, Nick Carraway besides), inexorably into the past. That father, Maury, had been poet-laureate of Feliciana Parish, busying himself with publishing vignettes of historical events and non-Roman churches. His library was filled with romantic English poetry, the Waverley novels, Episcopal Church history, southern history and biographies of Robert E. Lee. He loved Lee "the way Catholics love St. Francis" (116): the Confederate hero had become for him "as legendary and mythical as King Arthur and the Round Table." The books indicate the reasons for the name given him by his father:

> Do you think I was named Lancelot for nothing? The Andrewes was tacked on by him to give it Episcopal sanction, but what he really had in mind ... was that old nonexistent Catholic brawler and adulterer, Lancelot du Lac, King Ban of Benwick's son, knight of the Round Table and—here was the part he could never get over [or, it seems, get right]—one of only two knights to see the Grail (you, Percival, the other); and above all the extraordinariness of those chaste and incorrupt little Anglican chapels set down in this violent and corrupt land besieged on all sides by savage Indians, superstitious Romans, mealy-mouthed Baptists, howling Holy Rollers. (116)

"What's in a name?" all Percy's work would seem to ask. In this novel and in Lance's name there are, clearly, genes and destiny, the maddened living and killing, and the need both to tell and hear of it, the re-living of the whole after the fact.

Whether Lance's father and mother saw themselves in this romantic light, or Lance chooses to recall them in this way is unclear. But the romance dissolved in each case as the young Lance made his first discoveries of evil. The first took the form of an ill-gotten $10,000 found under the argyle socks in Maury's drawer. Lance recalls his sense of delight as his eyes devoured the money, "the sweet shameful heart of something, the secret." The reader has an early clue to his later quest: "There is no secret in honor. If one could but discover the secret at the heart of dishonor" (213). While his father had been tending to such business, Lance's mother Lily had been having a kind of courtly love relationship with "Uncle" Harry Wills, a Mardi Gras krewe knight in a Duke's costume, who gives Lance gifts of a glass pistol with candy inside and a Swiss army knife. Thus, Maury, a cuckold, a sorrily trivialized Arthur, became a sort of role model for his son, precursor of Lance's own cuckolding. And Lily, a clear parody of the maid of Astolat, was "like a lovebird. She lived for love. Literally. Unless she was loved, she withered and died" (212). In this mix love seems to join money as twin bitch goddesses in Percy's postmodern American culture.

It is Lance's mysterious Cousin Callie who, appearing from out of the hurricane at the end of the novel, wearing an out-of-season camellia, like Dumas' Camille, pinned to her shoulder, provides us with Lance's reminiscence of Lily. In fact, Lance begins to confuse the two, perceiving them both as fallen women. He remembers Lily in a picture of a VMI military wedding, prankishly "proffering an unsheathed sword" to the photographer (225): "The sword is upright, the blade held in her hands, the hand guard making a cross." There he sees her as a Joan of Arc, but his ultimate mental picture of Lily has her with Uncle Harry "in the linoleum-cold gas-heat-hot tourist cabin" (216). Are these two his mother and father? The reader, with Lance, wonders. With all his rich heritage of names, Lance literally—and spiritually—does not know, cannot know whence he sprang. He must question his own paternity as he will later that of his daughter.

Continually within the point of view of his gnostic—even Manichean—hero's memory and current consciousness, Percy complicates these pictures of human evil with one of surd evil. Lancelot recalls that he was "in love" with Lucy Cobb. As a Louisiana football hero, from a state in which people valued fistfights and cockfights, Lance met the Georgian Lucy in Highlands, North Carolina, where the easy decorous manners of the eastern South prevailed. They were married, moved to Belle Isle and had two children. "Then," Lance says, "she died." Of Elaine, the Lily Maid of Astolet, who simply ceases breathing and dies of her love for Lancelot, Tennyson writes:

> She grew so cheerful that they deem'd her death
> Was rather in the fantasy than the blood.[9]

In Lucy the cause is leukemia and the fantasy in the mind and character of her husband, as Percy creates another, radically different version of the romantic Lily Maid.

Lance himself is unromantically discharged from the army, "not bloody and victorious and battered by Sir Turquine but with persistent diarrhea" (28). In the second generation Lance has witnessed not only the end of heroism but the decay of courtly love. The antithesis of the pure knight of the Grail, his son is no Galahad—consummate finder of the real grail—but bisexual and living in an old streetcar. And this Galahad has a sister seduced by a lesbian.

If Lucy was Lance's romantic past, Margot, his second wife, despite her infatuation with the crafts, the artifacts of the past, becomes his present. Belle Isle, fallen on hard times, opens its doors to tourists on the Azalea Trail, and Margot, from Texas with ten million, has become a "belle." Though it is impossible for new money to participate in the Comus ball, the Azalea Festival is a uniting of the oil rich and old, broke River Road gentry, the very same "rare royal betrothal" Margot and Lance will make. Less coy than Scarlett, Margot, Percy tells us, met the master of Belle Isle and promptly doffed her ante-bellum costume in order to become its mistress: "Damned if the hoop skirt didn't work like chaps" (75). Margot has a Morgan le Faye-like gift for transformations. Now, in his cell, Lance feels that he himself was transformed by Margot. He ponders what love is and speaks to Percival: "For by your dear sweet Jesus I did love her there for her droll mercinariness and between her sweet legs and in her mouth . . ." (81). The "there," where he first made love to Margot, is the pigeonnier of Belle Isle. Along with the hospital cell, the pigeonnier is a critically important place of discovery in the novel, at once the Oriel of Launcelot and Guinevere and the Chapel Perilous of a question to be answered. It is there that Lance and Percival had first read *Ulysses* and discovered sex and the anger of an Odyssean hero whose wife has other suitors.[10] Margot can (or could), however, be like Morgan, both helpful and malicious in her crafts. Lance describes how this "Texas magician" transformed Belle Isle with its Carrara mantelpiece, English antiques and slave chairs, back to its original state. In addition, she turned the pigeonnier into a kind of "hunting lodge"-office for Lance. But, Lance explains, when she was finished with Belle Isle, she was finished with him.

Margot's new project involves a film crew at work on the new enchantment, twentieth-century cinematic magic, which will employ Belle Isle as well as a miniature steamboat on False River as settings. Margot has only a bit part and acts as girl Friday to Merlin, the Hemingwayesque director; Lance, in the background off-stage, is adviser on matters of southern history. Margot, having transformed the ancestral home to a celluloid stage-set, has her future sights set on playing Nora in "A Doll's House" for Janos Jacoby, co-director and alter-Merlin, who seems actually to be in charge.

It is during the filming that Lance makes his great "discovery." He is in the pigeonnier where he first made love to Margot and will later have his vision of the Lady of the Camellias. What Lance discovered, in glancing at his daughter Siobhan's camp application, and now remembers so vividly, is the letter "O" (significantly grailshaped) in her blood type, which indicates that she cannot be both his and Margot's daughter. Old bills and a bit of figuring confirm that she was in Texas with Merlin during the time Siobhan would have been conceived. He has discovered his wife's infidelity. And it is at this point that the nature of the quest he is reliving with Percival becomes explicit. If "the greatest good," Lance says, "is to be found in love, so is the greatest evil" (139). Armed with this new knowledge, the gnostic Lancelot seems restored to health. No longer a victim of the malaise, he quits drinking and with a virtually insidious lucidity develops his plan to seek the ultimate sin. Margot had been his "absolute," his "infinite," his "feast," his grail: "That was my communion, Father—no offense intended, that sweet dark sanctuary guarded by the heavy gold columns of her thighs, the ark of her covenant" (171). Now he would seek sin in the same place. As he tells it, "So Sir Lancelot set out, looking for something rarer than the Grail. A sin" (140).

His decision has caused Lance to take a hard look at himself in the mirror. What he saw was a man gone to seed: "Do you remember the picture of Lancelot disgraced, discovered in adultery with the queen, banished, living in the woods, stretched out on a rock, chin cupped in both hands, bloodshot eyes staring straight ahead, yellow hair growing down over his brows? But it's a bad comparison. My bloodshot eyes were staring too but it was not so much the case of my screwing the queen as the queen getting screwed by somebody else" (64). He engages Elgin, a black MIT engineering senior and liveried tour guide at Belle Isle, to "watch" and to film the sexual encounters of the film crew at the motel. When Lance views Elgin's flawed films he sees tiny reddish figures in a Dantesque hell, with tiny Pentecostal flames flickering over each head. Percy readers will recognize in the delta shape of the Margot–Merlin–Jacoby *menage à trois* and the "rough swastikaed triangle" (192) of Raine Robinette and Troy Dana, the film's stars, and Lucy, Lance's daughter by his first wife, a ghastly parody in which perverted sex becomes the horrible inversion of Percy's own intersubjective theory of symbol which he describes in his essay, "The Delta Factor."[11] With his suspicions empirically validated, he devises his own plot—a marplot whose events, in initiating life's evils, totally outstrip them in their killing cruelty—by which the crew will move into Belle Isle and be blown up by leaking methane gas from the well upon which the old mansion sits. He sends away both his daughters as well as Merlin, with whom he shares a sense of perverse fellowship as cuckold. Ironically, it is the Christmas season, the tree is lighted in the living room, and the traditional bonfires are burning on the levee to celebrate the Incarnation. At the same time Lance is planning his elaborately staged destruction, a great hurricane is threatening the coast. Percy, a lover of puns and word games and jokes, names the hurricane "Marie." Raine, whose name may signify "rein" or "reign" or "raines," the fabric of Guinevere's shroud, insists that they take "champagne" up to the belvedere atop Belle Isle and "have a party named 'Goodbye movie, hello Marie' " (204).

As he relives the events with Percival, he recalls for the first time how he performed their old Bowie knife test, sticking the blade, supposed to have belonged to Jim Bowie himself, into the cypress wall and trying to withdraw it. The Excalibur of their youth would become Lancelot's instrument of an act by which he discovers, beyond envy and revenge, no secret but only the nothingness at the heart of evil.

Knowing understood as a gnostic grasp of esoteric fact and "knowing" in the biblical sense become one in his dark ritual; both are essential to Lance's plan as he visits the bedrooms of Belle Isle, where Elgin's concealed cameras convert living into mere acting, home into cinematic stage-set, and sex into sheer obscenity. In Raine's room, Troy Dana—the "faggot" as Lance calls him—lies stoned on the far side of the bed. Lance, seeing his daughter Lucy's sorority ring on Raine's hand, sodomizes the willing actress in order to discover her "secret." Then he finds Margot and Janos Jacoby in the great Calhoun bed whose design, complete with its buttresses, gargoyles and altar screen, resembles a Gothic cathedral. Lance the new knight sees the two as the new beast and squeezes them more tightly together: "Mashed together, the two were never more apart, never more themselves" (240). Then all three seem to float in the methane–filled air. They, in fact, replicate Dante's Paola and Francesca, destined to be inseparable and driven forever by the winds of the Inferno. Their sin?—their adultery, of course, which resulted from their having read the story of Lancelot and Guinevere.

Lancelot consummates his nihilistic quest in wreaking vengeful judgment on the new barbarians. He slits Jacoby's throat with his Bowie knife, given him years before by that ambiguously fallen woman, the

Lady of the Camellias, his Lady of the Lake. After the explosion in which Lance is blown free, he returns to the ruins, not to find the four bodies but to retrieve the knife. Later judged incompetent to stand trial, he will be freed when he is declared sane. Although guilt is not seen to be an issue for either the law or Lance, Percy's reader, like Percival, knows that this unholy knight's unholy grail is in himself.

And so a year later he carries on his curiously compulsive monologue with Father John, who makes him feel that he is overtaken by his past, by his self. Lance, having confessed to Percival, the hooded knight, senses that Percival still has a question: "Do you love?" Lance has an answer ready, though it is hardly the one Percival has in mind. Because he cannot stand the world as he finds it, Lance has been developing a Utopian vision of a new order and a theory of sexual love by which to defend himself against the barbarism and start the world over. Behavior will be based, he insists manically, not on Catholicism or any other ism but on a stern new code for "gentlemen," who will hold a "gentleness toward women and an intolerance of swinishness, a counsel kept, and above all a readiness to act, and act alone if necessary" (157). This third revolution will take place in Virginia and follow the other two—that of 1776, won because the British were stupid, and the second, in 1861, which failed because, as Lance says, "we got stuck with the Negro thing and it was our fault" (157). His new knight will look like the Virginian, with his gun across his shoulders standing on the Blue Ridge, a perfect reembodiment of the broad sword tradition.

Lance explains that such new men would "have felt at home at Mont-Saint-Michel, the Mount of the Archangel with the flowing sword, or with Richard Coeur-de Lion at Acre. They believed in a God who said he came not to bring peace but the sword" (157). As opposed to Christian *caritas*, Lance's code involves a "stern rectitude," a "tight-lipped courtesy toward men," and "chivalry toward women," who "must be saved from the whoredom they have chosen" (158). Women, for their part, will be either virgins or whores.

Lance's abstracted history of sex relates directly, if unbeknownst to him, to his own biographical revelations. First, there was the romantic period in which he "fell in love" with Lucy, the figure of light in the

Paradiso, whom he insists was a virgin. The current period, represented by Margot and the film company, is like a "baboon colony" or a "soap opera." The third stage he insistently predicts will be a clarification by way of catastrophe, a living death, when everything will become desert. This phase and the "new earth" that it will for him ensure is symbolized by the third woman in Lance's life, Anna, a young woman made autistic as a result of gang–rape with whom he communicates by tapping in Morse Code on the cell wall. From Lance's skewed perception, she is both whore, as a victim of rape, and virgin in that she is now like a ten–year–old. He will take her to Virginia and build a log cabin and they will be the New Adam and Eve of the third revolution—still another attempt, stupidly and self-righteously Utopian, to redefine a gnostically solipsistic Grail.

The film story within the novel depicts Lancelot's second phase, or the current state of sex in America. In addition, the film and its stars, in turn, constitute Percy's comic indictment of a particular scholarly work on the Grail legend. Perhaps the most fascinating parody related to Arthurian materials in *Lancelot* is the one Percy works on Jessie Weston's *From Ritual to Romance*.[12] Merlin believes, and rightly so, that he has "created" Troy Dana, whose name evokes both paganism and the heroic code of the Homeric epics. In himself Troy is "nothing, a perfect cipher," but with his helmet of golden hair he is perceived in the film as a "creature of light," (147) with a temperature "around 101. He actually glows." Everyone else in the film is "hung up" and, therefore, dead. Not only is Troy free in this universe of cinematic glare, he offers resurrection; he frees others, if only pathetically, for that false world. "Perhaps he is a god. At least he is a kind of Christ-type" (148). He frees Sarah, the librarian-initiate, played by Margot, in the stacks. "It is not just screwing," Merlin explains, "but a kind of sacrament and celebration of life. He could be a high priest of Mithras [in Weston, responsible for the initiation of women]."[13] Merlin expounds in postmodern doublespeak that the film will not treat love but be content with "the erotic which in any form at all, is always life-enhancing." The sharecropper of the vegetation-ritual film finds his celluloid Beatrice in the artistocratic girl. Jacoby explains: " 'It is the aristocrat in this case who has the life-embracing principle and not the sharecropper, as is usually the case, since he is usually shown as coming from the dirt.' 'Soil,' said Margot" (114).

If indeed the Grail legends, as Weston believes, have their kernel, their sole origin, in the Vegetation Ritual, the Life-Cult, what, Percy seems to ask, has become of the fertility ritual in the twentieth century? While Percy is, on the one hand, pronouncing judgment on the gnosticism, which Weston associates with the cults of Mithra and Attis, and the violence of his hero, much of Lance's critique of the American scene is the author's own—gone crazy, as the author knows. Percy would believe that the sort of Grail conception which is Weston's—divorced as it is from the source of the Grail, Christ—results in the very infertility that announces the true Wasteland of our time. Albeit through his unreliable narrator, he has provided a novel full of examples of desacralized sex so that the fiction may itself be read as a statement on Weston's theory: the discovery of the adulterous female symbol as sign of fertility in the letter "O," the ultimate impotence of both Merlin and Lancelot; the unerotically perverted sex of the film crew; the unspeakable rape of Anna; and, finally, the parodic rape in the film which takes place in the pigeonnier–Oriel of Belle Isle. *Lancelot* is Percy's fullest fictional dramatization of those conditions describing the character of postmodern American sexuality as seen by the noted American psychiatrist quoted by Percy: "In Harry Stack Sullivan's words, the mark of success in the culture is how much one can do to another's genitals without risking one's self-esteem unduly."[14] Joyous Gard or Camelot, clearly, Percy says, lies in a world elsewhere. Merlin's film satirizes Weston's pre-Christian ideas directly, as does Lance's own post-Christian story. In both love is divorced from spiritual as well as physical fertility and, therefore, from the source of love and life alike. Clearly, Lance has no genuine conception of authentic love, of caritas. His chauvinistic new chivalry is very old and very false, and it will not recreate a lost civilization. The role of Percival in the novel is to hold and transmit the secret that will.

For Percy, the existentialist, the question which still hangs in the air of this Chapel Perilous should not find its answer in an abstracted definition of love but in an act. What is the Grail? Whom shall it serve?

The seeming ambiguity of the structure and, in particular, of the open–endedness of the novel almost hides Percy's answers. In the first sentence of the novel Lancelot has said to Percival: "Come into my cell. Make yourself at home."[15] As the priest's visits go on, Percy, in the manner of Flannery O' Connor, has Lance address him by what might almost be termed "taking the name of the Lord in vain," in a coincidence of opposites. "Jesus, come in and sit down" (84). Lance has referred to Father John as one "obsessed with God" (216), as one who chose "the time-place god" (31). Twice the priest looks like Isaiah's "man of sorrows" (53:3) and, thus Percy implies, he must himself be "acquainted with infirmity." Lance sees Percival's sadness as nothing more than a "tolerant Catholic world-weariness" (131) which loses all distinctions and loves everything. But his cynical statement is precisely Percy's ironic affirmation of Percival as incarnate creature and of the need for participation in both the fall and the healing Incarnation. Percy has conceived of Percival, as Malory did, as one of the very few people who "believed in our Lord Jesus Christ ... who believed in God perfectly."[16]

In his final visit, Percival wears what Lance calls his "priest uniform" (163). Lance asks if he is "girding for battle or dressed up like Lee for surrender" (163). In Lance's scheme the priest might join the third revolution or retain the old Stoicism, but Percival has his own ideas of spiritual battle and surrender, closer perhaps to the dark night of the soul and that surrender to the love of God described by the mystics. The time is still November, the month of All Souls, when the last meeting occurs, and Father John has now begun to pray for the dead, for himself and Lance, those knights whose wounds are secret. Lance will soon be leaving and he will stroll down Annunciation Street. Will there be a fullness of message for him, an annunciation of incarnation, in what has been the only partially seen billboard sign from the "little view" from his cell?

The question for this knight of the Unholy Grail may well have been formulated at the very beginning of the novel when Lance points out the fragmented "message":

Free &

Ma

B

The gnostic Lance has missed the significance of the phonetic hieroglyph that would tell him what Percival "knows," that each of them — and Percy's reader as well — is free and may *be*; to "be," for Walker Percy, is both to become and to believe. But Lance, feeling very cold, complains: "Why did I discover nothing at the heart of evil? There was no 'secret' after all. . . . There is no question. There is no unholy grail as there was no Holy Grail" (253). Percival gazes at him with his same steady sadness, and Lancelot once again formulates the priest's perennial question: "Do I think I can ever love anyone?" (254). Each knight must make a decision and a new beginning, because there is a secret.

Lance refuses to live in the world he sees as Sodom and seems perched to create his own world with Anna in Virginia, even if it takes an apocalyptic sword to protect his Utopia. Yet Percy's endings always leave his characters open to possibility, and in this novel Lancelot seems willing to "wait" and give Percival's God "time," as he says. Curiously, it is Lance who jocularly describes Percival's grail: "So you plan to take a little church in Alabama, Father, preach the gospel, turn bread into flesh, forgive the sins of Buick dealers, administer communion to suburban housewives?" (256). Then, as if he is only now realizing what he must do, Percival looks straight at Lancelot. Under that gaze of the hooded knight, Lance says, "You know something you think I don't know, and you want to tell me but you hesitate" (256). Then Percival, speaking for the first time in the novel, says simply, "Yes." And his continued affirmations, his "yeses" (he says "yes" twelve times in this final scene, "no" just once), project into the future, they stand over against the "no's," the deep negations of Lancelot that have been the structure of the past, of his unholy quest. The Grail question still remains in the final lines. Lancelot: "Is there anything you wish to tell me before I leave?" Percival utters the novel's final word: "Yes." Unlike his paradigmatic predecessor, Lancelot has not done penance and he does not love, but he is free and he "may," because in Percy's grace–filled, redeemed world, anything may "happen." Percival, who will find the Grail, knows that secret.

It is in Tennyson's and then again Toynbee's understanding of the failure of the Arthurian myth before the onslaught of the barbarians that Percy finds sanctions for his attack on Stoicism and the chivalric codes of courtly love and the broad sword as they have developed in the 1970's in America. As the concept of a second coming of Arthur was completely inadequate to the Britons before the onslaught of the barbarians, so are those Arthurian values inadequate to the barbarism of sexual abuse and modern violence which define the postmodern world of Lancelot Andrewes Lamar.

Arthur's Christian realm was destroyed by the barbarians within— the adultery and resultant blood feuds—as much as by Modred and the barbarians without. When his knights departed on their separate quests, Arthur sorrowed that he would not see many of them again and realized that the Round Table and its code were at an end. Percy, like Malory and Tennyson, is deeply concerned with "decline and fall"[17] and the available alternatives to that decline and fall. One is what Will Percy called "the unassailable wintry kingdom of Marcus Aurelius"; still another is Lance's apocalyptic third revolution of individualistic conservatism; the third is implicit in all Percy's work: "Compared to the fatalism of his artistocratic Uncle Will, and the messianism of Lancelot, Percy says he has much more hope. 'I'm a Catholic, and I believe that with all the difficulty it is having, the Judaeo–Christian tradition is the last best hope of sustaining democracies.' "[18] In that tradition Percy sees the world as full of signs: words (even on billboards), events, people, sacraments. Each work ends with sacrament, Walker Percy's Grail. In *The Moviegoer* Binx follows the Mardi Gras of his life with the penitential understanding of Ash Wednesday. Like Chrétien's Percival on Good Friday, he then has the potential to see the Grail. He can reject the "knowing" Stoicism of his Aunt Emily and begin to "do" the works of faith, to love and marry Kate, to care for his brothers and sisters, whom he has hitherto thought of only as his "half-brothers and -sisters." *The Last Gentleman* ends with a baptism in Santa Fe, *Love in the Ruins* with a Christmas Mass. *The Second Coming*, the novel which follows *Lancelot*, is as much about life as Lancelot is about death. It offers an answer to both the malaise and the old and new adulteration of love in the truly life-enhancing coming together and marriage of Will Barret and Allie, herself a sacrament for Will. The "Space Odyssey," the last chapter of *Lost in the Cosmos*, concludes with the ancient Abbot Liebowitz offering Mass for an extraordinarily ecumenical group of survivors as the world begins over again after the nuclear holocaust of the obscene year 2069. *The Thanatos Syndrome*, Percy's most recent fiction, concludes with a Mass of the Epiphany, the feast which celebrates Christ's being shown forth to the world. Walker Percy's grail is, quite simply, what it has always been in the Christian tradition, the cup of the last supper and the blood of the crucified Christ. Percy, both piously and parodically a new Joseph of Arimathea, would save it for the wasteland of the postmodern world.

University of Missouri, Columbia

NOTES

[1]Zoltán Abádi–Nagy, "A Talk with Walker Percy," (1973), *Conversations with Walker Percy*, eds. Lewis A. Lawson and Victor A. Kramer (Jackson, 1985), 73.

[2]Percy adopts this Thomistic term from Gabriel Marcel's title. Marcel's work, like that of Søren Kierkegaard and Martin Heidegger, has been a definitive influence in Percy's thought.

[3]Walker Percy, *The Moviegoer* (New York, 1967) (cited by page numbers hereafter within the text). The novel was first published by Alfred A. Knopf in 1961 and won the 1962 National Book Award.

[4]The epigraph to this essay is from D. C. Somervell's abridgement of Toynbee's multivolume work (New York, 1947) 1, 223.

[5]Walker Percy, "Stoicism in the South," *Commonweal* 64, 14 (July 6, 1956), 343–44.

[6]Walker Percy, *Lancelot* (New York, 1977) (cited by page numbers hereafter within the text).

[7]Sir Thomas Malory, *Le Morte D'Arthur* (London, 1906) 2, 190-91. Percy is clearly familiar with Malory and Tennyson, but any critic who knows his thoroughgoing habit of research may well imagine he has read older texts as well.

[8]Malory, 2, 271.

[9]*Idylls of the King*, in *The Works of Tennyson*, ed. Hallam Lord Tennyson (New York, 1931), 406.

[10]"Personified by the driven-to-murder Lancelot is 'what my Uncle Will used to call the broad-sword tradition, that goes back to Ulysses taking revenge on all the suitors who were hanging around his house when he got back from his long voyage to Troy. He doesn't just throw them out. He kills them all, you know. If somebody offends you, you kill them.' " (Percy in a 1977 interview with William Delaney in "A Southern Novelist Whose CB Crackles with Kierkegaard," *Conversations with Walker Percy*, eds. Lewis A. Lawson and Victor A. Kramer [Jackson, 1985], 154).

[11]Walker Percy, *The Message in the Bottle* (New York,1954).

[12]Jessie L. Weston, *From Ritual to Romance* (New York: Peter Smith, 1941). See also John Edward Hardy, *The Fiction of Walker Percy* (Urbana: University of Illinois Press, 1987), 146-49.

[13]Weston, quoting Cumont, describes Mithra as "le génie de la lumière céleste," 156.

[14]*The Message in the Bottle*, 100.

[15]The verb "come" resonates in Percy's fiction in the title of the novel that follows *Lancelot*, *The Second Coming*; in the final words of *Lost in the Cosmos*, "Come back." In his essay on faith, "The Message in the Bottle," Percy explains that the apostle who delivers the good news may, when "everyone is saying, 'Come!,'

when radio and television say nothing else but 'Come!,'" find that "the best way to say 'Come!' is to remain silent." *The Message in the Bottle*, 148.

[16]Malory, 2, 198.

[17]Delaney interview, 152.

[18]Delaney interview, 157.

Film Treatments of the Legend
of King Arthur

Kevin J. Harty

For more than eighty years, filmmakers have brought versions of the legend of King Arthur to the screen.[1] These films reflect both a general interest in medieval themes as a source for action and adventure films and a particular fascination with elements — friendship, love, betrayal, the quest, and a utopic ideal — embodied in the many-sided legend of the once and future king. In seeking Arthurian materials as possible sources for films, screenwriters and directors turned first to operatic treatments and then to nineteenth-century literary retellings of the Arthurian legend. Only later did medieval versions and original twentieth-century treatments of the legend — the latter, at times, only tangentially related to the matter of Arthur — become sources for screenplays.

Films Based on Operatic Treatments of the Legend of Arthur

The great success the first New York production of Wagner's *Parsifal* enjoyed as the highlight of the Metropolitan Opera's 1903-1904 season inspired Edwin Porter, Thomas Edison's principal director at the time, to attempt an ambitious and costly film version in 1904. The film employs trick photography and elaborate sets, but the acting is overly stylized to suggest that the actors are singing their parts. Edison himself hoped to use the film as the basis for an invention that would synchronize phonographic recordings with film, but such a venture was not yet technologically possible.

Problems with inadequate technology also plagued two early European attempts to bring to the screen operas based on Arthurian materials. In 1912, Mario Caserini directed an Italian film of *Parsifal* more detailed in its presentation of Wagner's opera than Porter's, and in 1920, the French director Maurice Mariaud filmed a version of *Tristan et Yseut*, consisting of six songs. Mariaud's film, while a mixed success artistically, does combine realistic outdoor settings — the cliffs of the Riviera as stand-ins for those of medieval Cornwall and Ireland — with a dramatic flare for the grand.

No one attempted another film treatment of the Arthurian legend based on a source in opera until 1972 when Yvan Lagrange went to Iceland to film his *Tristan et Iseult.* More than a straightforward film of the opera that is its source, Lagrange's film is a multi-media version of an oft-told tale that the director himself subtitled an "opera en scopecoleurs."[2] The film's chief interest lies in its use of cinematic effects to retell the legend of Tristan in terms of what Lagrange intriguingly sees as a conflict between love and war.

More successful, both artistically and commercially, has been Hans-Jürgen Syberberg's controversial 1982 film version of Wagner's *Parsifal.* Running slightly more than four hours, the film is set within a claustrophobic labyrinth, constructed out of an overblown model of Wagner's death mask. Syberberg has effectively used elaborate sets, puppetry, expert dubbing, and a doubling of the title character, who is alternately played by a man and a woman, to create what is for many *the* opera movie of all times.

Films Based on Nineteenth–Century Literary Treatments of the Legend of Arthur

The first Arthurian film to use a nineteenth-century source for its screenplay was Vitagraph's *Lancelot and Elaine.* Released in 1909, the film is a rather free rendering of Tennsyon's poem from the *Idylls of the King.* Successfully balancing action with narration in its attempt to do justice to its poetic source, the film is rich in cinematic innovations, including camera shots inside a dark cave and close-ups of knights on horseback doing battle.

The most popular nineteenth century Arthurian source for films remains Mark Twain's novel, *A Connecticut Yankee in King Arthur's Court* — which first came to the screen in 1921 in Fox Studio's production, *A Connecticut Yankee at* [sic] *King Arthur's Court*. The film was critically acclaimed as a comedic *tour de force,* proving that the medium was capable of serious comedy. The screenwriters miss no opportunity to add touches of contemporaneity to the film, but the novel's basic plot and satiric thrust remain intact — even if Twain himself might not, at times, recognize the film as a version of his novel. The success of this silent film led the studio in 1931 to make a talking version of Twain's novel released under the title *A Connecticut Yankee*. Again, the screenwriters take some liberties with incidentals — here, for instance, the Yankee's arsenal includes a fleet of automobiles, tanks, airplanes, machine guns, and sawed-off shotguns. Will Rogers plays the part of the Yankee with wit and sympathy, and Myrna Loy and Maureen O'Sullivan are convincing as Morgan Le Fay and Alisande. This second film version of Twain's novel also proved a success, and the studio rereleased it in 1936.

In 1949, Twain's novel returned to the screen for a third time in Paramount's *A Connecticut Yankee in King Arthur's Court*. Truer to the plot of Twain's novel in details as well as in intent than either the 1921 or the 1931 versions, this film, more a vehicle to display the musical talents of Bing Crosby in the title role than anything else, is nonetheless the least successful of these three screen adaptations of Twain's novel. In this version, the plot advances not by dramatic interaction between characters but by a mix of silly dialogue and song.

Most successful in matching the comic genius of Twain's novel is a 1979 Disney film released in the United States as *The Unidentified Flying Oddball* and in Great Britain as *King Arthur and the Spaceman*. The film adds a twist to the plot of the novel by having a NASA malfunction send astronaut Tom Trimble and a look-alike robot back to the sixth century at time-warp velocity. The adventures that follow have as their source some of the funniest scenes in the novel.

Films Based on Medieval Continental Treatments of the Legend of Arthur

In 1942, Jean Delannoy directed a compelling modernized version of the medieval story of Tristan and Isolde, *L'Éternel Retour*, from a screenplay by Jean Cocteau.[3] While retaining the main incidents of the legend, the film introduces a pathologically sinister family, the Frossins, who subvert at every turn the uncontrollable love that Patrice (Tristan) and Nathalie (Isolde) have for each other. Unfortunately, the film is at times less than subtle in its racism. The hero and heroine are blonde, while the Frossins, whose adult son Achille is a dwarf, are dark and by implication degenerate. The film's title suggests — and the final credits state — that legends live on to be reborn without the knowledge of their heroes.

Less successful in its treatment of the same legend is the 1979 film *Tristan and Isolt*, subsequently released on videotape under the title *Lovespell*, one of the movies Richard Burton (King Mark) made late in his career solely for financial reasons. While the setting looks medieval enough, the treatment is wooden, and the dialogue is at times downright ridiculous.

Veith von Fürstenberg's *Feuer und Schwert*, on the other hand, retains the medieval setting while also doing justice to the legend of Tristan and Isolde. The film is especially notable for its personal touches: Isolde knowingly gives Tristan the potion and later bears him a child. Unfortunately, the film has not been a commercial success despite the visual poetry of its images, which present a credible reading of a much-distilled tale of ill-fated love.

Von Fürstenberg's film is of a kind with what are perhaps the most artistically successful film treatments of the legend of Arthur, Robert Bresson's *Lancelot du Lac* (1974) and Eric Rohmer's *Perceval le Gallois* (1978). Originally entitled *The Grail*, Bresson's film, whose source is the Vulgate *Mort Artu*, is a meditation on the downfall of the Middle Ages. From Bresson's perspective, that downfall is directly linked to a loss of a sense of the spiritual, which the Grail — appropriately missing from the film — symbolizes. Critical reaction to the film has been sharply divided. *Lancelot* was awarded the 1974 International Critics Prize, but Bresson refused to accept the award.

Eric Rohmer's *Perceval*[4] is clearly the most authentically medieval example of Arthurian film. As Rohmer himself admitted in an interview, he set out to "rediscover the vision of the medieval period as it saw itself."[5] Rohmer's source is Chrétien de Troyes' *Le Conte du Graal*, from which he has cut the end of the text and substituted a version of the medieval passion play in which the hero, now truly united with Christ, takes the central role.

In 1980, the German director Richard Blank made a 90-minute film for West German television of a different version of the quest for the Grail, Wolfram von Eschenbach's *Parzival*. Blank's film abounds in references to the modern world and provides a more straightforward and accessible reading of the legend of the quest than previous Arthurian films were able to bring to the screen.

Films Based on Medieval English Treatments of the Legend of Arthur

As a number of the films just discussed indicate, Arthurian literature can successfully be translated to the screen. However, films based on medieval English Arthurian sources have had notably less success in translating their sources to the screen. By almost universal agreement, the fourteenth-century anonymous romance, *Sir Gawain and the Green Knight*, is the finest example of its genre. Yet two attempts, both directed by Stephen Weeks, to turn the poem into a film failed miserably. First, in a low-budget attempt, *Gawain and the Green Knight* (1973), Weeks consistently proved himself overwhelmed by his source and produced a film that is heavy on swordplay and light on plot. Then, in a bigger budgeted remake, *Sword of the Valiant* (1983), Weeks again failed, despite the presence of a stellar cast that included Sean Connery as the Green Knight and Trevor Howard as a much too old King Arthur, to make sense of his source. Instead, Weeks twice presents a curious jumble of scenes taken from various sources often at best vaguely Arthurian.

A number of other films have claimed Thomas Malory's great fifteenth–century retelling of the Arthuriad, *Le Morte Darthur*, as source. The first, MGM's *Knights of the Round Table* (1953), is, according to a souvenir booklet distributed by the studio for the film's release, based entirely on Malory's "studious work."[6] But despite such a claim of fidelity to its putative source, the film, more notable as the studio's first production in CinemaScope, presents yet another curious jumble of Arthuriana. In the film, Modred and Morgan are lovers, and much of the plot is given over to chase and battle scenes, whose ultimate sources are similar scenes in movie westerns. In *Knights*, though, the good guys wear white armor, and the bad wear black.

Only slightly more successful in its handling of materials from *Le Morte Darthur* is the 1963 film *The Sword of Lancelot*, released as *Lancelot and Guinevere* in Great Britain. *Sword*'s distinction lies in its being the first film to deal unhesitatingly with the adultery between Lancelot (Cornel Wilde, who also directed the film) and Guinevere (Jean Wallace). In *Knights of the Round Table*, the two only share soulful looks. In *Sword*, the treatment of the adultery is more explicit. Unfortunately, the film's Arthur (Brian Aherne) is too old. Indeed, he is a very old man married to a much younger woman, who clearly deserves Lancelot as her lover. Such a shift in characterization prevents the film from balancing fairly the conflict among the principals in the Arthurian love triangle.

Also claiming Malory's *Le Morte Darthur* as a source is *Excalibur* (1981), whose director, John Boorman, promised to tell "the whole story" of the work of England's "first hack writer."[7] His promise notwithstanding, Boorman has instead produced a film

that freely conflates Malory's *Morte* with other sources and strips
the Grail of any Christian associations. In a film where the king
and the land are one, the Grail is a not-always-clearly defined
fertility symbol, and events in *Excalibur* revolve around a trinity of
women — Igrayne, Guinevere, and Morgana — and their complex
relations with Arthur, Lancelot, and Merlin, who is the film's central character.

Arthur the King, a movie made for CBS television in 1982 but
not shown on network television until 1985, attempts to retell Malory's story of Arthur through the eyes of an American tourist who
falls Alice-in-Wonderland-like into a hole in the ground at Stonehenge and lands in an icy cave housing Merlin and his lover,
Niniana. Together, these three recreate the world of Arthur, a
world at best vaguely familiar to anyone who has read Malory. But,
except for a subplot involving Gawain and Dame Ragnell, here a
pig-faced woman, there is little to suggest a clear line from the film
back to Malory or to any other recognizably medieval source.

More interesting, if not always successful, is a BBC "silent
version" of Malory's work, aired in 1984 as *The Morte D'Arthur*.
Part drama, part mime, the film stars the Royal Shakespeare Company's John Barton as the knight-prisoner, Sir Thomas Malory,
who narrates the events of the last two books of the Morte. As
Malory speaks, his narrative comes to life in a series of choreo-
graphed scenes enacting the collapse of the Arthurian ideal.

More detailed in its use of plot lines from Malory's *Morte* is
The Legend of King Arthur, a coproduction of the BBC, Time-Life
Television, and the Australian Broadcasting Commission. The
program, a series of eight 30-minute episodes, was originally
shown on BBC 1 in October and November, 1979. More recently,
it was aired on the Arts and Entertainment Cable Network in 1988.
The Legend of King Arthur straightforwardly tells of the rise and
fall of the Round Table by focusing on the continuing jealousy of
Morgan and the continuing passion of Lancelot and Guinevere.

Films Based on Twentieth–Century and on Original Treatments of the Legend of Arthur

Prince Valiant, Hal Forrest's long running comic strip, came to the screen in 1954 in a film of the same name. This film reflects Hollywood's continuing fascination with medieval themes, but, as *Prince Valiant* proves, such a fascination does not always translate into a successful film — indeed, the director, Henry Hathaway, later disassociated himself from the film. In a screenplay weighed down by fairly wooden plot devices, the Viking Prince Valiant (Robert Wagner) fights his former countrymen to secure Arthur's throne and to regain his own. Twentieth Century Fox's first film in Cinemascope, *Prince Valiant* is most memorable for a series of battle scenes and a spectacular final fire scene where flames engulf and destroy a castle.

T. H. White's *The Once and Future King,* the twentieth century's most ambitious retelling of the Arthuriad, has twice come in part to the screen. Disney's *The Sword in the Stone* (1965) recounts the education of the boy Arthur at the hands of Merlin and his talking owl, Archimedes. An example of the art of Disney animation at its best, *Sword* nonetheless takes sufficient liberties with White's novel — most notably in the introduction of the character of Mad Madame Mim, an evil witch and Merlin's nemesis — to dilute the charm of its source.

Parts of White's novel were also the source for *Camelot* (1967), Joshua Logan's attempt to bring the Broadway musical of the same name to the screen. Critical reaction to the film was mixed, in large part because both the stage and film versions are generic oddities; they are musical tragedies. But Logan's film — which starred Richard Harris as Arthur, Vanessa Redgrave as Guinevere, and Franco Nero as Lancelot, none noted for an ability to carry a tune — does focus on the love of Lancelot and Guinevere and its tragic consequences, albeit on a one-dimensional level.

That Arthur is viewed in the twentieth century as once and future king is especially evident in those films that reinterpret the story of Arthur for their own purposes. In *King Arthur Was a Gentleman*, a 1942 film whose greatest debt may be to the British war effort, a sad sack soldier named Arthur King imagines he has found Excalibur. When ordered to the German front, King uses his sword in a series of heroic acts. In Columbia's *Adventures of Sir Galahad* (1949), the setting is vaguely medieval, but the plot is indebted to only bits and pieces of the legend of Arthur. Such a convoluted grab bag of sources is in a way appropriate to this fifteen-part serial enabling it to be true to its genre, the cliffhanger.

The Black Knight (1954) also has a vaguely medieval setting, but little about the film's rather contrived plot reflects any earlier retelling of the legend of Arthur. In this film, Arthur's kingdom is threatened by King Mark, himself in league with a band of Saracens who carry out human sacrifices at Stonehenge. Mark and the Saracens are eventually defeated by a blacksmith named John (Alan Ladd), who despite his humble origins rises to the rank of knight and saves the Round Table.

In *Siege of the Saxons* (1963), released in Great Britain as *King Arthur and the Siege of the Saxons*, marauding Saxons eagerly await the death of the aging Arthur. Early in the film, Arthur is murdered by a traitorous former champion, Edmund of Cornwall, but the throne of Camelot is secured by Katherine, Arthur's daughter, with the aid of a Robin-Hood-like character, Robert Marshall.

Equally silly in its treatment of the Arthurian legend is *King Arthur, The Young Warlord* — a film made in Britain in 1975 but never released commercially. This film, which is now available on videotape, pits the young Arthur, brother to Kai and son to Llud, against Saxons, Picts, and Jutes, as well as against Mark of Cornwall, in a not-totally-successful attempt to unite England.

Monty Python and the Holy Grail (1975)[8] is not so much a send-up of the Arthurian legend as it is a send-up of other film treatments of that legend. An at-times genuinely funny comic gem, the film borrows threads from earlier literary and cinematic treatments of the legend of Arthur and interweaves them with

Hollywoodesque scenes of swashbuckling adventure, spectacle, and fights to the death.

Finally, George Romero's *Knightriders* (1981) offers one of the most original film treatments of the legend of Arthur. Set in contemporary western Pennsylvania, *Knightriders* examines the values previously found in Arthurian society as they are practiced by a group of motorcycle stunt riders who perform at country fares. In this version of Camelot, crass commercialism and corrupt sheriff's deputies work together to threaten the world Billy (Ed Harris in the role of the film's Arthur figure) and his followers seek. Romero—best known as the director of cult horror films—clearly sees Arthur as once and future king, and *Knightriders* is his meditation on the possibility of recreating the Arthurian ideal in a troubled modern-day America.

La Salle University

NOTES

[1]This essay does not discuss two kinds of films. The first includes films such as the 1964 *Seven Faces of Dr. Lao* that treat Arthurian characters only in passing. Here one of the faces mentioned in the title is that of Merlin. The second includes films such as the 1984 film of Bernard Malamud's *The Natural*, where a Perceval-like Roy Hobbs joins the Knights, a baseball team managed by a "wounded" Pop Fisher. These films treat Arthurian themes only indirectly or analogously.

For an discussion of the influence of Arthurian literature on film in general, see Frank McConnell, *Storytelling and Mythmaking, Image from Film and Literature* (New York, 1979).

[2]André Cornand, "Review of *Tristan et Iseult*," *Image et Son* 284 (1974), 103-104.

[3]Jean Cocteau, *Three Screenplays,. trans. Carol-Martin Sperry. (New York, 1972).*

[4]The film's screenplay is available in *L'Avant-Scéne du Cinéma* 221 (February 1, 1979).

[5]Nadja Tesich-Savage, "Rehearsing the Middle Ages," *Film Comment* 14 (September-October, 1978), 51-52.

[6]*Knights of the Round Table* (New York, 1954), n.p.

[7]Harlan Kennedy, "The World of King Arthur According to John Boorman," *American Film* 6 (March, 1981), 32.

[8]The screenplay along with a number of production-related materials is available in *Monty Python and the Holy Grail (Book)* (New York, 1977).

APPENDIX: FILMOGRAPHY

An earlier version of the following filmography appeared in *Quondam et Futurus* (7 [Spring 1987], 5-8; [Summer 1987], 18). I am grateful to Mildred Leake Day, editor of *Quondam et Futurus,* for her continued support of my work on Arthurian film.

The filmography is arranged chronologically. Titles are given first — alternate titles are separated by a slash — followed by the names of the director — unknown for one silent film — and of the production company and the date of the production. Information on the availability of films for rental appears in parantheses; a simple notation of "V" indicates that the film is available on videotape in Beta or VHS formats.

Parsifal, dir. Edwin J. Porter, Edison, 1904.

Lancelot and Elaine, dir. ?, Vitagraph, 1909.

Parsifal, dir. Mario Caserini, Ambrosio, 1912.

Tristan et Yseut, dir. Maurice Mariaud, Nalpas, 1920.

A Connecticut Yankee at [sic] *King Arthur's Court,* dir. Emmett J. Flynn, Fox, 1921.

A Connecticut Yankee, dir. David Butler, Fox, 1931.

King Arthur Was a Gentleman, dir. Marcel Varnel, General Films, 1942.

L'Éternel Retour, dir. Jean Delannoy, Discina International, 1943 (V).

The Adventures of Sir Galahad (15-part serial), dir. Spencer Bennett, Columbia, 1949.

A Connecticut Yankee in King Arthur's Court, dir. Tay Garnett, Paramount, 1949 (V).

Knights of the Round Table, dir. Richard Thorpe, MGM, 1953 (V).

The Black Knight, dir. Tay Garnett, Columbia, 1954 (Williams Films, 2240 Noblestown Road, Pittsburgh, PA 15205).

Prince Valiant, dir. Henry Hathaway, Twentieth Century Fox, 1954 (Arcus Films, 1225 Broadway, New York, NY 10001).

The Siege of the Saxons / King Arthur and the Siege of the Saxons, dir. Nathan Juran, BLC Columbia, 1963 (Arcus Films, 1225 Broadway, New York, NY 10001).

The Sword in the Stone, dir. Wolfgang Reitherman, Disney, 1963 (V).

The Sword of Lancelot / Lancelot and Guinevere, dir. Cornel Wilde, Emblem, 1963 (Williams Films, 2240 Noblestown Road, Pittsburgh, PA 15205).

Camelot, dir. Joshua Logan, Warner Brothers, 1967 (V).

Tristan et Iseult, dir. Yvan Lagrange, Film du Soir, 1972.

Gawain and the Green Knight, dir. Stephen Weeks, United Artists, 1973.

Lancelot du Lac, dir. Robert Bresson, Mara Films, 1974 (New Yorker Films, 161 W. 61st Street, New York, NY 10023).

King Arthur, the Young Warlord, dir. Sidney Hayers, Patrick Jason, and Patrick Sasdy, Heritage Enterprises, 1975 (V).

Monty Python and the Holy Grail, dir. Terry Gilliam and Terry Jones, Python Pictures, 1975 (V).

Perceval le Gallois, dir. Eric Rohmer, Gaumont-New Yorker Films, 1978 (New Yorker Films, 161 W. 61st Street, New York, NY 10023).

The Unidentified Flying Oddball / King Arthur and the Spaceman, dir. Russ Mayberry, Disney, 1979 (V).

Tristan and Isolt / Lovespell, dir. Tom Donovan, Clar Productions, 1979 (V).

The Legend of King Arthur, dir. Rodney Bennett, BBC, Time-Life Television, and the Australian Broadcasting Commission, 1979. (Aired on Arts and Entertainment Cable Network in 1988.)

Parzival, dir. Richard Blank, West Deutsche Rundfunk, 1980.

Excalibur, dir. John Boorman, Orion, 1981 (V).

Feuer und Schwert / Tristan und Isolde, dir. Veith von Fürstenberg, Gence und von Fürstenberg Filmproduktion, 1981.

Knightriders, dir. George Romero, United Film, 1981 (V).

Parsifal, dir. Hans-Jürgen Syberberg, Gaumont-TMS Films, 1982 (V).

Sword of the Valiant / The Legend of Gawain and the Green Knight, dir. Stephen Weeks, Cannon, 1983 (V).

Arthur the King, dir. Clive Donner, CBS, 1982/1985.

The Morte D'Arthur, dir. Gillian Lynne, BBC, 1984.

Heroes in Four Colors:
The Arthurian Legend in Comic Strips and Books

Sally K. Slocum and H. Alan Stewart

Through the ages, the heroic ideals embodied in the Matter of Britain have been adapted by artists and writers to suit the tenor of their times. In popular art, one sees most clearly the prevalent image of the Arthurian hero in a particular culture. The medium of comic strips and books has tended to follow the lead of other art forms in its interpretations of Arthurian themes, but it has also interestingly adapted these themes to its own conventions and, in recent years, has exhibited a growing sophistication which has allowed for more personal expressions of the heroic Arthurian ideal.

The appearance of Arthurian characters and settings in newspaper comic strips occurs at least as early as 1933, when artist–writer Milton Caniff's *Dickie Dare* daydreams himself into the world of Arthurian romance.[1] Four years later, however, a much more significant work appears, as *Prince Valiant, in the Days of King Arthur*, created by Harold R. Foster, debuts in the Sunday comics sections of American newspapers on February 13, 1937.[2] Foster, an author–illustrator in the American tradition typified by Howard Pyle, begins his story when his titular hero is still a child, as Valiant's father, King Agnar of the legendary Nordic land of Thule, flees by sea from a usurper with his wife and son and loyal retainers, eventually coming to land in Britain.

In ensuing weeks, Foster relates how Agnar and his entourage settle on a desolate island in the midst of a great marshland, and how Prince Valiant grows from a child to a strong and brave youth. After visiting a witch who tells him he will know adventure but never contentment (April 17, 1937), the prince returns home to find that his mother has died. A year later, Val decides to leave the marshes and, Perceval–like, puts together some makeshift arms and armor and sets out to become a knight. He soon encounters Sir Launcelot and, later, Sir Gawain with whom he joins company. After adventures with a wicked knight and a dragon–like creature, in which Valiant plays as heroic a role as Gawain, the companions arrive at Camelot, "the city of marvel," where Val meets Arthur, Guinevere, and Merlin, and becomes Sir Gawain's squire.

Foster's Camelot is of course the idealized medieval castle–city that would be familiar to readers of Pyle or Sydney Lanier. However, Foster does not limit the scope of his Arthurian milieu to that of an imaginary kingdom of the High Middle Ages. Though he chooses to portray Arthur and his Round Table as they are known in romance, Foster also incorporates the real history of the fifth century by including not only the Saxon chief Horsa, but also such non–Arthurian figures as Attila and events such as Genseric's sack of Rome. Also, the characters eventually travel far beyond the familiar environs of medieval Europe, visiting Africa, India, and North America among other non–traditional locales. Foster's approach to combining history and legend may be unique in the Arthurian tradition; the care for authenticity helps create a sense of verisimilitude in which the heroics of the characters seem more plausible.

As regards the traditional characters of the legend, "merry Gawain" probably plays the greatest role in *Prince Valiant.* Merlin and Morgan le Fay are featured in early episodes but are less prominent later, as magic and fantasy become less important in the strip. When Prince Valiant finally goes on a quest for the Holy Grail, he discovers at Glastonbury only that the Grail may or may not exist. Modred appears occasionally in a villainous role. In general, Foster seems more interested in the Arthurian milieu and ethos as a whole than in particular characters or events.

During the early sequences of Valiant's adventures as Gawain's squire, leading up to his eventually being made a Knight of the Round Table, Foster develops what will be the essential visual and narrative style of *Prince Valiant.* He eschews many of the conventions of comic–strip storytelling, including sound effects and word balloons (the text is separate from the image but still enclosed in the frame of the illustration), with the effect that the work has less immediacy and more of a historical flavor than most comics. As an illustrator, Foster emphasizes authentic, realistic detail, but not at the expense of depicting the romantic nobility of his characters and epic grandeur of their world.[3]

As a writer, Foster also combines realism and romanticism in his characterization of Valiant; the hero is brave, self–confident, and honorable, but he is also rash and experiences failures, which are sometimes treated humorously and sometimes not. When he first fears he has lost his first love, "the fair Ilene," to a rival, Val puts on a show of high spirits before Camelot's knights, but later "quietly sobs out his heartbreak in the dark" (May 7, 1938). Prince Valiant is thus in the tradition of heroes of medieval Arthurian romance, courageous knights–errant eager for combat who nevertheless, in the words of Richard Cavendish, "are not bovine men, too stupid to feel fear and too stolid to be a prey to self–doubt. On the contrary, they tend to be highly–strung, emotional and sensitive."[4]

In the early years of *Prince Valiant* there is, in fact, an ominous undercurrent of tragedy, beginning with the marsh witch's prophecy and continuing through the deaths of the hero's mother and of Ilene, who is lost at sea despite the great efforts of Val and his rival, Arn. It seems that whatever actions Val may take, he is doomed to unhappiness, as Sir Balin in Malory is fated to die. While the story generally maintains the tone of youthful exuberance and high adventures, the tragic episodes and the ominous tone of the prophecy help to associate Prince Valiant's biography with its legendary antecedents. As the years go by, however, and Foster becomes more and more involved with the vicissitudes of his hero's life, this tragic element becomes less and less important; ultimately, the witch's prophecy is revoked, and Valiant is freed to find a happier destiny.

Such a destiny is presaged by Val's first encounter with Aleta, Queen of the Misty Isles. Believing for a time that she has cast an evil spell upon him, the prince eventually discovers that he has simply fallen in love with her. They wed (October 2, 1946), and before long Aleta conceives and bears a son, who is named Arn after Val's old rival and companion.

It is worth noting that Val and Aleta's marriage in 1946 and subsequent birth of Prince Arn coincide with the return of American soldiers to their sweethearts or wives in the United States, and the beginnings of the post–World War II "baby boom." As a popular medium, comics naturally reflect the concerns and preoccupations of the reading public, and as the first adventure strip hero to "settle down," Prince Valiant pioneers in this respect.[5] Foster's challenge at this point is to demonstrate that the introduction of marriage and family into his hero's life does not mean the end of romance or adventure.

In a 1969 interview, Foster is asked about his conception of "the Hero," and he replies:

> He has to lead a normal life. For instance, Val met Aleta.... The natural thing after that was marriage; and when you get married, you have children. So it was just a natural sequence. He does what we should do.[6]

Foster has no interest in the medieval custom of courtly love or in the chastity of a Galahad; his twentieth–century, American middle–class value system virtually requires that his hero marry and have children.

The introduction of the domestic element changes the strip, though adventure continues to be the major element. Foster gives Valiant and Aleta a volatile relationship; they have quarrels and passionate reconciliations, which helps sustain the sense of romance through the births of four more children. There is occasional tension between the demands of knightly (or queenly) duty and those of love and family, somewhat reminiscent of the story of Erec and Enide (Geraint and Enid); but generally the relationship is a happy one, and family squabbles are often simply a source for domestic comedy. as the children grow, the youthful exuberance of the early strips is regained, first with Prince Arn and then with his siblings.[7] While there is no ceasing of struggle and challenge, in the bosom of his family and in the service of King Arthur, Prince Valiant does come to know a large measure of contentment. His father having been restored to the throne of Thule, the middle–aged Val can look forward to his children inheriting two kingdoms. In a sense, Prince Valiant has come to live the American dream.

In 1971, Hal Foster turned the drawing of *Prince Valiant* over to John Cullen Murphy; in 1980 he ceased to write it as well, and in 1982 he died at the age of eighty–nine. His strip has continued without him in much the same vein, now written by Murphy's son Cullen. Foster's epic has been translated into numerous languages, has been reprinted many times, and has been adapted into a film. Like a medieval romance continued for decades by various authors, *Prince Valiant* goes on, possibly indefinitely.

Hal Foster's influence over the whole field of Arthurian comics is immense, to the extent that no other major Arthurian newspaper strips have appeared, and one must turn to the comic book format for further explorations of the mythos. Comic books have featured direct adaptations of the legend, such as "Knights of the Round Table" in the American *Classics Illustrated* 108 (1953), and "King Arthur and His Knights" serialized in the British weekly *Swift* (1955);[8] but though such adaptations have their place, the heroic image in American comic books has been dominated by the concept of the super–hero, as introduced with the character Superman in *Action Comics* 1 (1938). The super–hero's roots extend back to the superhuman protagonists of mythology and legend, and the knight–errant of medieval romance, who sets forth into the world to protect the innocent and avenge injustice, is one prototype of the comics' costumed adventurer who sets out to battle evil.

An exccellent example of the malleability of the figure of the Arthurian knight to the requirements of the super–hero comic book is the Shining Knight *(Adventure Comics* 66 [1941]). The hero, Sir Justin, is like Prince Valiant, a contemporary addition to the Knights of the Round Table; bearing an enchanted sword and suit of mail bequeathed him by Merlin, riding a winged horse named Victory, Sir Justin is transported into the twentieth century by virtue of being frozen alive in an icy crevasse. Revived in 1941, Justin immediately resumes his battle against evil, battling American criminals and aiding the Allied war effort. Sir Justin's reactions to contemporary life are treated with humor, and there are occasionally enjoyable flashbacks to the Shining Knight's adventures in and around Camelot.

Another knight added to the roster of the Round table by comics writers, Sir Percy of Scandia (*Black Knight* 1 [1955]), is not in his original incarnation an actual super–hero, but a medieval adventurer who poses as a cowardly fop to mislead Arthur's enemies, while striking for justice as the unknown Black Knight. In the twentieth century, Sir Percy's heroic spirit lives on in his descendant Dane Whitman, the present–day Black Knight (*Avengers* 48 [1967]) who battles injustice with the magical Ebony Blade forged by Merlin.

Merlin also plays a role in the empowerment of young Brian Braddock in *Captain Britain* 1 (1976). Brian is confronted by Merlin and an unnamed Lady (later revealed to be his daughter) at the Siege Perilous—here a magical ring of stones rather than a seat—and given the opportunity to become a costumed, super–powered champion of justice. In producing its first comic book specifically intended for the British market, the American publisher Marvel Comics perhaps inevitably turns to the Arthurian legend to create a nationalistic counterpart to their earlier hero, Captain America. In this first episode Captain Britain is specifically associated with the Knights of the Round Table, and in later stories he actually journeys with the Black Knight to an Otherworld Camelot and meets King Arthur. More recently, he has joined with a group of super–heroes in a "spin–off" of Marvel's popular *X–Men* series entitled appropriately enough, *Excalibur* (1987).

Perhaps the least typical of the Arthurian super–heroes is Etrigan, the Demon in *The Demon* 1 (1972), a creature of the imaginative artist–writer Jack Kirby. Etrigan is a survivor of the fall of Camelot — an infernal servant of Merlin, sent into the world in human guise to live through the centuries. As Jason Blood, demonologist, Etrigan uncovers the presence of supernatural evil and sheds his human form to become an embodiment of savage, elemental fury, seemingly only slightly less dangerous than his monstrous foes. Merlin himself makes several appearances in the course of the series, as does Morgaine Le Fey as the Demon's nemesis. DC Comics cancelled the series after twelve issues; a revival by artist–writer Matt Wagner in 1986 furthers the character's mystique with the revelation that Etrigan is Merlin's half–brother.

As a genre, the super–hero comic book is thematically and aesthetically limited, receiving much of its energy and impetus from the power fantasies of adolescent males. These heroes nevertheless possess an elemental, myth–like power in the contemporary imagination, and their juxtaposition with the older heroic ideals embodied in the Arthurian legends can produce interesting results.

All of the stories of modern Arthurian super–heroes, as well as the stories in which traditional characters interact with other heroes like Spider–Woman or the Defenders, speak in some way to the old theme of Arthur's survival and return; but there have been other approaches to this subject in comics. In an ironic vein, the popular European adventure hero, Corto Maltese, actually stands in for Arthur to foil a German ("Saxon") plot against Britain during World War One in Hugo Pratt's *Corto Maltese: A Mid–Winter Morning's Dream* (New York, 1987). The sardonic, dispossessed sea captain may be far from the traditional Arthurian ideal, but he accomplishes the mission laid out for him by Britain's Faery guardians — Oberon, Puck, Morgana, and Merlin.

It is in two recent American comic book series, however, that one finds the fullest treatments of Arthur's return. Both series reflect the growing sophistication of the American comic book, fueled by the growth of the specialty or "fan" market during the 1970's and 1980's. The first of these comics to appear, *Camelot 3000* (1982), features perhaps the most elaborate and thorough handling of Arthurian themes to appear in any comic, while the second, *Mage: The Hero Discovered* (1984) by Matt Wagner, takes a more personal and allusive approach to the materials of the legend.

In one sense, *Mage* is another super–hero comic; the hero, Kevin Matchstick, develops powers of super–strength and near–invulnerability at the beginning of the story, and through most of the series wears a sort of costume – a black t–shirt with a white lightning bolt emblazoned across it (a design inspired by the costume of 1940's comics hero Captain Marvel). A more personal theme is suggested, however, by creator Wagner's editorial revelation that Kevin is visually based upon himself. This hero, when first introduced, is a seemingly ordinary man in a contemporary urban environment, who only learns that he is actually the latest incarnation of the "eternal Hero" when he suddenly finds himself caught up in a war between supernatural forces of good and evil. Kevin is skeptical of this destiny and indeed actively resists it, but goaded and guided by his self–appointed companion and mentor, a whimsical figure called Mirth, the World–Mage, he reluctantly comes to accept his role as the reborn wielder of the power of Excalibur against the evil Umbra Sprite and his minions – or in Kevin's words, "Yeah. Right. I'm King Arthur" (*Mage* 14 [1986] 9, 10).

The appearance of Excalibur, and the open acknowledgement of Kevin's earlier existence as Arthur (as well as the unspoken but clear identification of Mirth with Merlin), comes in the series' thirteenth issue, but Arthurian motifs are used directly or subtly alluded to throughout the series. One of Matchstick's first supernatural opponents is called "the Marhault ogre," and a significant subplot involves the villain's attempt to find and kill a crippled mystical entity, the Fisher King. Other references to Celtic mythology and fairy lore enhance the Arthurian flavor. Kevin has no

Round Table, but he and Mirth gain two allies in the course of the series—a young woman named Edsel, who fights enemies with an enchanted baseball bat, and Sean Knight, the ghost of a public defender.

There is a considerable amount of humor in *Mage*, particularly in the early issues, as Kevin encounters one impossible thing after another, and as the incongruities of ancient magic and modern urban life are explored (for example, Mirth hides from the Umbra Sprite by "imprisoning" himself in an automated bank teller). The conflict is always presented as a serious one, however, and the tone of the work becomes grim in the later chapters as both Knight and Edsel die in battle with the Umbra Sprite's servants. It is in fact with Edsel's death that her own true nature, as well as Kevin's, are revealed: she is the reincarnated Lady of the Lake, the "carrier" of the Hero's weapon—the baseball bat is the modern Excalibur, and only when it comes into the Hero's hands does it, and he, attain their true power.

But before Kevin takes up his weapon to make a final stand against the Umbra Sprite, he must resolve his own reluctance to accept his identity as the Hero. "All I've ever wanted is to be alone...I'm no hero," Kevin tells Mirth, echoing his denials throughout the series. The mage's response is that no one is entitled to peace simply by the fact of his existence; that the isolation to which Kevin clings

> is in fact your fear of yourself, and the sacrifices that others have made around you. You fail to see that the Hero lives within us all. Your denial does not change it...
> (14 [1986] 17,18).

Here Mirth expresses Wagner's major thematic concern, that a heroic potential exists in each individual which can be actualized as each contends with his or her own life's circumstances.

Kevin's apotheosis comes at the conclusion of the fourteenth chapter, as he brings forth the glowing–white Excalibur–bat from the alley dumpster, in whose metal side he himself has embedded it in his rage at Edsel's death, thus reliving the Arthurian episode of the sword in the stone. The fifteenth and concluding issue details his assault on the Styx Casino, the Umbra Sprite's stronghold, and moves through phantasmagoric battles with dwarf–like Redcaps, a giant, a dragon, and the Wild Hunt before arriving at a somewhat ambiguous conclusion. The Hero's first war has been won, but his biography is to be continued by Wagner in two future series, beginning with *Mage II: The Hero Defined.*[9]

In style and tone, *Mage* is virtually at an opposite remove from *Prince Valiant.* While Hal Foster's art is stately and exacting in detail, Wagner's is darker, looser, and more expressionistic; and while Foster relies heavily on a text to convey his story, taking a literary approach, Wagner eschews captions entirely, reflecting the influence of film. Foster is more interested in history and realism, Wagner in myth and fantasy. Yet both convey their personal attitudes toward heroism in their work and creatively utilize the materials of Arthurian legend in their expression. These two series, along with *Camelot 3000*, give the clearest indication of the wide range of approaches possible within the comics form and suggest its potential to produce interpretations of the legend not possible in any other medium.

Though other comic depictions of the Arthurian world present ongoing adventures in the Arthurian spirit, *Camelot 3000* by Mike W. Barr and Brian Bolland (writer/co–creators and plotters/artist) is complete in twelve issues. DC Comic's first maxi–series and first comic to be printed on 45 Pound Baxter Stock, *Camelot 3000* is somewhat different from traditional comic books. The bright and deep colors and heavier paper provide a new look. Appended commentary to the first four issues informs readers of Arthurian sources. "Chapter Two: Many Are Called" presents a brief discussion of Sir Thomas Malory and a short bibliography; "Chapter Three: Knight Quest" includes a survey and bibliography on "The Real King Arthur"; "Chapter Four: Assault on the New Camelot" appends a select list of recent works based on Arthurian legend.

Following issues print fans' letters to the editor, revealing that interest in Arthurian materials is strong and widespread.

The heroic demands on King Arthur and his retinue in the comic book *Camelot 3000* are many, as the fellowship of the Round Table must save the earth from distant planetary invaders and restore order and law to the earth. The futuristic society of the year 3000 seems doomed: the earth is overpopulated and deficient in food and water; the earth's leaders are self–serving, concerned only with maintaining their individual power; the insect–like/saurian–like invaders take no prisoners of earthlings, who are powerless to stop them; there is no hope; the force behind the invasion is Morgan le Fay, working with the U.N. Security Director and his pawns, the four world leaders, to subdue the earth to their rule.

Into this dismal prospect King Arthur returns. Young Tom Prentice, pursued by aliens, seeks shelter in the Glastonbury Historical Dig, where he bumps into a large stone inscribed "Hic Iacet Sepultus Inclitis Rex Arthurus Rex Quondam. . . ." He pries open the tomb and Arthur rises asking "How long—how many nights has slept Arthur Pendragon, King of Britain, Lord of the Holy Roman Empire?" Arthur, battle ready, heroically slays the threatening aliens (*Whud! Shree!*), and he and Tom take an alien ship to Stonehenge to free Merlin from Nyneve's charm. Merlin transports them to the Salisbury Down Nuclear Plant, where he conjures Excalibur from The Lady of the Lake. The sword, through Merlin's magic, appears in the United Nations General assembly, lodged in an anvil with the familiar inscription "Whoso pulleth this sword..." (2, 2). Arthur once again (but this time on TV and witnessed by people all over the world) removes the sword—which none have been able to do—and "For the first time in a long time—they have a HERO again" (2, 11). He vows to unite the planet and free its people.

Merlin is crucial to Arthur's cause. It is he who locates the reincarnated knights—and Guinevere—and restores their former ancient memories. Barr and Bolland have captioned the maxi–series "Continuing Legends Chronicled by Sir Thomas Malory,"

and the continuity of characters of the Round Table, regrouped for
the struggle against these evil forces, relies heavily on Malory and
other medieval sources. Guinevere, now Commander of Earth
Defense Forces Joan Acton, is summoned to join Arthur. She is an
active warrior who courageously fights in the battles, using what
she can of her Defense Forces to aid the resistance. Now more
knight than queen, she observes: "In my last life, clinging Queen
Guinevere wouldn't dared have embarked on a quest of her own
...but Commander Acton wouldn't have it any other way" (3, 10).
Guinevere and Lancelot retain their medieval love as their past
memory is restored.

And Lancelot remains "the best knight of this world" (9, 20)
and a valiant and heroic fighter. In this life, Lancelot is still a
Frenchman and inordinately wealthy. His "orbiting asteroid retreat" (2, 19) serves as New Camelot where he presents Arthur
with a New Round Table. After Percival achieves the Grail, Lancelot is appointed guardian of the Grail, only to have it stolen. The
high spirituality of Lancelot is not overlooked in the comic book.
In Malory's "A Noble Tale of Sir Lancelot du Lake," Lancelot
heals the wounded and profusely bleeding Sir Melyot, and in "The
Book of Sir Lancelot and Queen Guinevere," he cures the be-
witched, wounded Sir Urry when he searches his wounds.[10] In
Camelot 3000, Merlin has counseled Arthur to wed Guinevere in a
public ceremony. Guinevere is slain in an assassination attempt on
Arthur. Lancelot kneels over the dead queen praying, "Take my
breath and make it hers. . . . still my heart but quicken hers. . . .
Take my life but let her . . ." (6, 20), and the queen is restored to
life. However, even his medieval memory of the devastating effects
of his adultery does not prevent him from repeating it. Warned that
his love for the queen may again destroy Camelot, Lancelot explains, "We are the best of friends, Arthur and I, and one would
give up anything for the other – anything but her" (5, 19). This
time, moreover, Arthur has "ocular proof" of their adultery and
banishes them from the court – for a time.

The other knights restored to Arthur are, at first glance, not promising. Reminiscent of the Beaumains and La Cote Mal Tale episodes in Malory, in which unlikely–looking knights are chided by Kay for their appearances, these future incarnations are not the perfect physical knights they were.

Kay is discovered in New Chicago while he is fleeing loan sharks. Down and out, Kay is greeted by Arthur: "My foster brother! In trouble as always, I see!" (3, 9). And in this setting, Kay is a churlish knight, insulting Percival and Sir Tristram and betraying the court to Morgan Le Fay, allowing her to return Merlin to Nyneve's spell. Kay dies taking a blast meant for Arthur, but Arthur had already sentenced him to death for his treachery (8, 15-20).

Percival is found at a penal colony in Australia, just when he is transformed into a grotesquely hulking Neo–Man – "Neo–Men! Criminals, dissidents and undesirables, genetically changed to loyal, virtually brainless servants of the powers–that–be" (2, 4). But for his hideous form, Percival retains his medieval memory and serves loyally. This time it is Percival's turn to achieve the Grail. Powerful in fights, Percival has no trouble smashing bad guys (*Skree!*); he recruits and leads a band of Neo–men (7, 15). His devout prayer leads him to find and "achieve" the Grail (9, 5-20). His heroic demeanor has not been altered by the transmogrification.

Perhaps the most unlikely knight, and most intriguing to the fans – if the letters are a true indication – is the reincarnation of Sir Tristan as a woman. With her memory restored, Sir Tristan – as she insists on being called – is miserable in her female form. She implores Merlin to transform her to her proper male body, and is tempted by Morgan to betray the court to regain a man's body. She is especially unhappy to be female when Isolde appears – a reincarnate, but still a woman. The love potion is apparently still in effect – to the dismay of young Tom Prentice, infatuated with the female knight. Tristan nevertheless fights side by side with the other knights and is fiercely loyal to Arthur, so loyal that on his orders she uses her hated womanly wiles to distract the enemy to allow Arthur's band another victory. The heroic nature of Sir Tristram is not a sex–linked characteristic.

Sir Gawain and Sir Galahad play lesser roles than they had in Malory but are nevertheless important. Gawain, in this life a black South African, is closely bound to his family. Reluctant to leave his wife and son, he responds without hesitation to the call to join Arthur and fights valiantly.

Sir Galahad's modern life as a failed Samurai warrior is redeemed by his self–sacrifice to save the rest of Arthur's company. In a similar spirit, Galahad leaves the Grail quest to Percival since Galahad had been "transformed" by the Grail in his previous life (9, 10).

The new fellowship is advised and guided by Merlin who retains his medieval powers and characteristics. Rosemary Morris observes that "The relationship [between Arthur and Merlin], which is everywhere consistent, has three strands. Merlin combines the brusquely hectoring attitude of a king-maker to his puppet, the father's protective affection, and the firm governance of a teacher. To all three Arthur responds with meekness, affection, gratitude and obedience."[11] Such is the relationship in *Camelot 3000*. It is through Merlin that Arthur's company is reassembled, and he offers guidance and strategy along with his wizard powers. As in Malory, Merlin is removed from the scene and ensnared by Nyneve. The future fellowship of the Round Table must rely on its own strength to save the beleaguered earth without Merlin's magic powers. Brian Bolland has depicted a serious, aged mage in drawings that satisfy most readers' concepts of Merlin. He is also a source of humor in his impatience with humans — he calls them "pets."

The character of Arthur is consistent with his most heroic medieval self. He leads his troop in battle, defends a helpless woman with her child — "Unhand her, Monster... I'll not stand by and see an innocent harmed — not while I live!" Swiftly, with a *BROK* and *KRAK* he saves the day (2, 5-6). He is a judge as well as a warrior. He banishes the adulterous Lancelot and Guinevere from the court (7, 22) and sentences the traitorous Kay to death (8, 13). This Arthur is a dispenser of justice. Arthur loves his company and is moved to distraction by the betrayal of Lancelot and Guinevere. Some medieval treatments of Arthur show a tendency "towards fits of abstraction. These build up a picture of a man very prone to fits of spiritual paralysis or *tristitia* from which he is powerless to emerge unaided, a man very prone, in fact, to the sin of sloth."[12] His depression brought on by his loss of his queen and best knight brings a halt to the struggle. Not until New Camelot is attacked and Squire Tom Prentice wounded does Arthur return to heroic stature.

Heroic stature of the whole fellowship is utterly necessary for the effort against the invaders, backed and commanded by Morgan le Fay and her ally Jordan Matthew—the reincarnated Modred. Morgan's sorcery has been enhanced during her sojourn on her tenth planet. Her "magicks" are the real strength of the bad guys, and to end the contest, Arthur must kill Morgan. In the final battle, Arthur vanquishes Morgan, but is himself destroyed, as Merlin says, "Until the cycle begins anew" (12, 24).

Arthurian material has been consistently reshaped to reflect the concerns of the era that produced it. The combination of futuristic science fiction with medieval faery in *Camelot 3000* is very successful. In the society of *Camelot 3000* there is faith and hope in scientific advancement but with the recognition that technology has failed to fulfill its promises. In the year 3000 earth is overpopulated, its populace powerless because of corrupt and greedy world leaders. For all of the apparent technological progress, there is great need for ancient heroes with a noble purpose:

> Through the history of this earth, the strong have had their way. . . . I pledge the dawn of a new day, when strength shall be used not for its own ends...but to protect the weak...to crush the strong...to serve the right! (7, 19-20).

This is Arthur's creed. Futuristic medical advances allow the wounded knights to heal fast (7, 2-3), but for radiation sickness, only the Holy Grail can effect a cure (9, 19). The misguided society that controls dissenters by electro–chemically transmogrifying citizens into huge, mindless Neo–Men is inspired by Arthur's drawing the sword from the anvil (2, 10-11). Excalibur can even power a spaceship (10, 12).

The medieval heritage of the legend is kept before the reader through flashbacks. For example, Arthur's effort to kill the baby Modred is recalled (9, 7-8); the young Arthur drawing the sword from the stone (2, 9), a version of the origins of the Grail (9, 3-4), the love of Elaine for Lancelot (10, 19), as well as the history of Morgan Le Fay (5, 9-12) are evoked and illustrated. Malory's *Mort D'Arthur* and a volume named *Geoffrey of Monmouth* are among the books on Merlin's desk (3, 1). This literate comic book, not limited to retelling the old stories, has nevertheless rendered some of them anew and pays homage to them. The comic book genre has its own powers.

The illustrations add depth to the characters and situations. Here we are not told of the anguish various characters suffer; we are shown. Descriptions are replaced by pictures that are at once revealing and demand interpretation. Since *Camelot 3000* was originally published in installments, the readers, as is revealed in letters, participated imaginatively in anticipating future issues.

If Arthur is lost in the final battle, he and his heroic entourage have won the war. Gawain returns to his family, Tristan and Isolde find happiness together (this comic book does not have the Comic Code Approval), and Guinevere is pregnant — possibly with Arthur's child. But the real significance of Arthur's brief return is the new hope experienced by human beings and their energetic reclamation of the earth with "a new standard to uphold" (12, 31) that Arthur, once King, bequeaths to the future.

Camelot 3000 has been reissued in book form (New York, 1988), and in that form it gains recognition as a twelve-chapter novel. The reprinting excludes the advertisements, appendices and letters. The preface "Epic Beginnings" by Don and Maggie Thompson explains the publishing history of the comic. Mike W. Barr has written a foreword, "Opening Knight," which surveys briefly the origins of the Arthurian legend and the life of Sir Thomas Malory. An Afterword profiles the work of co-creators Barr and Bolland.

Camelot 3000, like other comic book treatments, has made the Arthurian legend accessible to many who might otherwise not be exposed to it in a coherent way. Many who disparage "funny books" will be surprised by the mature approach of these works, and some will recognize that they bear comparison to other recent novels that embrace Arthurian materials. Renderings of the fellowship of the Round Table have been a part of the popular culture of their societies, and comics have made their contributions to Arthurian legend in a popular genre that is far reaching.

The University of Akron and Memphis, Tennessee

NOTES

[1]Milton Caniff, *The Complete Dickie Dare* (Agoura, CA, 1986), 59-72.

[2]Though much of Foster's *Prince Valiant* work has been reprinted over the years, there is as yet no compete edition of the strip in a permanent format, excepting newspaper collections on microfilm; thus, in this article individual strips will be identified by the date of their original publication.

[3]Dale Luciano, "The Princely, the Proud, and the Eclectic," *The Comics Journal* 95 (1985), 52; Greg Potter, "Panel Progressions: Hal Foster The Classicist," *The Comics Journal* 63 (1981), 285-86.

[4]Richard Cavendish, *King Arthur and the Grail: The Arthurian Legends and their Meaning* (New York, 1978), 60.

[5]Another example of *Prince Valiant* reflecting topical concerns occurs with a 1939 sequence in which Valiant, Gawain, and Tristram teach the peaceful inhabitants of the Tyrolean Mountains to defend themselves against the invading Huns. The identification of "the Huns" with Nazi Germany is clear in this episode. See Pierre Couperie et al., *A History of the Comic Strip* (New York, 1968), 85.

[6]Fred Schreiber, "A Candid, Unpublished Interview: The Master, Hal Foster," *Nemo: The Classic Comics Library* 9 (1984), 16.

[7]Arn Saba, "Harold R. Foster: Drawing Upon History," *The Comics Journal* 102 (1985), 63.

[8]Comic book series (and characters who appear in several series) will be identified by the issue number (if known) and the year of first publication.

[9]Besides its original publication in fifteen issues by Comico, *Mage: The Hero Discovered* has been collected in three trade paperback volumes by Donning. Kevin Matchstick has also appeared in a four–part "Interlude" strip intended to bridge the first and second *Mage* series, published in the comic book *Grendel*, issues 16-19 (1988).

[10]Sir Thomas Malory, *Works*, ed. Eugene Vinaver, 2nd ed. (Oxford, 1974), 663.

[11]Rosemary Morris, *The Character of Arthur in Medieval Literature* (Cambridge, England, 1982), 115-16.

AVALON TO CAMELOT:
An Ongoing Arthurian Quest

Freya Reeves Lambides

In writing his vast and complex novel *A Glastonbury Romance* John Cowper Powys intended

> to explore the effect of a particular legend, a special myth,
> a unique tradition, from the remotest part of human his-
> tory, upon a particular spot on the surface of the planet
> together with its crowd of inhabitants of every age and
> every type of character.... Its heroine is the Grail. Its
> hero is the Life poured into the Grail. Its message is that
> no one Receptacle of Life and no one Fountain of Life can
> contain or explain what the world offers us.[1]

The "spot on the planet" is Glastonbury, where the Grail and
Arthurian legends have gathered with a potency which is palpable,
drawing pilgrims for centuries. As one of those pilgrims, my
Arthurian studies have been not a literary investigation so much as
the *experience* of a "living myth" now spanning into its second
decade.

As Blake scholar and poet Kathleen Raine noted recently:

> There is in the treasury of every nation a body of mythol-
> ogy, legend, and folklore interwoven with history and pre-
> history—associated with certain places and the names of
> kings and heroes, with events natural and supernatural—
> preserved by tradition both oral and recorded. These le-
> gends and records belong to the *whole* people lending to
> each brief, unremarkable life a larger identity and par-
> ticipation; as if in some sense these stories are our *own*.
> They give us a place in history—and not only history—but
> in a story whose imaginative meaning goes beyond history

lending a sense of glory and cosmic significance, and a
beauty special to our own people and place on Earth.[2]

Raine suggests that Arthur and his court are a creation *of* and
a presence *in* the imagination, which we continue to adorn with all
those attributes which we would most wish to find in "the person
and circumstances of a perfect king. Arthur embodies the virtues
of justice, fortitude, prudence, and magnanimity. . . ." Far from
being an exercise in reductionism, this perception expresses the
power of the "Arthurian ideal" which has so deeply and authentically penetrated the period and culture in which we live. Our lives
are tempered with this ideal; its codes and values are woven both
subtly and boldly, with and without intent, into the fabric of many
of our twentieth-century lives. Echoes of this particular and potent
variety of chivalry are distinguishable in the dreams and language
of the civil rights, human rights, and peace movements and for
centuries have stirred the activism and attitudes of many who seek
to forge a civilization which strives for the common good. This
yearning is for a world in which the commitment is to improve
rather than to destroy, in which the courage to envision a new way
of life where power, wisdom, and gentleness co-exist are among
the powerful components which draw many into a life-long fascination with the Arthurian mythos. Certainly they were among the
factors which inspired me to become the founder and publisher of
Avalon to Camelot, a magazine devoted to exploring all aspects of
the Arthurian legends.

Though the inspiration was mine, *Avalon to Camelot* became
a reality through the enthusiasm and commitment of a nucleus of
students who gathered for an adult education seminar taught by
Debra N. Mancoff at Chicago's Newberry Library in the spring of
1982. The Newberry's fine collection of Arthuriana and its welcoming policy toward both independent *and* affiliated scholars
proved an ideal meeting ground for the thirteen men and women
brought together by their mutual Arthurian interests, who
᠁red around a long refectory table in the Newberry's Fellows
ᶾe for a half-dozen Saturday mornings.

By the following year, my original plan for an Arthurian newsletter of four pages had expanded to thirty-two pages, to include feature articles, columns exploring the legends from different perspectives, and departments which would then function as the newsletter was originally envisaged — as a mode for communication among Arthurians, on events, products, and publications. Included was the dream of illuminating the magazine with centuries of Arthurian imagery from manuscripts, paintings, books, and hopefully original works, thereby continuing the Arthurian illustrative tradition. All of the above ideas were actualized in *Avalon to Camelot*'s first issue, mailed in October of 1983, and have now expanded to fill forty-eight pages.

Between the Newberry seminar and first mailing, I had traveled to New York to present the ambitious prospectus developed by Debra Mancoff, Sara Boyle, Ted Drendel, Luke Matranga and me to Geoffrey Ashe. As the well-respected and popular author of several non-fiction Arthurian books and as the resident Arthurian expert of Glastonbury, Ashe's enthusiastic endorsement of our proposed publication provided us with increased confidence. We chose the Eighteenth Annual International Congress on Medieval Studies at Kalamazoo to test the idea further. It was a "vintage year" for Arthurian scholarship and several prominent Arthurian scholars whom we met soon agreed to join Mr. Ashe as the founding members of the magazine's advisory board. Among them was Mildred L. Day, whose fine Arthurian newsletter *Quondam et Futurus* so well complements *Avalon to Camelot*'s goals and content, with its timely news of events and publications. These scholars have supported our concept of a vehicle by which Arthurian scholarship could reach a broader audience in a format readable and intelligent as well as visually appealing. By mid-July 1983, as the editorial content came in, an eighteenth-century engraving of the Round Table at Winchester arrived from Portugal, sent by a friend who was unaware that a plan for a magazine existed — the ideal image for *Avalon to Camelot*'s first cover.

The contents of the first issue included a feature on arms and armor in the Arthurian age by Helmut Nickel, Curator of Arms and Armor for the Metropolitan Museum of Art, which was to evolve by the second issue into a regular column, "Arthurian Heraldry." Other columns included "The Quest for the Historical Arthur," which continues to explore various theories related to the search for the elusive figure behind the Arthurian legends, and "The Arthurian Legend in the Arts," which includes articles by experts in the spheres of music, architecture and film, as well as the more familiar visual arts. The first article was by Debra Mancoff, co-editor with William Hale, whose column shared his area of expertise, etymology. "Primary Works in Translation," was intended to examine the great medieval works of Arthurian literature from points of view ranging—for example—from a novice's response to a first reading of Malory to a translator's sharing of his craft. The first volume also included a column on methods and approaches to teaching Arthurian works which was subsequently dropped when we expanded the format and with input from among our readers who teach suggested that an increased number of features, and longer, more informative articles were even more helpful than a "how-to" column. Our focus was further refined when the generous mail following the second issue, which was largely devoted to the character Gawain and the incomparable *Gawain and the Green Knight*, came largely from scholars and those who teach the poem.

Luke Matranga, *Avalon to Camelot*'s guiding professional publishing spirit, thoughtfully withheld the fact that twelve to eighteen months is the "usual" time allotted for the birth of a magazine with major financial backing and a full-time staff, until the first issue of *A to C* arrived from the printer eight months after its conception. Through the two and a half years preceding his death in 1985, he never fully acknowledged how his participation guided our editorial standards and immeasurably enhanced the satisfaction the staff gained through his discipline and training. The distinctive look of the magazine, already apparent in that first issue, was shaped with the assistance of the magazine's graphic designers Theo Kouvatsos and Ted Drendel, and included numerous illustrations, calligraphy, and the use of decorative capitals to give each feature article and the columns a special touch. Also present from the beginning has been the authoritative, readable tone of the editorial content, something which academic authors have found a refreshing, if sometimes challenging, change from their usual academic writing.

Avalon to Camelot's editorial format has changed somewhat with various staff changes; our current editor Alan Lupack's "Free-Lancing" column has covered modern Arthurian poetry, the contrasting approaches of book illustrators to Tennyson's *Idylls*, and among others, a look at absurdities of character and situation in modern Arthurian fiction. Associate editor Dan Nastali's collecting of and interest in literary history bring an informed perspective to his "Lesser Known Works" column which explores the creative development and impact of Arthurian literature, high and low, in its cultural context. The late Barri C. DeVigne, a contributing editor since *A to C*'s inception, wrote an occasional column, "Arthur and Ancient Britain" in which he displayed his expertise on the myths, megaliths and folklore of Britain. DeVigne had been a friend since guiding me, some years before, to the site near South Cadbury in Somerset which is often associated with Camelot. We had walked the ramparts and huddled beneath a tree through a chilling rain atop the hill which may once have held the timbered Dark Age hall remembered in legend as Camelot. Years before, he had spent a Lammas Eve encamped with John Steinbeck at the same site, so that he might serve as a witness in the event that folklore proved true to life and Arthur and his knights indeed rode out from their sleeping cavern beneath the hill. Our subsequent years of correspondence led to Barri becoming "Our Man in Britain."

Early issues of the magazine featured articles which clustered around a central character—Gawain, Arthur himself—or a major theme such as the Grail quest. With the fourth issue, in which the contents were enlarged a full fifty percent, the editorial approach expanded as well. The theme of that issue was "Women and the Arthurian Tradition," and it celebrated women as Arthurian authors and patronesses, as characters in medieval and modern works, as historical and mythological figures, and more. The response to that issue confirmed our editorial direction towards themes that were centered on a point of major interest to Arthurians yet broad enough to permit unexpected approaches and to bring little known aspects to light. The Merlin one met in the pages of *Avalon to Camelot*, for example, might be found, in various articles, in the company of Joan of Arc, African storytellers, and Edgar Allan Poe, or in a medieval swordsmith's forge or an eighteenth-century architectural folly.

Avalon to Camelot's audience began to define itself with response to the first issue, and after several years of correspondence — as well as a readers' survey which elicited more specific information — a group self-portrait of that audience has emerged. And a diverse group it is, ranging in age from fifteen to eighty–four and in location from virtually every part of the United States to posts all around the globe. Not surprisingly, academics — both teachers and students — constitute almost half of the readership, and another substantial portion, almost twenty percent, are involved in arts and communications professions as writers, actors, broadcasters, musicians, novelists, poets, and authors of children's literature. But the rich diversity of the rest of the readers was an unexpected delight as individuals identified themselves as bankers, ministers, lawyers, physicists, folklorists, veterinarians, accountants, doctors, firefighters, computer programmers, and even homesteaders.

The readers have told us that *Avalon to Camelot* has reinforced their aspirations ranging from the wish to travel to sites associated with the Arthurian and Grail legends to such goals as becoming full-time Arthurian literary or historical scholars, archaeologists (the possibility of an actual Dark Age Arthur drew many of our readers of all ages to their Arthurian interest), poets, novelists, composers, and artists of pictorial works inspired by this timeless myth. While others expressed no professional ambitions related to Arthurian matters, few seemed to seek mere entertainment; nearly all appear to draw inspiration and sustanence from it on some level.

Almost sixty percent of our readers traced their Arthurian interests to early childhood—the single author most often cited as first inspiration was T. H. White, and indeed White was the writer most frequently mentioned as "favorite author." However, in this category as in others, the answers reflected the intellectual mixture of our readership. While many were drawn to modern authors, particularly White, Mary Stewart, Rosemary Sutcliff, Geoffrey Ashe, and Parke Godwin, many listed Malory—and several, Geoffrey of Monmouth, Wolfram, Chrétien, the *Gawain*- poet and the bards of *The Mabinogion*. And while childhood reading was the most frequently cited early association with the legends, others reported several different avenues to their interest: the operas of Wagner, the *Prince Valiant* comic strip, a vacation visit to Tintagel, and one of our favorites, a woman whose fourth–grade teacher made the entire 1934 school year an Arthurian experience for her class.

Readers also shared with us intensely personal experiences, such as a young Japanese woman who is taking a graduate degree in English after having been inspired by the Arthurian stories. With modern Arthurian works in English being difficult to come by in Japan, she began writing her own versions, and on her first trip to America she purchased three boxes of Arthurian books to study and enjoy on her return home. More than one reader, on discovering *Avalon to Camelot*, has told us that they previously believed that they were alone in their devotion to the stories, and their responses have been most gratifying:

> The Arthurian legend is more than a legend to me. It is love and hope for all the human race. It is tragedy which is universal and strength which survives. The characters offer me solace and friendship; the time excitement and

escape. Your magazine has become a vital part of all this...I owe you a debt I'll always hope to repay.

Another, a twenty-eight year-old graduate student appended an essay to his questionnaire in which he stated at greater length and with greater eloquence a faith manifested implicitly but unmistakably by many of our readers:

> Once a man leaves a legend, that legend develops a life of its own, separate from the historical person.... King Arthur is not a historical character then, but a mighty dream and vision, one that still convinces many that Right Makes Might and not the other way around, and that it is right to show courtesy and honour to every person until they prove that they do not deserve it, and that it is better to fight injustice and oppression than to merely accept it. This is the vision of Camelot which I try to bear into the twenty-first century.

Clearly, our readers are willing participants in what may be called "The Living Arthurian Tradition" — a continuity of themes, characters, symbols, stories, and values which remains vital in spite of the changes in the culture which embodies them. The art, poetry, music, popular novels, radio and television serials, films, and role-playing games of our present era are the cultural descendants of those first tales told centuries ago 'round the hearth of a winter's fire. Their abililty to awaken the full range of human feeling — from tragedy and despair to courage and spiritual aspiration — is not diminished by the fact that it is transmitted through the media of the modern era. The range and variety of Arthurian "experiences" available to lovers of the Arthurian tradition in the late 1980s is extraordinary indeed. Surely this demonstrates something beyond a nostalgic longing for the return of the "once and future king." It is more likely an expression of the form in which Arthur *has* returned in civilization's moment of need.

Richard Harris, the actor who portrayed Arthur in the 1968 screen version of Lerner and Lowe's *Camelot* (based on

T. H. White's *Once and Future King*), and who has played the role repeatedly on stage since the film in 1968, said in a recent interview,

> . . . it all suggests that Camelot is there to be touched; it's in the heart. They either dream of it, they wish for it, or whatever. And that's why I think the love affair of America with *Camelot* still exists. [3]

The "love affair" is actually shared by countless numbers in America and beyond — wherever a resonance with the full range of archetypal human experience so vividly expressed in the Arthurian and Grail legends is felt. Readings by popular modern Arthurian novelists and papers discussing their works increasingly appear on the programs of science fiction/fantasy conventions world-wide. Medieval events based on Arthurian themes are mounted at universities, perhaps at the demand of their students who enroll in substantial numbers for the growing number of Arthurian literature — even history — seminars which are now available. Others encounter Arthurian subjects in adult education seminars and through the entertainments of medieval festivals and theme restaurants which serve medieval fare accompanied by music — and occasionally jousts. Role playing games such as *King Arthur Pendragon*, draw on the entire Arthurian mythos to channel imaginative exercises and research into a sophisticated blend of strategies, ethics, and the expression of long-range cooperative goals requiring an understanding of both Arthurian literature and the chivalric code. Taken as a whole, these disparate yet overlapping audiences reveal a broad popular phenomenon; each enhances the others in a creative cross-fertilization. And as modern Arthurian novelists and artists are imaginatively influenced by the growing world of Arthurian scholarship — be it literary, psychological, or historical — so is that scholarship itself enlivened by the numinous quality of the ongoing legend and its weavers.

This burgeoning creative activity overlaps to some extent — and is additionally supported by — a long tradition in America,

England, and on the Continent of individuals and groups who are particularly interested in the psychological, mythological, esoteric, and spiritual approaches to the Arthurian saga, especially (but not limited to) those aspects related to the Grail legend. As with those who prefer the approaches of literary, historical, and/or archaeological scholarship and those who merely seek momentary entertainment, these less "mainstream" groups also gather for conferences, seminars, study tours, and artistic events, and support a specialized publishing market. For example, in the years 1986-88, three Merlin Conferences were held in London which approached the Arthurian material largely through what might be called active imagination, meditation, and mythological thinking, looking to the symbolic aspects of the legends.

Concurrent with this multifaceted Arthurian renascence, there is also an emerging spiritual movement which emphasizes a deep concern for expanding perspectives in seeking creative solutions to the current world crisis. Its aim is to establish a balance, harmony, and wholeness between the Earth and her inhabitants, and to honor the body, mind and spirit of both the individual and the Universe, engendering a world view with heightened awareness of "the spiritual radiance which shines through the world." As Kathleen Raine put it,

> Our society is forever thinking about changing outer circumstances; Blake's 'revolution' will come about when we change *ourselves* — from inner awakening outer changes will follow. We cannot treat a living and holy Earth as we would a lifeless mechanism, nor human beings in whom the Divine Humanity is manifested in all its myriad forms as the mortal worm born in a night to perish in a night — an expendable part in the mechanism of the world. We have created our nightmare world in the image of our ideologies, but with the awakening of our humanity we will see a different would and create a different world.[4]

Depth psychologists—particularly Jungians—are using Arthurian and Grail symbolism to explore modern psychological and ethical concerns. The numbers and influence of those who approach the Arthurian mythos in ways other than the traditional are sometimes overlooked by segments of the academic Arthurian establishment. However, each of these sometimes disparate viewpoints sheds light on the process of myth-making and its impact on the souls of nations and humanity.

Jean Shinoda Bolen, a Jungian analyst and author of several books on mythic aspects of modern life, has recently completed *The Grail and the Goddess*, a book which in part chronicles a pilgrimage to England and Scotland on which I acted as her guide in "Grail country." Significantly incorporating archetypal Grail imagery, the book explores the interlacing paths of four "Sister Pilgrims" and others whose lives have intersected with them. It is a case where the Grail quest has proven to be a perfectly appropriate representation of the experiences of contemporary women, including recovery from sickness, the expansion of understanding, the increased courage to speak of inner realities—all potentialities which are, in truth, part of the human experience, and not just that of women.

Among others whose works seek to broaden our understanding of the Arthurian mythos are such poets, painters, musicians and visionaries as William Blake, Richard Wagner, many of the Transcendental and Romantic poets, T. S. Eliot, Charles Williams, C. S. Lewis, Fiona Macleod, Rudolph Steiner, John Cowper Powys, Dion Fortune, and a number of more contemporary writers including Kathleen Raine, David Jones, Joseph Campbell, Heinrich Zimmer, Alan Garner, John Boorman, John and Caitlin Matthews, R. J. Stewart, Gareth Knight, Edward C.Whitmont and Robert Johnson. Their books, music, and films have not only pleased a broad audience, but many have influenced other creative artists.

Increasingly, writers and scholars with a feminist persp⎯ ⎯ are providing an evolving view of the Arthurian tradition v tempered by the authenticity of female experience, ir

individual autonomy and an increased awareness of the influence
of roles and self-perception in shaping one's world view. Women,
of course, from Eleanor of Aquitaine to Jessie L.
Weston and beyond, have been major creative and critical forces in shaping the
Arthurian tradition. In our time, Marion Zimmer Bradley—among
a host of women authors who have recently reworked the legends—attracted the admiration of many women readers by presenting the stories from the perspective of the major female characters in *The Mists of Avalon* (1983). Not only are modern readers
gaining an increasingly vivid image of the texture of Dark Age life
and relationships in these new Arthurian stories, but also they are
recognizing the characters as potential guides to that inner transformation which ultimately offers the individual participation in
the modern world with renewed hope and vision.[5]

Edward C. Whitmont, author of *The Return of the Goddess*
speaks in the introduction of the book of his Orthodox Jewish
childhood in Austria during the First World War where he rebelled
at an early age against his "parochially narrow family" and learned
"from early years to go my own lonely way.... I was attracted to
myths and fairytales. I imbued myself in them. The Germanic
myths impressed me very much."[6] He began studying the piano at
age four or five and intended to be a professional musician; until
the age of fifteen or sixteen he "lived in the world of Wagner,"
especially *The Ring* and *Parsifal*. He became keenly aware of the
perversion of these works and the myths which inspired them by
the Socialist and Nazi regimes before he fled at age twenty-six to
America after his parents were killed in the Nazi gas chambers. He
became a medical doctor, and eventually one of the founding
members and the chairman of the C. G. Jung Training Center in
New York. Whitmont feels that the lessons and symbols within the
Grail legend may provide a model for the healing of modern
Western society—beginning with the development of the individual, building to a new collective consciousness.

The first function of mythology according to Joseph Campbell,
the pan-cultural mythologist, is "to initiate the individual into

cultural forms that speak to the deeper level of the psyche . . .The function of 'elemental ideas' is to lead us inward. . . ." [7] Arthurian and Grail legends are linked by some authors (such as Wolfram von Eschenbach in his twelfth-century masterpiece, *Parzival*) to Eastern traditions. Such works furnish a metaphoric framework which bridges the boundaries of Western cultural roots and the yogic mystical world view, which utilizes similar metaphors and emphasizes techniques and study leading to the direct *experience* of the Divine. Campbell has noted that contemplatives and practitioners of both the Eastern and Western traditions have "no difficulty understanding each other." Cultural historian William Irwin Thompson supplies further insights in his 1982 work *The Time Falling Bodies Take to Light: Mythology, Sexuality, and the Origins of Culture.*

In an interview a few months before his death in October of 1987, Campbell responded to the question of how we as a culture might find our way out of the spiritual chaos of modern times to discover the "next mythology" with a metaphor inspired by Arthurian legend:

> Whenever a knight tried to follow a path made by someone else, he went altogether astray. Where there is a way or a path, it is someone else's footsteps. Each of us has to find his own way, and this is what gives our Occidental world its initiative and creative qualities. The images that mean something to you, you'll find in your dreams, in your visions, in your actions — and you'll find out what they are after you've passed them.[8]

Campbell believed that for most people this awakening came through the symbols of their own culture, though it was also his belief that the next myth must be one which expands to include the whole planet. In such a context, the Grail quest can be understood as neither solely a Christian quest, nor as one which is *necessarily* religious, but as a universal symbol of "the possibility of approaching the universal Mystery—of opening the mind to the mystery of the universe — to the mystery of oneself . . . if you understand what the symbol connotes, it can become a justifying and guiding principle in your life."[9]

T. S. Eliot wrote of such experience in his *Four Quartets*: "We had the experience but missed the meaning / And approach to the meaning restores the experience / In a different form, beyond any meaning / We can assign to happiness."[10] Eliot understood that the goal of the quester is not so much to find the Grail as to comprehend the *meaning* in the experiences met along the Quest — and beyond even this to experience "the bliss of being" in participating in a world wherein the Grail is ever-present, though it may pass among us unseen until our vision is opened to the presence of Eternal things in the "intersection of the timeless with time."[11] In *The Power of Myth*, a now-best-selling book based on interviews between Bill Moyers and Joseph Campbell in the final year of his life, Campbell stated his belief that it is not meaning we are seeking, but "an experience of being alive, so that our life experiences on the purely physical plane will have resonances within our own innermost being and reality, so that we actually feel the rapture of being alive. That's what it's all finally about, and that's what these clues help us find within ourselves."[12]

What is it about the Arthurian stories in particular which exercises such a deep and immediate hold on so many readers? Heinrich Zimmer provides an answer in his interpretive study, *The King and the Corpse*: "The aim of this recreation is simply to let the old symbolic personages and adventures work upon and stimulate the living imagination, to revive them, and to awaken in ourselves the old ability to read with intuitive understanding this pictorial script that at one time was the bearer of the spiritual sustenance of our own ancestors. The answers to the riddles of existence that the tales incorporate — whether we are aware of the fact or not — are still shaping our lives."[13]

Zimmer feels that despite the intervening centuries since the writing of the great medieval Arthurian romances, their messages are very close to us, although we have stored them away with "the bric-brac of childhood and of former centuries — having outgrown them."[14] Zimmer suggests that:

> the generations that fashioned these romances are not merely our spiritual ancestors, but to some extent our physical as well. They are inside our bones — unknown to us; and when we listen, they are listening too. As we read, some dim ancestral ego of which we are unaware may be nodding approvingly on hearing again its old tale, rejoicing to recognize again what once was a part of its old wisdom. And if we heed, this inner presence may teach us, also, how to react to these romances, how to understand them and put them to use in the world of everyday.[15]

How exactly do we establish contact with or an awareness of this inner presence in order to enter the Arthurian world and join it to our own? The routes are many, the approaches varied, as can be seen from *AtoC*'s "Personal Journeys" columns in which several of our staff have shared the beginnings of their Arthurian interests.

Helmut Nickel, for nearly thirty years the Curator of Arms and Armor at the Metropolitan Museum of Art in New York, who was raised near Dresden before WW II was, like Edward Whitmont, drawn by Wagner:

> Actually, my interest in my professional field of arms and armor and in the Arthurian legends started at a very early stage. In fact, I do not remember a time when I was *not* interested in these two subjects. It seems to have started on a family hiking trip when we passed a farmhouse near the village of Graupa near Dresden. Intriguingly, the house had two white swans wrought into its green-painted gate and two lengthy inscriptions chiseled into its sandstone pillars. I must have been about four years old, because I could not read yet, and asked my mother to tell me about them. She explained that this had once been the summer retreat of Richard Wagner, who had written *Parsifal* and *Lohengrin* in this house. She told me the stories

of the Grail and the Swan–Knight in condensed form.... During my student days I earned my thinly buttered bread as an illustrator, specializing as an adaptor for comic strips of classic adventure stories.... Alas, my truly great love, the Arthurian stories, were a field already preempted by Hal Foster's *Prince Valiant* ("Prinz Eisenherz" in his German editions), and thus I never had a chance to illustrate a romance of chivalry.

Debra Mancoff, wrote in the third issue of how the Arthurian legend became for her "a bridge between my childhood dreams and my scholarly pursuits." She recalls playing "a daring Lancelot or Arthur to my sister's rather demanding Guenevere," and fonder memories playing the Queen, herself. She grew up on a Chicago street bounded by "avenues with the evocative names Arthur and Albion," gained a visual aspect to her flights of imagination in the movie version of *Camelot,* began searching for the special meaning in the saga by reading Tennyson and Malory, and wrote her doctoral thesis on *The Arthurian Revival in Victorian Painting.* The closing sentence in her "Personal Journey" reads, "From childhood fantasy to my current academic endeavors, the legend has been an essential thread in my life and its meaning a tangible part of my present reality." It was with a share of amusement and a feeling of "good omen" that she disembarked the night before the interview for her present job in the Department of Art History at Beloit College in view of the sign for the restaurant in her lodging—The Sword in the Stone.

Sara Boyle, *AtoC's* Managing Editor, who was a member of the Newberry class and like Ted Drendel has been part of the magazine since its inception, wrote in her characteristically terse style in the first issue what is evidently not an uncommon experience:

Blame it on Richard Burton. Used to listen to my employer's cast album of *Camelot* repeatedly while babysitting. Took my copy of *The Once and Future King* along on other jobs. Read Mary Stewart's "Merlin" books with relish in college. Afterward, on to Edison Marshall and Rosemary Sutcliff. Charles Squire's *Celtic Myth and Legend* added new insights. In spring of 1982 attended a seminar at the Newberry Library entitled "From Avalon to Camelot." There I fell in with a motley crew of other die-hard enthusiasts and my fate was sealed. No rescue seems imminent.

Ted Drendel was "hooked" by the legend in early childhood. He created the magazine's logo calligraphy, is involved in the art direction of the magazine, adds a note of levity with his cartoons, and provides occasional original illustrations. Ted is a goldsmith by vocation, which bridges his childhood castle and armor building from "discards of the adult world." A portion of his journey follows:

> One aspect of the legend which has long interested me is the sense of pathos throughout. All the heroes are in a sense failed heroes. They all have pure motives, a strong sense of moral and ethical idealism, and strive to live by these standards—but at some point they all fail. Alhough they have failed, they are still heroes. Perhaps *because* they have failed they are even greater heroes—certainly they are more human. I would suggest that the nobility of spirit evidenced by these heroes lies within the grasp of each of us. Maybe it is just *that* which has made me return to Arthur so many times.

Dan Nastali, the magazine's associate editor, already had a well-established Arthurian interest nearly twenty-five years ago when he embarked on what he saw then as the managable task of creating a comprehensive bibliography of Arthurian literature. The compilation of the bibliography continues, has given birth to a library overflowing with Arthuriana, and has opened dozens of doors for him into the literary history of Europe and America. He share his easy authority and the scope of his knowledge in his regular column, "Lesser Known Works."

William C. Hale, *AtoC's* other co-editor for the first volume, was a student of the Malory scholar, R. M. Lumiansky at the University of Pennsylvania. He recalls being initially drawn to study Arthurian literature more by "the Great Man" than by the subject matter, but after hearing Prof. Lumiansky "intone Malory as though he were reading scripture in Church" he was "taken by the power and tragic drama of the story."

Our current editor, Alan Lupack, has had the opportunity to directly observe and appreciate the current international range of contemporary Arthurian works, including Henryk Tomaszewski's 1982 mime theater production of *The Knights of King Arthur* which he saw during the impending establishment of martial law in Poland, during which time he was forced to vacate his teaching post at the University of Wroclaw. Through his teaching Arthurian literature, writing a sequence of Arthurian poems and an Arthurian novel, editing an anthology of poems on Arthurian themes, and editing and publishing with his wife Barbara Tepa Lupack a journal of poetry and short fiction entitled *The Round Table* (which contains occasional Arthurian works), Alan has been made aware of "the range of values embodied in the legends":

> I find that the material has wide appeal—perhaps wider than any other course taught— because it contains so much of truth, so much of life.... Although I have experienced and written stories and poems about such harsh contemporary realities as Vietnam and martial-law Poland, I find the Arthurian legends' romantic stories no less effective (and in some ways more effective) a means of dealing with the troubles of the modern world. In a volume of Arthurian poetry, I treated the problems of war, the dangers and rewards of idealism, and the grievous results of the abuse of power, which to me is at the heart of many contemporary ills.

His "Journey" closes: "I am fascinated by a legend which has inspired so many works of art and so many people for so many centuries. I find in those legends a wealth of values and ideals, of understanding, of humanity."

Those who are concerned that immersion in Arthurian literature is an escape from, or way of avoiding reality, might adopt the poetic perception wherein the world of symbols and of the imagination are *timeless* realms within which the analagous, rather than the linear reigns; the great storytellers of all times and their creations exist simultaneously and with meaning in one's inner life, that ineffable region which is the source of myth, renewal, and sustenence.

The road from *Avalon to Camelot* has gradually led me to a kinship with numerous others, to inner and outer journeys, and to extraordinary experiences such as these described by Joseph Campbell:

> Furthermore, we have not even to risk the adventure alone, for the heroes of all time have gone before us. The labyrinth is thoroughly known; we have only to follow the thread of the hero path. And where we had thought to find an abomination we shall find a god. And where we had thought to slay another we shall slay ourselves. Where we had thought to travel outward we shall come to the center of our own existence. And where we had thought to be alone we shall be with all the world.[16]

Publisher, *Avalon to Camelot*
Evanston, Illinois

NOTES

[1]John Cowper Powys, "Preface," *A Glastonbury Romance* (London: Macdonald, 1951), xi.

[2]Kathleen Raine, "Blake and King Arthur" (Transcript of address at the Second Merlin Conference, June 13, 1987, London).

[3]Richard Harris, "Lerner and Loewe: Broadway's Last Romantics" (Transcript of PBS Television program aired Chicago, Illinois) April, 1988.

[4]Raine.

[5]Jack Zipes, "Preface," *Don't Bet on the Prince: Contemporary Feminist Fairy Tales in North America and England* (New York, 1986), xi–xiv.

[6]Edward C. Whitmont, "Introduction," *The Return of the Goddess* (New York, 1982), xi.

[7]Joan Marler, "Introduction," "The Mythic Journey: An Interview With Joseph Campbell," *Yoga Journal* 77 (1987), 58.

[8]Marler, 58.

[9]Marler, 61.

[10]T. S. Eliot, "The Dry Salvages," *The Four Quartets,* in *The Complete Poems and Plays: 1909–1950* (New York, 1952),133.

[11]Eliot,136.

[12]Joseph Campbell, *The Power of Myth,* with Bill Moyers, (New York,1988), 5.

[13] Heinrich Zimmer, *The King and the Corpse,* trans. Joseph Campbell (Princeton, 1956), 96–97.

[14]Zimmer, 97.

[15]Zimmer, 97.

[16]Joseph Campbell,123.

Index to Volume II